Economic Complexity and Evolution

More information about this series at http://www.springer.com/series/11583

Georg D. Blind

The Entrepreneur in Rule-Based Economics

Theory, Empirical Practice, and Policy Design

Springer

Georg D. Blind
University of Zurich
Zurich, Switzerland

ISSN 2199-3173 ISSN 2199-3181 (electronic)
Economic Complexity and Evolution
ISBN 978-3-319-62778-6 ISBN 978-3-319-62779-3 (eBook)
DOI 10.1007/978-3-319-62779-3

Library of Congress Control Number: 2017948233

Printed on acid-free paper

This Springer imprint is published by Springer Nature
The registered company is Springer International Publishing AG
The registered company address is: Gewerbestrasse 11, 6330 Cham, Switzerland

There is a discipline adapted to the schools, and which it is profitable to have studied, but which has no direct bearing upon action.

Francis Edgeworth (1889)
on Walras' "Eléments d'économie politique pure".

Foreword

While many economists will contend that understanding the nature of the entrepreneur is a key to understanding what is going on in an economy, little research on the issue has come forth up to now. It is a pleasure to introduce a book that makes a major contribution to filling the gap.

The particular aim of the book is to develop a theoretical approach for the study of entrepreneurship that is sufficiently general to ensure its applicability to a wide range of empirical cases and yet still sufficiently specific to allow for the formulation of a set of interesting and testable hypotheses.

The book combines what belongs together but what mostly is considered to be like fire and water: a unified theory of entrepreneurship and down-to-earth empirical work. The author demonstrates that integrating the various scattered pieces into a whole and the most detailed work at the empirical level is in no way self-contradictory but rather represents highly complementary aspects of a scientific effort to cope with this issue. The approach is entirely at odds with recent claims to achieve integration by featuring concepts such as "Universal Darwinism" and the like and instead trusts unreservedly the inductive power of empirical facts as a guide for devising the basic theoretical structure. The book succeeds persuasively in demonstrating that gaining the most general theoretical insights requires doing research at the lowest level of detailed empirical facts. The analysis stands faithfully in the tradition of Charles Peirce who proposed that the methodological tool most adequate for any evolutionary analysis is "abduction": the continuous interplay between induction and deduction in an ongoing process of theorising.

The book builds on and feeds the present discourse of a rule-based approach (RBA) in economics. It adapts the RBA with a view to use it for empirical analysis of the entrepreneur and of entrepreneurship in general and for investigating the Japanese case in particular. In this frame, entrepreneurship is an entrepreneurial rule, a particular way of doing things, whereas the entrepreneur is a carrier and propagator of such a rule.

Taking an evolutionary perspective, the entrepreneur is viewed as either an equilibrium-disturbing Schumpeterian entrepreneur or an equilibrium-creating entrepreneur. The diffusion of the rules of entrepreneurship is seen to influence the size and structure of a response rule population, or what the author calls the "founder force". The interactions between the entrepreneur and the economic environment are discussed at both the level of functions and personality of the entrepreneur (as a carrier of rules) and the nature and kinds of rules governing the entrepreneur's operations.

The factor rules are associated with the CBST rule taxonomy that distinguishes between cognitive, behavioural, social and technical rules as factors governing entrepreneurial action. It is shown how factor rules interact with each other on the one hand and how the composite of interacting factor rules impacts on the set of response rules on the other hand. The illuminating theoretical discussion sheds light on perennial issues like causality and validity of quantitative and qualitative measurement. Empirically, a set of factor rules is seen to constitute a full explanatory system of rules that contains all rules considered to be causally relevant in an investigation period. On this basis, a rich empirical picture of the role of entrepreneurs and the kind of entrepreneurship in the Japanese economy is portrayed.

While the new empirical findings are interesting in their own right, the main contribution of Dr. Blind's work may be seen to lay in presenting an approach that enables us to respond to major challenges of theory construction and of theory validation in new ways. The study brings home the point persuasively that when it comes to realism, a rule-based approach is far superior to the approach adopted by mainline economists. The RBA approach brings up for discussion formal-analytical rigour and empirical validity as criteria for validation in theorising, and, unlike neoclassical theory, it takes position for the latter. But let us listen to the author himself:

> While neoclassical theory has achieved a formally complete system at the cost of limited empirical validity, the RBA eschews formally complete and invariant theorising in favour of local hypotheses that—through testing—can be transformed into locally valid theorems. In essence, the RBA offers researchers the freedom to extract locally valid theorems without the binding constraint of a fixed formal theory but does so in exchange for their commitment to strive for greater empirical realism (p. 47).

The upshot of this is that it is not just the poor empirical base of neoclassical economics that accounts for its lack of realism but rather its defunct underlying scientific structure that makes impossible doing adequate empirical research in the first place.

This book offers a sumptuous smorgasbord with dishes for scholars interested in the construction of evolutionary economic theory generally, delving deeply into the nature of different personalities of entrepreneurs and various rules governing their decisions, the multilevel outcomes of factor rules and response rules, and it will inspire practitioners that move in the realms of policy and management in Japan that serves as an empirical showcase.

Bon appétit!

University of St. Gallen, Switzerland Kurt Dopfer

Preface

There is arguably no need to motivate a volume on entrepreneurship in economics. If any, William Baumol's famous quote on the absence of the Prince of Denmark in the discussion of Hamlet should well enough serve the purpose. Any reader browsing these first pages will arguably agree that the entrepreneur needs to be brought back to the discussion of economics.

In contrast, only some among the many individuals sharing Baumol's view will already be familiar with the rule-based approach. Rules as devices for economic analysis have increasingly earned recognition since Eleanor Oström's pioneering work was awarded the 2009 Nobel Memorial Prize in Economic Sciences. While Oström's understanding of rules was predominantly informed by her empirical work, she has also engaged in methodological discourse on the use of rules. One of her last articles "Crafting analytical tools to study institutional change" (2011) presents "an overview of a new diagnostic tool for analysing institutional dynamics, mainly changes in rule systems". The concluding discussion matches her own inductively derived rule methodology to what she sees as the most relevant among a number of "very interesting approaches to the study of the evolution of human societies" (ibid: 333). What follows is a minute introduction to the essentials of the rule-based approach (RBA), a synthetic analytical framework for the study of economic evolution originating from the works of Kurt Dopfer (2001, 2004, 2005, 2006; Dopfer and Potts 2008).

While Oström is very positive about the RBA in general, I have since long shared her concerns that it "does not provide us with enough details about the nature of rules and rule configurations [...] to inform how changes might take place and how these changes could be measured" (Oström and Basurto 2011: 334). The volume at hand aspires to answer Oström's call for methodological guidance on how to use the BRA in empirical research and to provide as exemplar a complete empirical study of entrepreneurship.

Thus, the three parts of this volume combine three distinct purposes. Part I demonstrates how a reasoning with rules may be employed for theory building. Part II aims at providing the methodological guidance that Oström has been asking for by proposing a template for empirical investigations guided by the RBA. Its third part, in turn, puts the proposed methodology to an empirical test by conducting a study of entrepreneurship in Japan.

At first sight, the choice of Japan as empirical test ground might not seem obvious. It is, however, an ideal choice for demonstrating how rule-based analysis allows for bringing to light specific characteristics of an economy, which received approaches typically fail to capture. Thus, our choice of Japan predominantly originates from the potential of showcasing the integrative power of the rule-based analysis. Coincidentally, entrepreneurship in Japan has hardly been investigated so far in spite of the alarmingly low and constantly declining levels of latent and actual entrepreneurship. Thus, our choice kills two birds with one stone.

Parts of this volume follow some earlier work (Blind 2012; Blind and Pyka 2014). Nevertheless, this volume does not originate from a collection of essays but represents a dedicated monograph. As such, individual parts intimately build on each other. Aiming at increasing convenience to readers, the author has included a considerable number of cross-references for enhancing the cohesion between parts of the volume.

Zurich, Switzerland Georg D. Blind

References

Blind GD (2012) Investigating entrepreneurial spirit with the rule approach: why self-employment is on the decline in Japan. Evol Inst Econ Rev 9(1):183–198

Blind G, Pyka A (2014). The rule approach in evolutionary economics: a methodological template for empirical research. J Evol Econ 24(5):1085–1105

Dopfer K (2001) Evolutionary economics – framework for analysis. In: Dopfer K (ed) The evolutionary foundations of economics. Kluwer Academic Publishers, Boston, pp 1–44

Dopfer K (2004) The economic agent as rule maker and rule user: Homo Sapiens Oeconomicus. J Evol Econ 14:177–195

Dopfer K (2005) The evolutionary foundations of economics. Cambridge University Press, Cambridge

Dopfer K (2006) The origins of meso economics – Schumpeter's legacy. Papers on economics and evolution. Max Planck Institute, Jena, p 610

Dopfer K, Potts J (2008) The general theory of economic evolution. Routledge, London

Oström E, Basurto X (2011) Crafting analytical tools to study institutional change. J Inst Econ 7(3):317–343

Acknowledgements

Most of the inspiration to write this book stems from the works of Kurt Dopfer and his pioneering efforts in reconstructing economic theory. Adding to the intellectual stimulus that led to the writing of this book, Kurt Dopfer constantly encouraged my endeavours and was most helpful with any down-to-earth matters such as obtaining funding. Last but not least, he was supportive of my research interest in "Things Japanese"[1] right from the start, based on his own experience in this country from 1972 to 1976.

Much in the same spirit, Andreas Pyka, Harald Hagemann and Marco Lehmann-Waffenschmidt were kind enough to advise on some research that diverges from the "received canon" of economic inquiry in a number of respects. First, its theoretical foundations are somewhat remote from what still is to be considered the centre stage of contemporary economics. Second, this book is not only an economics one but touches base with other disciplines such as management science, sociology and cultural studies. Equally open to interdisciplinary inquiry and discourse David Chiavacci, Raji Steineck, and Stefania Lottanti von Mandach have contributed most valuable criticism and advice.

Kiichirō Yagi most significantly contributed to the making of my research fellowship at Kyoto University in 2008–2009, where he kindly introduced me to the Japanese research community in Evolutionary Economics, and successfully supported my funding efforts with the Japan Society for the Promotion of Science (JSPS) providing generous research funding.

Collecting the data used in the applied part of this research meant a considerable amount of work, a task that I could never have accomplished alone. The merits for the completion of this endeavour are all those of Dr. Kuniaki Makino, of Takahiro Semba and—after my return to Europe—of Dr. Yoko Nakamura.

As much as I have to thank the Japan Society for the Promotion of Science providing the funding of Mr. Makino and Mr. Semba, I would like to express my gratitude towards the Foundation of the German Industry (SDW), which has supported this project with a full 3-year grant.

[1]"Things Japanese", probably *the* classic in Western studies of Japan, is a comprehensive glossary written in 1890 by Basil Hall Chamberlain 17 years after his arrival in the country.

Contents

List of Figures

List of Tables

Chapter 1
Introduction

Abstract The nature of the entrepreneurial role can be clarified by raising three central questions: who is an entrepreneur, what does an entrepreneur do and how does an agent eventually become an entrepreneur? This helps to understand of the Schumpeter–Knight distinction of equilibrium-disturbing versus equilibrium-creating entrepreneurs as an empirical question that only can be researched *ex post*. Building on this, the entrepreneur is defined as a newly self-employed individual. We further explain how the inclusion of matters conventionally associated with disciplines other than economics may increase the explanatory power of analysis. We further introduce the subject matter, motivate the choice of the case study presented in Part III, and conclude with an outline of the structure of the book.

This book combines three purposes. First, it aims to develop a theoretical approach to the study of entrepreneurship that is (a) sufficiently general to ensure its applicability to a wide variety of empirical cases, (b) sufficiently specific to allow for the formulation of locally relevant hypotheses and (c) informed by reality to a degree that enables empirical testing of these hypotheses. Second, it aims to provide a methodological framework that guides enquiries from theoretical considerations through the formulation of hypotheses and on to their empirical verification. Third, in applying the theory via the proposed methodology to entrepreneurship in Japan, it aspires to answer two specific questions—what factors have been determining changes in entrepreneurial spirit and what has been driving the levels of latent and actual entrepreneurship over the past two decades? The three purposes of this volume are reflected in the order of its parts.

This introduction discusses a number of fundamental questions. It first clarifies diverging perspectives on the nature of the entrepreneurial role, before demonstrating that the enquiries of this volume represent essential economic research, while also embracing a number of aspects conventionally associated with other disciplines. The choice of entrepreneurship as the subject matter for an empirical investigation in general is discussed, as well as the geographical choice of Japan in particular. The introduction concludes with an outline of the structure of the book.

G.D. Blind, *The Entrepreneur in Rule-Based Economics*, Economic Complexity and Evolution, DOI 10.1007/978-3-319-62779-3_1

1.1 What Makes an Entrepreneur?

This seemingly simple question can be read in different ways. First, it asks for the definition of "entrepreneur", or what an entrepreneur actually *is*. A second reading leads to the question of what an entrepreneur actually *does*? Finally, a third reading asks what causes an individual to *become* an entrepreneur.

In essence, all answers to the first and second readings can be reduced to the distinction between an equilibrium-disturbing Schumpeterian entrepreneur and an equilibrium-creating entrepreneur (compare, e.g. Grebel et al. 2003; Egashira 2006: 52). Evolutionary and neo-Schumpeterian economists lay particular emphasis on the innovative capacity of the equilibrium-disturbing entrepreneur. While fully acknowledging that there are a small number of entrepreneurs who cause an economy to undergo fundamental change, it is safe to claim that the vast majority do not. Still, this "army of unknown entrepreneurs" undoubtedly plays an important role in an economy. While the former determine the qualitative nature of economic change, the latter shape the dynamics ensuing from disturbances of equilibrium. A corresponding observation in business studies distinguishes first- and second-mover strategies.

Obviously, the two questions of what an entrepreneur *is* and what he or she *does* are closely interrelated and have given rise to a great many answers. These are only briefly discussed in this book, which settles on a pragmatic definition of the entrepreneur as *a newly self-employed individual*. This notion, to which the vast majority of contemporary entrepreneurship research adheres, essentially implies that the distinction between the disturbance and the creation of equilibrium can only be made through empirical investigation. In the vast majority of cases, there is no conscious choice between becoming an equilibrium-disturbing or an equilibrium creating entrepreneur. Typically, markets—and to some extent chance—will dictate this. Consequently, the distinction can only be made in an ex post appraisal.

As any economist will agree, both equilibrium-disturbing and equilibrium-creating entrepreneurs make substantial contributions to the development of an economy. In order to generate such contributions, an economy needs a sufficient number of individuals willing to become self-employed. Accordingly, this book seeks to provide conclusive answers to the third reading of our initial question: what causes individuals to become self-employed. From an individual perspective, this implies a choice between self-employment and dependent employment. From the national economy's perspective, understanding the underlying mechanisms will be key to controlling the size of what we may label its "founder force" and hence to influencing its potential for economic development.

1.2 Is This an Economics Piece of Research?

The empirical part of this research aims at investigating how the determinants of business formation have evolved in Japan since the burst of the country's "bubble economy" in the early 1990s. Naturally, the investigation of the Japanese case could also be the subject of an enquiry in the social science branch of Japanese studies. Similarly, the study of business formation might suggest that this research is a business studies enquiry. Yet, the study of business formation in Japan only serves as a *means* of corroborating general theoretical propositions originating from the domain of economics. The following section refines this argument.

First, the phenomenon of self-employment in Japan should be of equal interest to both economics and Japanese studies. In that sense, the empirical part of this volume definitely represents an end in itself. While the overarching methodology is entirely informed by economic thought, a number of techniques employed in the empirical part—such as field interviews and the study of local language materials—stem from the methodological core of the social science branch of Japanese studies. However, these techniques are used in this research with the sole purpose of increasing the explanatory power of economic analysis and therefore act merely as an auxiliary to economic enquiry. This type of "external insight" is an essential condition for developing meaningful economic explanation.

To date, orthodox economics has strongly resisted any attempt to develop localist theoretical approaches. This stands in stark contrast to the neighbouring discipline of business studies. For instance, business scholars have developed an entire canon of literature on "Japanese-style management" (e.g. Abegglen 1958; Imai 1986; Ohno 1988; Womack et al. 1990). But, apart from a growing consensus against the universalist claims of orthodox economics, what arguments could possibly support the proclaimed need for more localist approaches? The most abstract definition of an economy is the totality of economically relevant activities in a society. Naturally, ways of thought, custom and habit strongly influence the nature of these activities. Consequently, two countries might show as many differences in their national economies as in religion, history or other elements of culture. While a "Japanese-style economics" still remains to be developed, a growing minority of scholars are seeking new methods of economic theory and analysis. Interestingly, one of the most enthusiastic advocates of an "economics of Japan" is not himself a Japanese national (Katzner 2008, see also the discussion in Blind 2012a).

Most Japanese economists are not aware of any disparity between received economic models and the economic realities of Japan. When Western models of explanation eventually fail to produce conclusive evidence, Japanese researchers, rather than blaming the models, tend to argue that in respect of some structural factors, Japan unfortunately "does not yet fit the model". It is here that a localist approach scholars can make a significant contribution, bringing to the discussion aspects that are neglected by or unknown to economists adhering to Western paradigms of explanation, both in the West and in Japan. Such venturing into the "cultural domain", however, comes with considerable risk of faulty interpretations if the analysis includes simplistic culturalist explanations (compare the discussions in Blind and Lottanti von Mandach 2013, 2017). To avoid such trap, Part II of this volume develops an empirical methodology for working with localist argument (also presented in Blind and Pyka 2014). As important prerequisite, any sound localist study implies the inclusion local language materials, an issue that has come to be neglected in much of contemporary economic research.

Approaching the empirical part in this way may suggest a circular rationale of deduction and induction. However, I would like to suggest the image of a spiral: selective deductive points of departure are used to build a *general* theoretical torso; in turn, the empirical world analysed in this study and then used to substantiate the theoretical part is *distinctively specific*. In essence, theoretical premises, such as that universalist economic theories are prone to failure in a great many local contexts, can be corroborated by theoretical and empirical insights from a concrete empirical case.

Second, the use of terms such as "entrepreneurship" and "business formation" might suggest our subject matter belongs to the domain of management studies. This would be true if the purpose of our enquiry was a quest for "how-to" guidelines via the identification of best practices. However, our research focuses on the function and the functioning of self-employment in an economy and is therefore an economics piece of research.

It is true that management studies has long been fascinated by the creative capacity of the entrepreneur. Besides obvious questions such as how to become a successful entrepreneur, business scholars have produced a wide array of literature centring on the characteristics of the entrepreneur. Along the same lines, empirical studies in entrepreneurship research frequently investigate the chances of becoming an entrepreneur, a perspective that is clearly close to the third reading of our initial question of what makes an entrepreneur. Yet there is an important difference. While business studies look into the characteristics that make an individual become self-employed—as evidenced by the use of binary dependent variables—this volume focuses on a different perspective: what determines the size of the "founder force"? In other words, the empirical aim of this volume is to explain the size of the group of individuals that opt for self-employment over available economic alternatives in an economy.

In the case of the present research, *external insights* are a means to the end of furthering economic theory. In essence, although this volume draws on methods from Japanese studies and on concepts from business studies and other disciplines, it does so in the service of economics. I hope, however, that it will also offer a number of valuable insights to scholars from neighbouring disciplines.

1.3 Why Entrepreneurship? And Why Japan?

As emphasised above, the choice of entrepreneurship as explanandum in an empirical piece of research seeks to assist a reconsideration of the entrepreneur in economic theory. The entrepreneur has been largely absent from orthodox economics for many decades. This is in spite of the frequent assertion that he or she is a missing key figure in economic theory, as epitomised by William Baumol (1968), who wrote of the necessity "to bring the Prince of Denmark back into the discussion of *Hamlet*". His critique was taken up in the same year by yet another prominent figure: "The answer is that the standard competitive theory hides the vital function of the entrepreneur" (Leibenstein 1968). For evolutionary economists, the entrepreneur represents *the* central phenomenon that makes for economic development. In this respect, evolutionary economics derives much from the Schumpeterian concept of the entrepreneur as a "creative destructor". Given the entrepreneur's crucial role in overall economic development, an enhanced view of the evolution of the determinants of an economy's "founder force" will help to refine economic theory and policymaking. With respect to the latter in particular, a long-term view is indispensable.

The next step for a study exploring the determinants of business formation as the outward manifestation of entrepreneurship is to delimit the analysis to one specific economy in accordance with the localist arguments presented above. A few considerations will suffice to highlight the advantages arising from the choice of Japan.

First, the subject of entrepreneurship is yet to receive the attention in Japan that it enjoys elsewhere. So far, few studies have tried to explain business formation ratios for Japan (Ohe and Ohe 1996; Harada 2002, 2005), all of which rely on cross-sectional data, that is, they do not investigate potential change over time. A recent paper by Masuda (2006), however, does provide some descriptive data on historical trends but mostly focuses on examining the determinants of latent entrepreneurship across regions. The use of longitudinal data in this research seeks to offer new insights into the origin of the current state of affairs and to develop more targeted policy recommendations.

Second, some specific characteristics of the Japanese *economy* suggest both modelling advantages and particularly interesting features. For instance, its history of low interest rates during the last two decades attributes higher explanatory power to other determinants of business formation. In addition, the comparatively smooth, long and low-amplitude business cycles of the Japanese economy facilitate the extraction of other underlying processes. As a general observation, Japan remains under-researched relative to its economic relevance with major phenomena being poorly understood (compare Blind and Lottanti von Mandach 2012). What is more, Japanese statistics cover an extremely wide variety of topics and can be considered some of the most complete and reliable sets of data internationally available.

Third, cultural and social factors specific to Japanese *society* are promising points of departure for an empirical analysis. For instance, the shift in the relative importance of seniority and performance and of lifelong employment and a hire-and-fire mentality in the country's corporate culture that has reportedly evolved over the last 20 years may prove a significant influence on our subject matter. The same is true of what Hofstede (1980) dubbed "uncertainty avoidance" in his dimensions of culture, a category in which Japan occupies an outlier position.

1.4 Terminology

Enterprise formation by individuals as the outward expression of entrepreneurship is the subject of this investigation. Hence, entrepreneurship is to be understood as the creation of self-employment at the expense of dependent employment or of unemployment. An important distinction has to be made between enterprise formation and firm formation. While the former describes the act of starting a new business, the latter merely refers to the act of incorporation or registration of a business. This is an important distinction to keep in mind as much existing research starts off with data from commercial registers.

Due to its geographical focus on Japan, this volume contains a number of specific terms. A bilingual glossary providing references in alphabetical order is included for readers not familiar with Japan. For practical reasons, all terms are listed both by the pronunciation of the romanised Japanese term and by alphabetical order of its English translation. The original notation in Japanese characters is also given.

1.5 Structure of This Book

A valid theoretical approach to the phenomenon of self-employment as the outward manifestation of entrepreneurship is provided in Part I, which starts with an outline of the rule-based approach (RBA) as proposed by Dopfer (Dopfer 2001, 2004, 2005, 2006; Dopfer and Potts 2008). This analytical framework regards influencing factors as "rules" and their relative relevance in terms of "rule populations". The RBA builds on Veblen, Nelson-Winter, and Ostrom (compare Blind 2016) for the development of a *general* rule-based approach to the theory of entrepreneurship.

Part II then develops a methodology for constructing *specific* models in rule-based economics as introduced in Part I. It provides detailed guidance on what Erich Schneider recognized as being possible, namely how "both stationary and evolutionary phenomena may be subjected to a static as well as to a dynamic analysis" (Schneider 1953[1949]:194; compare the discussion in Blind and Pyka 2015). Having introduced a method for establishing the system of influencing factors for a given response item, it then proposes a procedure for reducing a thus conceived model to its causal core. The extent to which hypotheses developed using this methodology can be tested by existing techniques is also briefly discussed. In conclusion, an integrated case study exemplifies the use of this methodology in empirical research. Part II thus provides what Ostrom and Basurto have called for, namely "how changes might take place and how these changes could be measured" in the RBA (Oström and Basurto 2011: 334). The essentials of this methodology is also presented in Blind and Pyka (2014).

Part III applies the general theoretical approach of Part I to the case of entrepreneurship in Japan, employing the methodology developed in Part II. More specifically, the general approach to entrepreneurship is amended with factors specific to the Japanese case in order to establish a valid localist model. The model thus developed is reduced by a causality check of alleged influencing factors to its causal core, and the evolving nature of this model core is investigated using statistical methods. A number of findings documented in Part III are also presented in Blind (2012b).

Part IV, the final part of this volume, starts with a summary of findings in its theoretical, methodological and empirical parts. It builds on the evidence gathered in developing policy recommendations for the case of Japan. It reviews the challenges and merits of the rule-based approach experienced in the course of the empirical investigation of entrepreneurship in Japan.

References

Abegglen J (1958) The Japanese factory: aspects of its social organization. Free Press, Glencoe, IL
Baumol W (1968) Entrepreneurship in economic theory. Am Econ Rev 58(2):64–71
Blind GD (2012a) Culture and economic explanation: economics in the US and Japan. By Donald W. Katzner. New York: Routledge, 2008. 184 pp. $39.95 (paper). J East Asian Stud 12(1): 150–153
Blind GD (2012b) Investigating entrepreneurial spirit with the rule approach: why self-employment is on the decline in Japan. Evol Inst Econ Rev 9(1):183–198
Blind GD (2016) Behavioral rules: Veblen, Nelson-Winter, Oström and beyond. In: Frantz R, Chen S-H, Dopfer K, Heukelom F, Mousavi S (eds) Routledge handbook of behavioral economics. Routledge, Milton Park, pp 139–151
Blind G, Lottanti von Mandach S (2012) Ansichtssache: Zum Zustand der japanischen Wirtschaft nach Doppelschlag und Dreifach-Katastrophe. In: Chiavacci D, Wieczorek I (eds) Japan 2012. VSJF, Berlin, pp 131–149
Blind G, Lottanti von Mandach S (2013) Bescheidene Managementgehälter und sich schliessende Lohnscheren: Neue Einblicke in den japanischen Arbeitsmarkt. In: Chiavacci D, Wieczorek I (eds) Japan 2013. VSJF, Berlin, pp 203–228
Blind GD, Lottanti von Mandach S (2017) Not a coincidence: sons-in-law as successors in successful Japanese family firms. Crit Finance Rev (forthcoming)
Blind G, Pyka A (2014) The rule approach in evolutionary economics: a methodological template for empirical research. J Evol Econ 24(5):1085–1105
Blind GD, Pyka A (2015) Erich Schneider: the admiring disciple who did not become a follower. J Evol Econ 25(1):239–252
Dopfer K (2001) Evolutionary economics – framework for analysis. In: Dopfer K (ed) The evolutionary foundations of economics. Kluwer Academic, Boston, pp 1–44
Dopfer K (2004) The economic agent as rule maker and rule user: Homo sapiens oeconomicus. J Evol Econ 14:177–195
Dopfer K (ed) (2005) The evolutionary foundations of economics. Cambridge University Press, Cambridge
Dopfer K (2006) The origins of meso economics – Schumpeter's legacy. In: Papers on economics and evolution, No 610. Max Planck Institute, Jena
Dopfer K, Potts J (2008) The general theory of economic evolution. Routledge, London
Egashira S (2006) A present appreciation of evolutionary economics – a historical characterization of the alternative thoughts of economics in the light of evolutionism. Evol Inst Econ Rev 3(1): 47–69
Grebel T, Pyka A et al (2003) An evolutionary approach to the theory of entrepreneurship. Ind Innov 10(4):493–514
Harada N (2002) Potential entrepreneurship in Japan. JCER discussion paper, No 81
Harada N (2005) Potential entrepreneurship in Japan. Small Bus Econ 25(3):293–304
Hofstede G (1980) Culture's consequences. International differences in work-related values. Sage, Beverly Hills
Imai M (1986) Kaizen: the key to Japan's competitive success. McGraw-Hill, New York

Katzner DW (2008) Culture and economic explanation: economics in the US and Japan. Routledge, New York

Leibenstein H (1968) Entrepreneurship and development. Am Econ Rev: Papers and Proceedings of the Eightieth Annual Meeting of the American Economic Association 58(2):72–83

Masuda T (2006) The determinants of latent entrepreneurship in Japan. Small Bus Econ 26: 227–240

Ohe S, Ohe T (1996) Three key experiences of Japanese entrepreneurs during their elementary and secondary school years. Frontiers of entrepreneurship research (Conference Proceedings). Wellesley (MA). Available at: http://fusionmx.babson.edu/entrep/fer/papers96/ohe/

Ohno T (1988) Toyota production system: beyond large-scale production. Productivity Press, New York

Oström E, Basurto X (2011) Crafting analytical tools to study institutional change. J Inst Econ 7(3):317–343

Schneider E (1953[1949]) Einführung in die Wirtschaftstheorie II. J.C.B. Mohr (Paul Siebeck), Tübingen

Womack JP, Jones DT et al (1990) The machine that changed the world: the story of lean production. Rawson Associates, New York

Part I
A Theory of Entrepreneurship Through the Rule-Based Approach

Acknowledging that "there is still no theory of entrepreneurship" (Ripsas 1998), this first part seeks to develop a theoretical approach to entrepreneurship that can serve as the basis for empirical research. The approach must fulfil a number of conditions. First, it has to be general enough to ensure applicability to a wide range of cases. Second, it has to be specific enough to enable the full explanatory core to be extracted in an empirical study. Third, and perhaps most importantly, it needs to respect the reality of empirical research, that is, it needs to ensure that its constituent concepts can be applied effectively. But is a theoretical approach to entrepreneurship needed? Should received economics eventually have failed to answer this question? The following paragraphs show why I believe that both questions can be answered in the affirmative.

Let us start with what is still the most widely accepted definition of economics as a field of study: "Economics is the science which studies human behaviour as a relationship between ends and scarce means which have alternative uses" (Robbins 1945[1932]). If we apply this definition to entrepreneurship we find that (a) enterprise formation represents an act of human behaviour, which (b) depends on the ends an agent pursues and on his or her means in terms of endowments. In its neoclassical reading, our subject matter can be viewed as a microeconomic allocation problem faced by an individual agent when deciding how to optimally allocate available resources between self-employment and corresponding economic alternatives in order to maximise their self-interest.

Whilst this reading of entrepreneurship derived from Robbins' definition of economics is fully compatible with mainstream argument, closer inspection reveals a number of shortcomings. First, let us consider business formation as "an act of human behaviour". According to a frequently raised critique, neoclassical economics has reduced *Homo oeconomicus* to a decision-making machine, endowed with perfect rationality, with supernatural capabilities in marginal calculus, and with the maximisation of self-interest as a uniform end: in short, to a creature devoid of human traits.

With empirical evidence on the human character of *Homo oeconomicus* (e.g. Fehr and Gächter 2002) adding to years of theoretical objections, Dopfer reintroduced humanity into the conception of economic man, proposing *Homo sapiens oeconomicus* (2004). Accepting the *sapiens* property of human behaviour requires reconsideration of ends and means as used in Robbins' definition. First, in order to understand the behaviour of humans, one needs to reflect on the diverse nature of human ends. This requires an understanding of what "utility" means to *Homo sapiens*. If we believe any of the findings of social psychology, human needs go way beyond what may be measured in terms of "pay-offs". Consequently, any motivation causing economic action has to be considered relevant in economic analysis. An analysis of ends must therefore go beyond economic pay-offs to include aspects such as reputation, happiness and even instincts and beliefs. Second, the same is required for an analysis of means. Modern *Homo sapiens oeconomicus* relies on more than mere financial and human capital. Accordingly, aspects such as the institutional environment and cultural and intellectual endowments must also be included in a systematic fashion.

Unfortunately, the characteristics represented by the received *Homo oeconomicus* are not only incomplete—as outlined above—but are also seen as being invariant in time and space. Yet, *Homo oeconomicus* as a theoretical concept merely represents a local historical snapshot: *Homo oeconomicus* as conceived during the latter half of the nineteenth century arguably formed a reasonably appropriate portrait of the vast majority of economic actors facing subsistence conditions. But is a local snapshot sufficient for creating a model of human behaviour to be used in different historical stages and in different cultural spaces? Cultural, as opposed to biological, evolution has reached a pace to be measured in decades or centuries rather than in millennia or geological time. If we conceive of economic interaction as a cultural phenomenon in humans, the historicity of economic behaviour must be taken into account even for relatively short periods of investigation. The same holds true for the influence of local specificities. For instance, would *Homo oeconomicus* with his implicit Protestant ethic (Weber 1904/1905) actually lend itself to a sound analysis of Latin America in the twentieth century? In essence, we must accept that there are substantial differences in the causes of economic behaviour, including the decision to become self-employed or not, according to time and space.

To this specific critique of the received treatment of the entrepreneur as an exponent of *Homo oeconomicus*, a more general observation can be added. It is clear from an examination of other branches of economic sciences that they follow quite distinctive theoretical approaches to the investigation of the entrepreneur. For instance, neoclassical microeconomics would look into the cost of capital (the interest rate), Ordo-liberal scholars will tend to investigate market forms and aspects of the legal framework (Eucken 1932: 298) and Keynesian macroeconomists are likely to associate entrepreneurial activity with aggregate investment. In turn, management scholars may concentrate on "business sentiment", "access to finance" (Cressy 2002) or "business networks" (Davidsson and Honig 2003).

All these approaches are indisputably relevant to specific cases. However, when researching a concrete case in an empirical study, it is imperative to determine just which of the many approaches are actually offering explanatory power. An appropriate umbrella theory is indispensable to that assessment and to the consistent integration of relevant approaches into a theoretical whole. As the rule-based approach (Dopfer 2004; Dopfer and Potts 2008) not only represents such an umbrella theory but also provides a means to capture the essence of economic change, we start with the introduction of its main building blocks (Chap. 2). These elements are used to discuss the *function* of entrepreneurs in a rule-based economy (Chap. 3). We then develop a theoretical reading of entrepreneurship as an *analytical object*, that is, how entrepreneurship and its determinants can be conceived of in terms of rules (Chap. 4).

References

Cressy R (2002) Funding gaps: a symposium. Econ J 112:F1–F16

Davidsson P, Honig B (2003) The role of social and human capital among nascent entrepreneurs. J Bus Ventur 18:301–331

Dopfer K (2004) The economic agent as rule maker and rule user: Homo sapiens oeconomicus. J Evol Econ 14:177–195

Dopfer K, Potts J (2008) The general theory of economic evolution. Routledge, London

Eucken W (1932) Staatliche Strukturwandlungen und die Krisis des Kapitalismus. Weltwirtschaftliches Arch 36(2):299–321

Fehr E, Gächter S (2002) Altruistic punishment in humans. Nature 415(6868):137–140

Ripsas S (1998) Towards an interdisciplinary theory of entrepreneurship. Small Bus Econ 10:103–115

Robbins L (1945 [1932]) An essay on the nature and significance of economic science, 1st edn. MacMillan, London

Weber M (1904/1905) Die protestantische Ethik und der 'Geist' des Kapitalismus. Archiv für Sozialwissenschaft und Sozialpolitik 20, 21(1):1–54, 51–110

Chapter 2
The Rule-Based Approach in the Analysis of Economic Change

Abstract While there exist a great many of important cues to the understanding of the phenomenon of entrepreneurship, these are scattered across time and the entire landscape of sub-disciplines in economics. Adding to these, insights from neighbouring disciplines also suggest a wide variety of factors affecting the propensity of agents to eventually become entrepreneurs. In order to integrate these factors into a consistent model, this chapter presents the rule-based approach (RBA) as an umbrella theory of socio-economic change. Centre stage in rule-based economics is *Homo sapiens oeconomicus* (HSO), a heterogeneous agent open to learning and with the capacity to adapt his decision logic to individual circumstances. HSO is a "rule maker and rule user". We illustrate how the concept of rules and corresponding operations allows tracking the "life cycle" of an idea across the analytical levels of micro, meso and macro.

Although the rule-based approach of Dopfer and Potts has recently received increasing and most significant recognition (Oström and Basurto 2011), a brief introduction to its main elements is desirable at this point because it is fundamentally different from many received approaches in various respects as will become evident in the course of the following discussion.

The RBA takes its inspiration to a large extent from a desire to embrace the nature of economic change, and it can be presented as an answer to the theoretical void in explaining economic change. As we shall see, it offers a general analytical framework for the analysis of change in social systems.

2.1 Change as Reflected in Economic Thought

Economic change is most often publicly recognised when the macroeconomy takes an unexpected turn (compare Shackle 1979). Events such as the recent financial crisis spur public and scientific discussions on "how the rules of the game have changed". But economic change is by no means restricted to the macro domain. Changing industry structures, technology diffusion, and lock-in phenomena are of equal importance. Moreover, researchers have gathered ample evidence of significant change in key areas of microeconomics. For instance, recent experimental studies in behavioural economics have identified considerable heterogeneity among agents with regard to the

G.D. Blind, *The Entrepreneur in Rule-Based Economics*, Economic Complexity and Evolution, DOI 10.1007/978-3-319-62779-3_2

motivations that drive their action. This points to a fundamental change in the views about the mindset of agents compared with the received *Homo oeconomicus*.

Observations of economic change such as those mentioned above have come to challenge the predominant theoretical apparatus of orthodox economics that continues to perpetuate its quest for universal and invariant laws. While orthodox theory provides satisfactory tools for the analysis of economic operations in stationary environments, its set of assumptions and restrictions precludes the analysis of economic change. Examples include the complete absence of entrepreneurial opportunities in an equilibrium economy (as noticed by Grebel et al. 2003), the predominance of rational choice as the only endogenous source of explanation or the disregard for explanatory variables such as institutions. Amendments to the neoclassical canon to meet these challenges have considerably complicated its formal apparatus, yet eventual improvements have failed to suffice for the analysis of economic change as it can be observed in real-world economies.

Discontent with this situation has led to the emergence of several heterodox branches within the discipline of economics. Among these, it is evolutionary economics that most explicitly concentrates on the nature of economic change. Since its inception in the early 1980s with the seminal work of Nelson and Winter (1982), scholars in evolutionary economics have sought ways to delve into the nature of economic change. Although its focus is on economic change, evolutionary economics has never excluded the realm of economic operations from its analysis. However, as the objects of analysis are entirely different—orthodox scholars investigating economic operations within a given system and the evolutionary community enquiring into the change of this very system—a proper theoretical concept embracing both objects is indispensable.

In recent years, heterodox economists have produced many important concepts of the different manifestations of economic change (Foster 1987; Loasby 1991; Witt 1993; Metcalfe 1998). Building on these, *The General Theory of Economic Evolution* (GTEE; Dopfer and Potts 2008) introduces the rule-based approach (RBA) as an analytical framework embracing most of the former and combining them into a consistent framework.

By virtue of its object, the reasoning implied by the RBA as the analytical core of GTEE necessarily differs from traditional economic theories. While the neoclassical canon aims to identify universal and invariable laws, GTEE opposes this view in two fundamental ways. First, it recognises heterogeneity among agents and across geographies, denying the universality of "economic laws" and endorsing "localist" approaches (Katzner 2002). Second, since the knowledge base of agents is never the same at two different points in time, it denies the invariability of economic laws and endorses the recognition of "historic time". Ironically, one of the founding fathers of neoclassical economics once entertained quite similar views. In *Principles of Economics*, Alfred Marshall notes:

> The term "law" means then nothing more than a general proposition or statement of tendencies, more or less certain, more or less definite. Many such statements are made in every science: but we do not, indeed we cannot, give to all of them a formal character and name them as laws.
>
> (Marshall 1920 [1890]: I.III §4)

While Marshall only raises certain doubts as to the universality ("more or less certain") and the invariability ("more or less definite"), GTEE clearly states the opposite: there are neither universal nor invariable economic laws. It argues that all Marshallian "tendencies" are ultimately subject to change. With the premises of heterogeneity and historic time in mind, it becomes evident that GTEE does not offer any lawlike statements on economic phenomena that could be likened to the "principles" of the neoclassical canon. GTEE represents a generalised theory of change in social systems.

For the researcher, GTEE offers the rule-based approach (RBA) as analytical device for deriving locally specific hypotheses suitable for testing in empirical investigations. Through the testing of such hypotheses, researchers will eventually be able to develop locally valid theorems by way of induction. In that sense, GTEE represents what computer scientists might call an open-source theory: it provides the RBA as a programming language. In contrast, the neoclassical canon may rather be likened to proprietary software as it largely precludes any amendments.

In this research, rule-based reasoning comes with three specific advantages. First, it helps to develop an understanding of entrepreneurship that allows us to assess and eventually accommodate existing theoretical views of the subject. Second, it introduces a much needed dynamic perspective enabling an analysis in "historic time". And third, the construction of a locally valid model of entrepreneurship in Japan becomes feasible.

2.2 Building Blocks of the Rule-Based Approach

With important roots to be found in the work of Veblen, Nelson-Winter and Ostrom (see Blind 2016 for these linkages), the rule-based economics has evolved from within a spirited community of scholars of evolutionary economics. Its authors share many important insights from the recent discussion around "Universal Darwinism", a discussion that has undoubtedly delivered an important element in the development of evolutionary theory for economics (Hodgson 1993; Aldrich and Hodgson 2008). However, Dopfer and Potts rightly note that "Universal Darwinism has made a systematic error in overlooking the human mind as an emergent carrier domain, leading it to an unrestricted view of replicators" (2008: 5). We observe that the concept of an agent functioning as a replicator bears a calamitous similarity to the conceived *Homo oeconomicus* in his limited capacity to apply but a single rule to his actions: rational choice.

In contrast, Dopfer acknowledges the creative mind of *Homo sapiens*, his intellectual heterogeneity and his capacity to discriminate the use of rules according to the context. Consequently, Dopfer has since introduced the notion of *Homo sapiens oeconomicus* (HSO) presented as a rule maker and rule user (2004) where rules serve as "organizing principles" (Steineck 2013:351). The concept of a rule-making and rule-using economic agent serves as a cornerstone for the subsequent *General*

Theory (Dopfer and Potts 2008). In the following, we introduce key elements of their rule-based approach: the distinction of rules versus operations; the analytical domains of micro, meso and macro; and the taxonomy of classes and orders of rules.

The starting point for any evolutionary economic analysis is human knowledge: it represents the space in which economic activity takes place. Acknowledging the fact that the total knowledge base of all agents is never the same at two different points in time, the RBA introduces a two-level, multidomain analytical concept. The two levels consist of a deep mode of rules and a material mode of operations executed based on rules. The distinction of these two levels allows for a constructivist worldview, in which the cognition of individuals represents the basis for their actions as follows:

1. Level of rules that determine the nature and quality of economic operations
2. Level of economic operations enquiring variables such as prices and quantities

When employed for the purposes of empirical research, it is important to note that the primary object of rule-based analysis is not economic operations (2), but the structure and change of rules on the basis of which economic operations are conducted (1). This distinction into a primary and a secondary focus does not imply a value judgement but simply reflects the insight that an analysis of operations needs to be based on an understanding of the underlying rules. For example, rules such as tariff exemptions in international trade do not directly translate into fully liberated trade operations (Chiavacci et al. 2012; Blind and Ziltener 2014). In this sense, the distinction does not imply a hierarchical but rather a sequential order.

The focus of an analysis of rules on the deep level (1) depends on the respective analytical domain (Dopfer et al. 2004). Analytical domains include micro, meso and macro, which are not to be confused with micro and macro analysis in traditional economics (Dopfer and Potts 2008: 15–26). Contrary to received approaches, higher-level domains cannot be conceptualised by the aggregation of lower-level domains.

The micro domain addresses agents and agencies, that is, individuals and businesses, and enquires into the creation of new and the use of existing rules. The meso domain of rule populations—agents and agencies adopting a rule—looks into the diffusion of a rule into the public sphere. In turn, the macro domain analyses the interdependence and co-evolution of rules and their respective rule populations. Rule-based economics thus covers the following objects within its three domains:

1. Micro: Origination of a novel idea by an agent or by an agency, its eventual adoption as a rule; the agent as a rule carrier and locus of rule retention
2. Meso: The diffusion of a novel rule from one to many carriers; collective of adopters of rule *a* as population of rule *a*; institutions as rule populations with meta-stable entry and exit rates of carriers
3. Macro coordination: Integration of the novel rule population (i.e. institution) into the deep structure of existing knowledge

   Macro dynamics: Auto-generating mechanism of novelty creation through interaction between rule populations

Evolutionary micro analysis enquires into the evolution of knowledge within agents and agencies as the carriers of knowledge. It does so by distinguishing three phases: origination (Micro 1), selective adoption (Micro 2) and retention (Micro 3). Analysis of the origination of novelty is not restricted to previously nonextant ideas. On the contrary, it also includes concepts that are new to participants in the relevant market (Blind 2003: 17). The embedding of new rules in agents or routinisation in agencies leads to the retention of a rule in a carrier (Dopfer and Potts 2008: 43).

Meso analysis starts when the first transmission of a rule from the original carrier to another agent or an agency takes place, i.e. when the formation of a rule population commences (Meso 1). Conceived as diffusion (Meso 2), the concept of a meso trajectory maps the development of a rule population in time. Origination in Meso 1 refers not to an invention (as in Micro 1) but to an innovation as the latter necessarily requires the involvement of multiple agents in a market. The diffusion process in Meso 2 can follow quite different patterns depending on the type of diffusion, for example, via peer-to-peer transmission or via mass media, and on the availability of support by vested interests, for example, venture capital in the case of technological innovation. When the rule population reaches a saturation level in Meso 3, it attains *institutional* status.

The macro domain enquires into the consequences that the emergence of a rule population and the eventual attainment of institutional status may have for the overall economic system. The domain is subdivided into two fields. First, macro coordination analysis deals with change in the structure of the economy-wide knowledge base caused by the integration of a new rule population. Second, macro dynamics analyses how such integration itself eventually triggers new novelty and how this overall process is reiterated. Although both fields actually analyse dynamic processes, there is an important difference, which can be captured by distinguishing "adaptation dynamics" and "auto-generating dynamics".

When researching the effects of the emergence of a new rule population (a meso element) on the overall system of rules, the choice between a macro coordination analysis and an analysis of macro dynamics can be informed by looking into the effect exerted by the new rule population on associations between extant rules. If the emergence of the new rule population causes existing associations to vary by *intensity* only, the system is merely reacting and a macro coordination analysis will be sufficient. However, if existing associations vary by *quality* (i.e. breaking up or arising newly), the system has obviously evolved, which calls for a macro dynamic analysis.

In its most general reading, a rule represents a condition–action statement linking a condition to a specific outcome. Rules can be formulated in the form: "in order to…, do…". To conceive rules in a consistent way, Dopfer and Potts propose a taxonomy of rule classes and orders (Dopfer and Potts 2008: 6–10) that allows for a wider notion of rules than earlier approaches (e.g. Hodgson 1997).

Dopfer and Potts propose *four classes of rules* grouped into the categories of subject rules and object rules. Subject rules relate to the thinking and behaviour of economic agents. When subject rules address the cognition (theories) of agents, they are referred to as "cognitive rules"; when addressing the behaviour of agents (patterns of conduct), Dopfer and Potts refer to them as "behavioural rules". In contrast, object rules address the organisation of "things" including technical objects and humans alike. Object rules are referred to as "social rules" when governing the interaction of agents (the organisation of humans), while they are referred to as "technological rules" when addressing the arrangement of things.

To the distinction of rule classes, add *three orders of rules*. They help to understand the different ways in which rules are active in the economic system. At the centre of orders, 1st order operational rules provide the direct basis for operations (e.g. patents as technological rules for the operation of production) as well as for interactions (e.g. an auction rule as a cognitive rule for transactions).

In turn, rules controlling the overall functioning of an economy are designated 0th order constitutive rules. They represent the constituent basis on which all economic activity takes place and define the "opportunity space of permissible 1st order operations" (Dopfer and Potts 2008: 9). For example, law and legislation in a Hayekian reading (1973) represent a very important type of 0th order rules.

Finally, there are rules affecting the propensity to create, adopt and retain new rules, that is, to invent and to innovate in a social system. These are defined as 2nd order mechanism rules, where "mechanism" refers to the effect that 2nd order rules are having on other rules. Examples of 2nd order rules include aspects of the education system or a society's tolerance of failure. Likewise, the phenomena analysed in Witt's "learning to consume" (2001) can be understood in terms of 2nd order rules. In order to build a bridge to orthodox economics, the analysis of resources (such as capital or the present value of economic alternatives) corresponds to the study of operations conducted according to 1st order rules. Table 2.1 summarises the rule taxonomy.

It is instructive to compare this taxonomy with the empirically derived categories of rules in Oström and Basurto (2011: Table 2). "Boundary rules" and "payoff rules" closely correspond to 0th order constitutional rules, "choice rules" and "position rules" are a near equivalent to 1st order rules in the RBA, and the first "information rule" in Ostrom and Basurto could be conceived as a 2nd order rule (a rule pertaining to other rules). "Scope rules", however, would not be considered "rules" in the RBA but as outcomes of operations conducted according to specific technical rules. More details on these analogies can be found in some earlier work (Blind 2016).

Table 2.1 Taxonomy for the rule-based approach

Classes of rules			
Subject rules		Object rules	
Cognitive	Behavioural	Social	Technical
Orders of rules			
0th order constitutive rules:	Social, legal, political, cultural and other constituent rules		
1st order operational rules:	Rules originated, adopted and retained for operations		
2nd order mechanism rules:	Rules for changing the way of origination, adoption and retention		

Source: Rearranged from Dopfer and Potts (2008: 8, 9)

Distinguishing orders of rules also demonstrates the need for a history-friendly approach. For example, changes in 0th order rules, such as relevant elements of a culture's value system, need to be traced back beyond the respective investigation period in order to account for possible time lags caused by slow diffusion processes. Similar considerations apply to 2nd order rules where these exert influences through an education system. For instance, it will take a generation for the consequences of conceiving of an entrepreneur negatively as an "exploiting capitalist" or positively as a "creative adventurer" to play out. What is more, the blend of 0th and 2nd order rules is culturally conditioned and, therefore, highly regionally specific. Only by taking into account this background can one fully grasp local specificities in economic life. For instance, in the case of Japan, it would otherwise be difficult to understand the origins of particular 1st order rules such as LifeTime Employment or the Seniority Principle.

References

Aldrich HE, Hodgson GM (2008) In defence of generalized Darwinism. J Evol Econ 18:577–596

Blind GD (2003) Statistical methods for a dynamic analysis of meso-trajectories in evolutionary systems. M.A. Thesis, St. Gallen University

Blind G, Ziltener P (2014) Free trade live: insights from the Switzerland-Japan free trade and economic partnership agreement. In: Mottini R (ed) Yearbook 2014. Swiss Japanese Chamber of Commerce, Zurich, pp 53–63

Blind GD (2016) Behavioral rules: Veblen, Nelson-Winter, Oström and beyond. In: Frantz R, Chen S-H, Dopfer K, Heukelom F, Mousavi S (eds) Routledge handbook of behavioral economics. Milton Park, Routledge, pp 139–151

Chiavacci D, Blind G et al (2012) Ist das Freihandels- und wirtschaftliche Partnerschaftsabkommen (FHWPA) zwischen der Schweiz und Japan (bereits) eine Erfolgsgeschichte? Hauptergebnisse einer empirischen Analyse zu Umsetzung und Wirkung. Asiat Stud 66(1):19–56

Dopfer K (2004) The economic agent as rule maker and rule user: Homo sapiens oeconomicus. J Evol Econ 14:177–195

Dopfer K, Potts J (2008) The general theory of economic evolution. Routledge, London

Dopfer K, Foster J et al (2004) Micro-meso-macro. J Evol Econ 14(3):263–279

Foster J (1987) Evolutionary macroeconomics. Georg Allen Unwin, London

Grebel T, Pyka A et al (2003) An evolutionary approach to the theory of entrepreneurship. Ind Innov 10(4):493–514

Hayek FA (1973) Law, legislation, and liberty: rules and order. The University of Chicago Press, Chicago

Hodgson GM (1993) Economics and evolution: bringing life back into economics. Polity Press, Cambridge

Hodgson GM (1997) The ubiquity of habits and rules. Camb J Econ 21:663–684

Katzner DW (2002) What are the questions. J Post-Keynesian Econ 25(1):51–68

Loasby B (1991) Equilibrium and evolution: an exploration of connecting principles in economics. Manchester University Press, Manchester

Marshall A (1920 [1890]) Principles of economics. Macmillan, London

Metcalfe JS (1998) Evolutionary economics and creative destruction. Routledge, London

Nelson R, Winter S (1982) An evolutionary theory of economic change. Harvard University Press, Cambridge

Oström E, Basurto X (2011) Crafting analytical tools to study institutional change. J Inst Econ 7(3):317–343

Shackle GLS (1979) Imagination and the nature of choice. Edinburgh University Press, Edinburgh

Steineck C (2013) Truth, time, and the extended umwelt principle: conceptual limits and methodological constraints. In: Parker JA, Harris PA, Steineck C (eds) Time: limits and constraints. Brill, Leiden, Boston, pp 350–365

Witt U (1993) Evolutionary economics. Edward Elgar, Aldershot

Witt U (2001) Learning to consume – a theory of wants and the growth of demand. J Evol Econ 11(1):23–36

Chapter 3
The Rule-Based Economy and the Function of the Entrepreneur

Abstract Concrete examples are needed to illustrate the concept of rules and corresponding operations as key elements of a rule-based economy. Importantly, we demonstrate how the understanding of rules is a prerequisite for understanding corresponding operations. We then explore the role of the entrepreneur in an evolving rule economy. Taking reference to technological rules, we illustrate the function of the entrepreneur across analytical levels (micro, meso and macro) and then achieve generalisation of the entrepreneurial function for all classes of rules. Building on these insights, we propose a general definition of the entrepreneurial function in terms of a "propagator role", which involves the diffusion of new rules by linking makers to users.

This chapter has three aims: first, it uses concrete examples to illustrate the key elements of rule-based analysis in their capacity as part of a rule-based economy; second, it explores the role and function of the entrepreneur in an evolving economy; and third, it uses insights thus gained to develop a general definition of the entrepreneurial function in terms of a "propagator role".

3.1 Rules in an Evolving Economy

The study of technology can help us to understand the idea of an economy evolving with its "rule configurations" (Oström and Basurto 2011; Blind 2016). In the innovation dynamics literature, the notion of a "technological trajectory" has been widely adopted since its introduction (Dosi 1982) and can help to illustrate our purposes. In evolutionary industrial economics, differential growth has been explained as the consequence of differential growth rates of the underlying knowledge (Metcalfe 2005). An even more explicit distinction can be found in the work of Hirooka. He conceptualised the number of patents as a "technological trajectory" and the number of appearances of new products as a "developmental trajectory" (2006). This corresponds to the distinction between evolutionary and orthodox analysis: patents as rules are an object of evolutionary analysis, while products developed from them are tradable physical goods open to orthodox analysis. In rule-based economics, the distinction between rules and economic operations embraces this view.

G.D. Blind, *The Entrepreneur in Rule-Based Economics*, Economic Complexity and Evolution, DOI 10.1007/978-3-319-62779-3_3

It is difficult to grasp the difference between macro coordination analysis and the analysis of macro dynamics. Again, technological rules offer the best real-world examples. For macro coordination analysis, imagine a technical apparatus such as the Anti-Skid System, which turned out to complement existing technology. While new associations arose, existing associations did not break up but merely changed in intensity. On the operational level, there are still brake pads and friction plates. In contrast, the invention of the combustion engine and its ensuing market penetration caused many existing associations to be disentangled or even to reverse. The combustion engine, of course, "crowded out" the steam engine over the course of several decades.

Technological rules, as one important rule class, refer to the organisation of "things". Although technological rules are undoubtedly important drivers of economic growth and development, evolutionary economics tries to also integrate insights from other social sciences as well as from natural sciences (Nishibe 2006: 8; Dopfer and Potts 2008: 32). Here, the RBA defines "social rules" as referring to the organisation of humans. Imagine, for instance, a novel social rule that designates performance as the determiner of pay, and let this rule of PERFORMANCE PAY enter a system where a rule of SENIORITY PAY applied previously. If this new social rule is added as a bonus system, the rule turns out to be complementary to the existing set. Macro coordination would then suffice to investigate the effects on extant rules such as the behavioural rule of cooperation or the cognitive rule of trust. If, however, PERFORMANCE PAY were to entirely replace the existing SENIORITY PAY, existing associations would break up. Such a phenomenon would necessitate a macro dynamic analysis that would also explore how the disruption this would involve eventually triggers the emergence of a novel rule (such as salary insurance with the premium pegged to business cycle fluctuation).

In contrast to technological and social rules that refer to physical objects, behavioural and cognitive rules are internal to the minds of individuals. In spite of this different point of reference, analytical consequences of the emergence of a new rule population are the same. Imagine, for instance, the behavioural rule of a FAREWELL GIFT becoming popularised as an element of etiquette. While this might eventually reduce the importance of welcome gifts, it will not render them unappreciated. Hence, macro coordination analysis would suffice to gain an understanding of how the intensity of existing associations might change. If, however, a new pattern of social conduct such as premarital cohabitation emerges in a society, it may cause many existing associations to be broken or even to reverse, bringing about new novelty. The spread of this behavioural pattern, for example, caused new legislation to be introduced during the 1960s and 1970s.

The same distinction also applies to cognitive rules, which—for the sake of simplicity—we may call "theories" at this point. Consider, for instance, how quantum mechanics has emerged since the 1920s. In its relation to laser physics and to nuclear physics, it has led to new associations, yet it did not imply the falsification of the pre-existing theoretical body. Analytically, this could be captured as a macro coordination process. In an example from a more familiar domain, that of monetarism and its opposition to Keynesianism, we can see that some associations broke up or even went into reverse. Hence, this would be a subject to be studied through an analysis of macro dynamics.

3.2 The Function of Entrepreneurs in a Rule-Based Economy

By tracing the analytical path of a rule along its trajectories through the domains of micro, meso and macro, it becomes possible to illustrate the function of the entrepreneur in a rule-based economy. In this section, we outline the entrepreneurial function with implicit reference to technological rules. This will serve as a basis for the subsequent generalisation of the function for all classes of rules.

In the micro domain, the analytical focus is the origination of new rules. While entrepreneurs may effectively invent a rule, many rules originate from non-entrepreneurial agents such as scientists (Grebel 2013). It is also important to note that both a deliberate quest for novelty and fortuitous circumstances may equally well lead to the emergence of new rules. What follows has been aptly described by Hagemann: "The mainspring of economic progress is invention, which causes an impulse that works its way through the profit mechanism" (2008: 346).

It is in this profit mechanism, analysed in the meso domain, that the entrepreneur becomes a central figure. Using his imaginative capacity—not calculus—the entrepreneur assesses the market potential inherent in a new rule. Where this assessment delivers a positive image of market potential, the entrepreneur starts his or her mission. In doing so, he or she assumes two decisive functions: (1) persuading financiers to sponsor the marketing of the novelty and (2) persuading market participants to pay for access to the novelty. From the perspective of a rule-based economics, markets are the mechanisms regulating the frequency of rule use for operations. This holds equally for all types of markets from—albeit unrealistic—perfect competition to the monopolies granted by patent protection.

Yet such distinction of market types provides important guidance for understanding the role of rule entrepreneurs. For instance, the marketing of patent-protected products relies on pure market penetration strategies for the goods concerned. Such strategies require managerial skills but are of no interest to the rule entrepreneur. In this type of market, the role of the rule entrepreneur is that of an intrapreneur who (1) persuades superiors to sponsor his pitch and (2) competes on the internal market for novelty. In contrast, the external licencing of patents entirely fits the mission of a rule entrepreneur.

The emergence of a rule population represents a meso phenomenon. For instance, firms that have adopted a certain technology are referred to as carriers of the underlying rule. In this knowledge diffusion process, entrepreneurs are key as they broker access to the novel rule. The revenues from granting such access—referred to as "generic profits" (Dopfer and Potts 2008: 36)—are shared between entrepreneurs and financiers.

As a rule population grows, that is, as more agents acquire access to the rule, the smaller generic profits become, and the more likely this process is to affect the existing structure of rules. At this junction, rule-based macro analysis investigates how the system of extant rules reacts (macro coordination) or how it eventually evolves (macro dynamics). If the system of rules happens to evolve, it does so either because the disturbance to the existing rule structure has triggered the origination of yet another new rule or because the depletion of "generic profits" forces entrepreneurs to search for new novelty.

The economics discipline has been preoccupied with a discussion centring on the function of the entrepreneur. Often referred to as the "Kirzner–Schumpeter divide" (compare, e.g. Grebel et al. 2003), it centres on the distinction between an equilibrium-creating and an equilibrium-disturbing entrepreneur (e.g. Metcalfe 2004; Douhan et al. 2007; Roininen and Ylinenpää 2009), essentially drawing a line between stationary and evolutionary perspectives of the economy (Schneider 1953[1949]:194; Blind and Pyka 2015:247).

At the *rule level*, this distinction becomes obsolete, because a "rule equilibrium" would contradict the very principle of evolution. Admittedly, the emergence of a new rule population may stabilise the current macro rule structure and may even cause an economy to temporarily enter a meta-stable state where no novel rules emerge and no existing rules cease to apply. Yet, where chance fails to produce new novelty, entrepreneurs will work on finding it. This is because the generic profits accrued from granting access to the rule they are exploiting are continuously on the decline. Yet, until they find new novelty, an economic system may temporarily enter a meta-stable state.

At this point, it is important to note that even where the emergence of a rule population leads to a temporary stabilisation of the macro structure of rules, the *level of operations* may experience the kind of phenomena described by Schumpeter as evidence of creative destruction, such as fierce competition or the decline of an industry. What is more, the operational exploitation of an existing rule may also cause the emergence of a novel rule. From this we can infer that a clear-cut distinction between rule and operational levels of analysis is essential. From the vantage point of rule-based economics, the entrepreneur acts as a broker between the two levels, enabling the conduct of operations on a specific rule and striving for new novelty once generic profits from an earlier rule become depleted.

3.3 Generalised Roles of Inventors, Entrepreneurs and Financiers

The roles of inventors, entrepreneurs and financiers in the diffusion of a rule in a market apply in full to technological rules, but only partially to the other three classes of rules. With cognitive rules, for instance, entrepreneurs and financiers will only assume

Table 3.1 Functions of originators, propagators and supporters in rule diffusion

	Rule class			
Function	Cognitive	Behavioural	Social	Technological
Originator	Philosopher, theorist	Trendsetter, avant-garde	Social reformer, scholars	Inventor
Propagator	Entrepreneur, social entrepreneur, politicians, managers			Entrepreneur
Supporter	Rational and/or normative stakeholders			*Financier*

their roles if applying the rule yields a directly marketable product or service. However, this will often not be the case. As similar considerations apply to behavioural and social rules, it is necessary to develop a role typology for these three classes of rules. Building on Blind (2003) Table 3.1 uses the umbrella terms of originator, propagator and supporter to designate the three functions. It also gives a number of examples of the type of individuals that might assume these roles for the four classes of rules.

In essence, the four rule classes enable the entire diversity of a society to be captured. This general social science view turns into economic analysis whenever the rules under scrutiny enable operations that have direct or indirect implications for the economic sphere. From a methodological viewpoint, integrating cognitive, behavioural and social rules into the analytical framework allows insights to be easily accommodated in an economics enquiry as they are available from various social science disciplines.

The function of the entrepreneur in a rule-based economy is thus the propagation of new rules through the brokering of rule access. Where agents assume their *propagator* role, they cause the emergence of new rule populations via the diffusion of the rules into the public sphere. As we have seen, the entrepreneur is just one of the figures that may lend themselves to the role of *rule propagator*. Note that rules propagated by other figures should also be integrated into economic analysis where they cause economic consequences.

References

Blind GD (2003) Statistical methods for a dynamic analysis of meso-trajectories in evolutionary systems. M.A. Thesis, St. Gallen University

Blind GD (2016) Behavioral rules: Veblen, Nelson-Winter, Oström and beyond. In: Frantz R, Chen S-H, Dopfer K, Heukelom F, Mousavi S (eds) Routledge handbook of behavioral economics. Routledge, Milton Park, pp 139–151

Blind GD, Pyka A (2015) Erich Schneider: the admiring disciple who did not become a follower. J Evol Econ 25(1):239–252

Dopfer K, Potts J (2008) The general theory of economic evolution. Routledge, London

Dosi G (1982) Technological paradigms and technological trajectories. Res Policy 11:147–162

Douhan R, Eliasson G et al (2007) Israel M. Kirzner: an outstanding Austrian contributor to the economics of entrepreneurship. Small Bus Econ 29:213–223

Grebel T (2013) On the tradeoff between similarity and diversity in the creation of novelty in basic science. Struct Chang Econ Dyn 27:66–78

Grebel T, Pyka A et al (2003) An evolutionary approach to the theory of entrepreneurship. Ind Innov 10(4):493–514

Hagemann H (2008) Capital, growth, and production disequilibria: on the employment consequences of new technologies. In: Scazzieri R, Sen A, Zamagni S (eds) Markets, money and capital. Cambridge University Press, Cambridge, pp 346–366

Hirooka M (2006) Innovation dynamism and economic growth: a nonlinear perspective. Edward Elgar, Cheltenham

Metcalfe S (2004) The entrepreneur and the style of modern economics. J Evol Econ 14:157–175

Metcalfe S (2005) Evolutionary concepts in relation to evolutionary economics. In: Dopfer K (ed) The evolutionary foundation of economics. Cambridge University Press, Cambridge, pp 391–430

Nishibe M (2006) Redefining evolutionary economics. Evol Inst Econ Rev 3(1):3–25

Oström E, Basurto X (2011) Crafting analytical tools to study institutional change. J Inst Econ 7(3):317–343

Roininen S, Ylinenpää H (2009) Schumpeterian versus Kirznerian entrepreneurship. J Small Bus Enterprise Dev 16(3):504–520

Schneider E (1953[1949]) Einführung in die Wirtschaftstheorie II, 2nd edn. JCB Mohr (Paul Siebeck), Tübingen

Chapter 4
The Entrepreneurial Process in Terms of Rules

Abstract This chapter discusses the rule of entrepreneurship as an object of study in empirical research. It illustrates how agents eventually become carriers of that rule and under what circumstances they use it in the operation of starting a business. First, a definition of the "entrepreneurial process" in terms of rules is developed. In a nutshell, ENTREPRENEURIAL SPIRIT qualifies as a 2nd order rule that moderates the odds of becoming a latent entrepreneur or, in rule terms, of adopting the 1st order rule of INDIVIDUAL ENTREPRENEURSHIP. Next, we show how this understanding enables an integrated account of latent and actual, necessity- and opportunity-driven entrepreneurship and of entrepreneurial attitudes. Reviewing a number of important earlier theoretical approaches we synthesise these into a series of propositions. Importantly, specific empirical information is required for developing these propositions further into a locally valid theorem.

While the previous chapter proposed a generalised theoretical view of the propagator role frequently assumed by entrepreneurs in an evolving economy, we now consider the rule of entrepreneurship as an object of study in rule-based empirical research. We need to understand how agents eventually become carriers of that rule and under what circumstances they use it in the operation of starting a business.

From a micro perspective, this chapter first explores how different dimensions of entrepreneurship can be conceived in terms of rules. Based on that understanding, we discuss the conditions that may trigger the operation of becoming self-employed as an application of the entrepreneurship rule. Next, for a triangulation of our approach, we mirror it against a non-exhaustive number of received theoretical propositions pertaining to the entrepreneur. The final section of the chapter discusses the limits to general theory building implied by the decisively localist stance of rule-based economics.

G.D. Blind, *The Entrepreneur in Rule-Based Economics*, Economic Complexity and Evolution, DOI 10.1007/978-3-319-62779-3_4

4.1 Dimensions and Forms of Entrepreneurship

The relevant entrepreneurship rule reads: "To create income, be self-employed". When reasoning with rules, an agent adhering to the idea of earning income from self-employment represents a carrier of the entrepreneurship rule. The correct designation of the self-referential nature of the rule—the adopter as point of reference—is Individual Entrepreneurship (henceforth: "IE"). Starting a business by becoming self-employed is obviously an economic operation. As all economic operations originate from the application of a rule, we can identify IE as the underlying 1st order rule. Thus, the action of becoming self-employed equals an operation conducted on the basis of the IE rule.

Note that recent empirical entrepreneurship research in the business studies filed has made an almost equivalent distinction between "latent" and "actual" entrepreneurship (Storey and Johnson 1987). From the perspective of a rule-based economics, a latent entrepreneur is an agent who has adopted the IE rule, that is, who has become its carrier, but who has not yet conducted an operation based on that rule. In that sense, we may define as latent entrepreneur any agent–carrier of the IE rule prior to initial rule use for the operation of becoming self-employed.

Obviously, the business studies view makes an equivalent distinction between the wish to become self-employed and the actual operation of becoming self-employed. However, this view does not trace the rule of individual entrepreneurship independently: the latent entrepreneur ceases to exist when he or she turns into an actual one. In contrast, conducting an initial operation does not cause the carrier to abandon the IE rule. On the contrary, the agent continues to retain that rule.

Another recent concept developed within applied business studies that can equally be systematically conceptualised in a rule-based economics is "entrepreneurial attitudes and perceptions" (Global Entrepreneurship Monitor 1999–2013), recently also analysed as "entrepreneurial identity" (Obschonka et al. 2015). Here, rule-based reasoning suggests that these attitudes, perceptions, or identity may be captured as the population of agents that believe entrepreneurship represents a desirable and respected career option. We define these individuals as carriers of an Entrepreneurial Spirit rule (henceforth: ES). Population size, in turn, essentially corresponds to the general appreciation of self-employment in a society. As a 2nd order cognitive rule, ES impacts positively on the 1st order rule of individual entrepreneurship. In other words, the more positively entrepreneurship is regarded in a society (i.e. the larger the ES population), the more the number of latent entrepreneurs will grow.

Taking this reasoning one step further, the economic operation of actually becoming self-employed is directly influenced by the 2nd order ES rule. In business studies language, there would be "positive entrepreneurial attitudes as increasing the likelihood of conversion from latent to actual entrepreneurship". Joining these parts into an integrated view, we can note that actual business start-ups as economic

Table 4.1 The entrepreneurial process in terms of rules

RBA terminology	Entrepreneurship terminology	Definition
2nd order cognitive rule ENTREPRENEURIAL SPIRIT (ES) *Operation based on* ES	Entrepreneurial attitudes *NA*	General appreciation of self-employment *Any action or act of cognition derived from this conviction*
1st order behavioural rule INDIVIDUAL ENTREPRENEURSHIP (IE) *Operation based on* IE	Latent entrepreneurship *Actual entrepreneurship*	Individual wish to become self-employed *Becoming and being self-employed*

operations will depend on the size of the 1st order rule population of INDIVIDUAL ENTREPRENEURSHIP, with the latter being influenced by 2nd order ENTREPRENEURIAL SPIRIT. Table 4.1 summarises this reasoning and shows the terms used in the rule-based analysis and in business studies.

4.2 Reasons to Apply Individual Entrepreneurship in a Start-Up Operation

To understand how start-up operations come about, it is helpful to analyse the various interactions between the rules of INDIVIDUAL ENTREPRENEURSHIP and ENTREPRENEURIAL SPIRIT (IE AND ES). Here again, we can draw some inspiration from empirical research in business studies, which makes a distinction between "necessity-driven entrepreneurship" and "opportunity-driven entrepreneurship" (Swett Mansfield 1927; Dennis 1996; Global Entrepreneurship Monitor 1999–2013). While the latter refers to the choice of self-employment as an occupation where alternative sources of income are available, the former characterises a situation where becoming an entrepreneur results from the absence or loss of alternative sources of income.

The central question of whether or not a particular business start-up is the result of a deliberate choice does not affect the distinction between the IE rule and the operation of actual entrepreneurship. While opportunity-driven entrepreneurship is clearly a deliberate choice, the link between necessity-driven entrepreneurship and latent entrepreneurship might be less obvious. At this point, a case-by-case analysis of the process quality in "rule configurations" (Oström and Basurto 2011: 318, Blind 2016: 149) helps to reflect on the conditions that make an agent adopt the IE rule.

We start with what we might call "true necessity entrepreneurship", where an agent who was neither a carrier of ES nor of IE at time $t = 0$ finds himself without sufficient income at time $t = n$. This necessity effectively forces the agent to adopt the idea of "earning income through self-employment", which is the IE rule. Applying the IE rule by conducting a corresponding operation in $t = n + 1$ equates to putting into practice the best business idea that he or she can think of. Business scholars refer to insufficient income as the "push hypothesis" in explaining entrepreneurship.

Next, imagine exactly the opposite situation of "unrestricted opportunity entrepreneurship", where a carrier of ES newly adopts IE after assessment against the existing set of rules that he is retaining at $t = 0$. In this second case, the agent will seek to establish his/her business immediately at $t = 1$. As this case implies the deliberate adoption of the IE rule, such cases are analysed in business studies as a "pull hypothesis".

Both 0th order rules and 2nd order rules might effectively inhibit the adoption of IE, resulting in two further distinct cases in addition to the two described above. The third case might be termed "time-lagged opportunity entrepreneurship". In this case, an existing carrier of ES adopts IE in $t = 0$ but, due to restrictions imposed by a 0th order rule such as trade regulations, does not commence his business in $t = 1$. However, if that restriction eventually becomes obsolete in $t = n$, start-up can be expected for $t = n + 1$. Entrepreneurship studies do not as yet have a concept corresponding to this type of business formation.

Finally, the fourth case is "necessity-induced opportunity entrepreneurship". Imagine an agent who adopts ES at $t = 0$ and deliberates about also adopting IE. At this point, his set of 2nd order rules inhibits the adoption of IE. Accordingly, he decides in favour of an alternative source of income. In the event where the agent is short of this alternative source of income at $t = n$, he will see the event as an opportunity. Accordingly, he will cease to retain inhibiting 2nd order rules and will start his business at $t = n + 1$. While clearly a hybrid situation, it differs from the first case of "true necessity entrepreneurship" in regarding the drying up of an alternative source of income either as an opportunity or as a necessity. As with the third type, entrepreneurship research has not yet conceptualised this type of business formation. Table 4.2 summarises the four cases identified.

Table 4.2 Rule-based analysis of the entrepreneurial process

Time t	True necessity entrepreneurship	Unrestricted opportunity entrepreneurship	Time-lagged opportunity entrepreneurship	Necessity-induced opportunity entrepreneurship
0	*ES* not adopted *IE* not adopted	*ES* retained *IE* newly adopted	*ES* retained IE newly adopted	*ES* newly adopted 2nd order rule(s) either inhibit adoption of *IE* or conduct of operations on *IE*
1	–	Operation on *IE* (start-up)	Operation on *IE* inhibited by 0th order rule	No operation on *IE*
n	*ES* and *IE* newly adopted by necessity		0th order rule becomes obsolete	*IE* newly adopted as inhibiting 2nd order rule (s) are relinquished by necessity
$n + 1$	Operation on *IE*		Operation on *IE*	Operation on *IE*

Note: *ES* ENTREPRENEURIAL SPIRIT, *IE* INDIVIDUAL ENTREPRENEURSHIP

4.3 Propositions on Entrepreneurship

We are ultimately to enquire the determinants of business formation rates, that is, the rate at which carriers of the IE rule are using that rule in the operation of starting a business. Within the micro–meso–macro framework, the analysis of the IE rule population and its determinants corresponds to a study of the population of carriers of the IE rule in its macro structural environment, that is, the nexus of rule populations associated with it. While this includes a meso perspective on the IE rule population and a macro perspective on its determinants, it does not mean to exclude the micro perspective of the RBA architecture. On the contrary, conducting a meso study requires an understanding of the micro process of rule adoption and retention because the size of the IE rule population, that is, the number of carriers of the IE rule, depends on the rule choices of individual agents. At the operational level, we are interested in how often carriers of the IE rule are applying the rule by starting a business.

The following summary seeks to match the approach to entrepreneurship that we have developed so far with a number of key theoretical views on entrepreneurship, keeping in mind the three questions formulated in the Introduction: what *is* an entrepreneur (definition), who *becomes* one (occupational choice) and what does an entrepreneur *do* (entrepreneurial activity)?

Starting with the *definition*, we agree with Stanley Metcalfe (2004) "that it is presumptuous to conceive of a simple, unifying approach". What is arguably already presumptuous in purely theoretical reasoning might ultimately turn out to be impossible when put into empirical practice. We therefore resort to an empirically viable definition of the entrepreneur as "anyone who starts a business". Current entrepreneurship research practice (Brockhaus 1987) implies that the operation of becoming self-employed is an application of the IE rule. The underlying idea reads as follows: "In the pursuit of earning income, one shall create one's own employment".

In one of Schumpeter's discussions of the entrepreneur, we find the following definitional statement that endorses the empirical definition used in this research: "it is leadership rather than ownership that matters" (1939: 102). In a modern reading, we would understand leadership as "process ownership" or, in more general terms, as "decision-making power". As the notion of self-employment involves the entrepreneur taking all relevant decisions, our definition conforms not only with Schumpeter's but also with the view of Marshall who equally stresses the importance of leadership for entrepreneurs: "in his rôle of employer he must be a natural leader of men" (Marshall 1920[1890]: 297).

On entrepreneurial risk-taking, Schumpeter argues: "it is the capitalist who bears the risk. The entrepreneur does so only to the extent to which, besides being an entrepreneur, he is also a capitalist, but qua entrepreneur he loses other people's money" (1939: 102–103). In light of our empirically inspired definition of entrepreneurs as self-employed individuals who take a substantial equity stake and hence risk, we refine our definition to exclude both corporate entrepreneurship (implicit already in Tuttle 1927; also referred to as "intrapreneurship") and the few special cases where business ventures receive full non-collateralised external funding.[1]

Our view of a risk-taking self-employed (capitalist) entrepreneur coincides with a much older observation made by Johann Heinrich Thünen as early as 1826. In a passage also identified by Engelhardt (2008: 149), Thünen notes[2]:

> At times, when the vicissitude of economic conditions leads to losses and the fortune and honour of the entrepreneur are at stake, the mind of the entrepreneur is engaged with the one single thought on how to fend off disaster—and sleep will escape from his layer.
> (Thünen 1990[1826]: 336)

Rule-based economics holds that the future is essentially open. This is because the emergence of new rules cannot be predicted and because fluctuations in extant rule populations can hardly be anticipated. In modern economies, where most risks can be insured, Knight's concept of uncertainty—denying the possibility of making profits in the absence of "universal foreknowledge" (Knight 1964 [1921]: 36)—becomes essential. This concept allows for profits even in an equilibrium economy where all *risks* can be fully priced. Some 30 years later, Mises specifies the nature of operational uncertainty that any self-employed individual faces: "The ultimate source from which entrepreneurial profit and loss are derived is the uncertainty of the future constellation of demand and supply" (Mises 1998 [1949]: 291). Against that background, we note that self-employment entails relatively larger operational uncertainty than dependent employment.

In summary, we can note that the empirically inspired definition of the entrepreneur as a newly self-employed individual is in line with the central arguments of Marshall and Schumpeter. What is more, Schumpeter's distinction between the entrepreneurial function and the capitalist function of the entrepreneur corresponds to the propagator and supporter roles introduced earlier (see Table 3.1). Empirical observation shows that self-employment typically involves elements of both functions as most entrepreneurs are facing uncertainty pertaining both to income and to their equity stake.

Occupational choice is guided by the individual rule sets of agents and by their personal circumstances. Having recourse to the individual rule set of agents enables us to explain what orthodox economics would label "irrational behaviour". From their perspective, agents opting for self-employment with unpredictable profits do behave irrationally. With the concept of rules, we have a powerful analytical tool to explain what Schumpeter hinted at when he referred to entrepreneurs as "acting differently than one would expect according to the static laws" (Schumpeter 1912). Many years later, Shackle phrased this more pointedly: "How

[1]Even within the venture capital industry, this is an exceptional case as entrepreneurs typically have to contribute a significant equity stake.

[2]The German original reads: "In solchen Zeiten, wo durch die Wechselfälle der Konjunktur das Geschäft große Verluste bringt und das Vermögen und die Ehre des Unternehmers auf dem Spiel stehen, ist der Geist desselben von dem einen Gedanken, wie er das Unglück von sich abwenden kann, erfüllt – und der Schlaf flieht ihn auf seinem Lager".

can choice be based on foreknowledge of what that choice is called on to create?" (Shackle 1979: 58).

From the perspective of a rule-based economics, a significant number of actors do not follow the cognitive rule of EXPECTED VALUE MAXIMISATION in their economic choices. A hallmark of rule-based economics, it allows for heterogeneous agents, and this heterogeneity refers to the set of rules that they have adopted. Where an agent decides in favour of self-employment, the IE rule has obviously overridden all other rules including EXPECTED VALUE MAXIMISATION.

It is clear from these considerations that we need to understand what makes for the differences in the rules that individual agents have adopted and that they are retaining. In order to be able to adopt a rule, agents need to be open to learning, an insight documented much earlier by Hayek when he identified markets as a learning process with "individual participants gradually learning the relevant circumstances" (1948: 100). In rule-based economics, "relevant circumstances" refer to agents adopting rules that are new to them (for an example of rule adoption as reaction to relevant circumstance, compare the "Visitors to Rome-effect" modelled in Blind and Lottanti 2017). Synthesising this into a theoretical statement, we note that agents are not born as (latent) entrepreneurs, but that they will eventually adopt the IE rule over the course of their lives.

Having seen how differences in rule sets between agents make for heterogeneity, we need to understand next what makes agents adopt a rule in general and the IE rule in particular. In essence, the adoption of a rule requires a cognitive process. As such, it is strongly influenced by perceptions, education and experience. In an economics context, the significance of these factors has been emphasised, for example, by Drucker who referred to the perception of market opportunities (2002 [1985]) or in Schultz's human capital theory (1975). In rule-based theorising, the story starts with education as one major source of 2nd order rules from the perspective of individual agents. Perceptions, then, are strongly guided by 2nd order rules. Experience, in turn, corresponds to the history of selective rule adoption and retention.

At this point, we have to look deeper into the cognitive process of selective rule adoption. When an agent comes to know about a rule, he will assess its compatibility with his extant set of rules. If it contradicts a rule that he already retains, a direct comparison is required. Through this process, 2nd order rules may strongly influence the propensity to adopt or reject a novel rule (where "novel" relates to the perspective of the individual agent). Whether or not a specific 2nd order rule impacts on the adoption of a 1st order rule in an individual case depends upon the retention of that 2nd order rule by the agent concerned. As the extant set of rules differs between agents, the outcome of this assessment cannot be inferred ex ante. However, the size of the respective rule population directly translates into a corresponding probability function. Therefore, an empirical study on the frequency of start-up operations can be conducted using a multi-population approach.

We are now in a position to discuss a number of examples of 2nd order rules impacting on the likelihood of adopting the IE rule. For a start, we might point to the operation of "uncertainty avoidance" in Hofstede's discussion of the dimensions of culture (1980) as a frequently cited factor diminishing the propensity to self-employment (compare George and Zahra 2002: 36). From a rule-based perspective, avoiding uncertainty represents the operation associated with an underlying cognitive rule, which—in the case of Japan—can be identified as the 2nd order cognitive rule Stigma of Failure. With this in mind, we can understand how the rule directly impacts on the process of selective adoption of the IE rule. Carriers of Stigma of Failure will perceive as an incalculable risk what noncarriers might perceive as entrepreneurial opportunity.

We have already identified Entrepreneurial Spirit (ES) as another directly relevant 2nd order rule for the eventual adoption of the IE rule. As a 2nd order rule, it is acquired through the influence of both kin and non-kin educators. Hence, the ES rule population also depends on the education system, which may teach the concept of entrepreneur rather negatively as a "capitalist exploiter" or positively as a "creative adventurer". Or, as Shapero and Sokol put it, "in a social system that places a high value on the formation of new ventures, more individuals will choose that path" (1982: 83).

Likewise, the adoption of the IE rule depends on Business Sentiment, a 2nd order cognitive rule impacting on the judgement of entrepreneurship as a viable economic option. This was observed by Marx during his studies of the British economy in the late 1840s. He saw *Unternehmungsgeist* as depending strongly on the business cycle (2004: 482). It is due to this kind of mechanism influencing perception that Dopfer and Potts have chosen to label 2nd order rules as "mechanism rules" (Dopfer and Potts 2008: 9).

In a population of agents, the probability of an agent adopting a specific rule will naturally be conditional upon certain characteristics of the agents. In analogy with *milieu* studies in sociology and with the analysis of customer segments by marketing scholars, we argue that the "social environment" specific to distinct subgroups of agents is an important factor in explaining the adoption of the IE rule. These characteristics may relate to various aspects of (a) the individual socio-economic profile and (b) the narrower (family) or wider (community) social environment.

With regard to the former, empirical studies have actually found that skill level or asset endowments are discriminating factors (Meager 1992). With regard to the latter, Alfred Marshall noted: "progress is most rapid in those parts of the country in which the greatest proportion of the leaders of industry are the sons of working men" (Marshall 1920 [1890]: 212). An analysis of the socio-economic profile of the "founder force"—the group of agents conducting start-up operations on the IE rule—will suggest which factors are relevant to establishing subgroups of agents.

In a nutshell, the occupational choice of self-employment equals irrational behaviour or—paraphrasing Schumpeter—behaviour deviating from "the static laws". The process of choice involves learning the relevant rules, where the critical learning of the IE rule depends on the set of rules already retained by the agent concerned. While this set cannot be known for the individual agent, the population approach helps to identify corresponding probabilities. As the latter varies with the socio-economic characteristics of agents, such as Marshall's reference to the "sons of working men", the consideration of subgroups is essential for the study of the adoption of the IE rule.

Turning finally to the level of operations—what the entrepreneur *does*—we hold that the application of the IE rule through the operation of a business start-up is the moment when "latent" entrepreneurship turns into "actual" entrepreneurship. We have further argued with Dopfer and Potts that 0th order rules of permissible operations tightly control the frequency with which 1st order rules are applied (Dopfer and Potts 2008: 9). This view, which implies that local laws and institutions impact on the frequency of business formation, is variously mirrored in the literature. For instance, government-led innovation promotion (Audretsch 2004), bankruptcy law (Armour and Cumming 2008), available funding sources (Mayer et al. 2005) or administrative complexities (Grilo and Thurik 2008) are among the topics frequently raised.

Equilibrium-disturbing Schumpeterian entrepreneurship has been contrasted with equilibrium-creating Kirznerian entrepreneurship, giving rise to a heated debate for decades. The distinction is theoretically most important. Specifically, it becomes relevant in evolutionary macro dynamics, which conceptualises how the emergence of a new rule population may cause the creation of new novelty. As we have seen, bringing a *new* rule to the market requires a "propagator" (see Table 3.1), a role frequently assumed by entrepreneurs. Equilibrium-disturbing entrepreneurship involves the bringing to the market of the products obtained from conducting operations on a novel rule. In turn, equilibrium-creating entrepreneurship refers to the exploitation of extant rules. In business terms, this distinction will be frequently recognised as a "first mover versus second mover or follower" strategy.

Once the business is started, the question as to what an entrepreneur actually *does* changes to: "How does an entrepreneur run his or her business?" A wide range of issues around the growth and development of firms have been discussed under the label of entrepreneurship (compare, e.g. Witt 2000). Yet, the very question itself implies that the story of the entrepreneur in its original sense comes to an end when he changes from founder to manager. This coincides with our empirically inspired definition of the entrepreneur as "anyone who starts a business", but not as "anyone who starts or *runs* a business".

In the section above, we have investigated the rule-based reading of entrepreneurship against a non-exhaustive number of received notions of certain aspects of the entrepreneurial process. We now convert our findings into a series of theoretical propositions. Heterogeneity of agents and historic time, that is, the ability of agents to learn, enter the argument as premises.

Proposition 1: The opportunity-driven start-up of a business by an individual agent corresponds to an operation conducted by applying the previously adopted rule of INDIVIDUAL ENTREPRENEURSHIP (IE) and implies the taking of significant risks that cannot be insured.

Proposition 2: Adoption of IE may originate from complementarity with the extant rule set and/or from necessity, i.e. when the agent is short of an alternative source of income.

Proposition 3: The likelihood that the rules of ENTREPRENEURIAL SPIRIT (ES) and of IE will be adopted is strongly influenced by 2nd order rules conditioning agents' perceptions as a result of education, the social environment and other experiences.

Proposition 4: The 2nd order rule of EXPECTED VALUE MAXIMISATION (EVM or "rational choice") may only be prevalent among entrepreneurs for whom the adoption of IE and eventual subsequent start-up operations were caused by absence or loss of alternative sources of income.

Proposition 5: Both 0th order and 2nd order rules may significantly impair the rate of conversion from IE to actual entrepreneurship through start-up operations.

Proposition 6: Where an agent conducting an operation on the IE rule brings new rules to the market, this disturbance makes the economy evolve and creates entrepreneurial opportunities for fellow agents; in turn, when no new rules are brought to the market, the economy approaches an evolutionarily stationary state.

4.4 The Limits to Generality as Imposed by Localism

The six propositions above suffice to explain (a) how entrepreneurship may come about in spite of uncertainty, (b) how agents aspiring to self-employment are influenced, (c) how institutional arrangements may inhibit latent entrepreneurs from becoming actual ones, (d) how the distinction between necessity and opportunity entrepreneurship is playing out, and (e) how entrepreneurs may ultimately contribute to the evolution of an economy.

While this might seem little in terms of a general theoretical appraisal of entrepreneurship, it not only unites much existing thought but also provides an integrated version of previously scattered arguments. Although it offers only limited potential for the formulation of hypotheses that directly lend themselves to empirical testing, we point out the need to build locally specific theorems on this general outline. By its very nature, rule-based economics implies that specific theorising is necessarily limited in time and space and that it needs to be empirically informed.

The vast majority of recent applied entrepreneurship research is directed towards international comparison (compare, e.g. Global Entrepreneurship Monitor 1999–2013). As a consequence, most research designs and underlying theoretical approaches follow a distinctively universalist approach. Yet, if we are to accept one of the most fundamental premises of the rule-based approach, namely, the diverse nature of individual agents' rule pools (the selection of rules that they are retaining as a carrier), a universalist approach must be considered impossible. While the orthodox model of the economic agent being exclusively driven by self-interest might still work comparatively well in the Anglo-Saxon world and in some continental European cultural environments, there is evidence that it fails to produce much analytical insights for economies differing more fundamentally, such as the economy of Japan (Blind 2012a). So, in acknowledging that *Homo oeconomicus* or rather HSO—*Homo sapiens oeconomicus* (Dopfer 2004)—reasons differently in different environments, we understand that applying a universalist theory to the study of locally specific economic phenomena cannot produce a sound analysis.

Against this background, it is obvious that we need to develop an understanding of HSO in its native habitat, in this case in Japan, for the purposes of our research. To answer our central questions, we need to develop a model that is customised for the properties of HSO *japonicus* (Blind 2012b) and the local characteristics of his socio-economic environment. Part III elaborates the general theoretical torso developed here with the local characteristics of Japan.

***

We have demonstrated that the entrepreneur is grossly at odds with the received concept of Homo oeconomicus: *the former is absent where the latter is put to work. Work from neighbouring disciplines suggests that a wide variety of factors affect how individuals eventually become entrepreneurs. In order to integrate these into a consistent model, we suggest having recourse to the rule-based approach as an umbrella theory. Centre stage in rule-based economics is Homo sapiens oeconomicus (HSO), a heterogeneous agent open to learning and with the capacity to adapt his decision logic to individual circumstances. HSO is a "rule maker and rule user". In his generalised role, the entrepreneur is a propagator of new rules linking makers to users and acting as a change agent in the economic system. As a rule, user HSO bases all operations on rules. Accordingly, understanding rules is a prerequisite for understanding corresponding operations.*

In the same vein, a sound analysis of business formation requires an antecedent analysis of latent entrepreneurship. We have shown how the "entrepreneurial process", or the "making" of an entrepreneur, can be conceptualised in terms of rules. We understand ENTREPRENEURIAL SPIRIT as a 2nd order rule that moderates the odds of becoming a latent entrepreneur, or, in rule terms, of adopting the 1st order rule of INDIVIDUAL ENTREPRENEURSHIP. We have shown how necessity- and opportunity-driven entrepreneurship can be conceptualised in terms of different sequences of rule adoption. In examining the reasons why carriers of INDIVIDUAL ENTREPRENEURSHIP eventually apply that rule to the operation of becoming self-employed, we argue that causation originates from the set of rules retained by individual agents. Given that entrepreneurship is associated with uncertainty, i.e. with incalculable risk, agents are not following the rule of EXPECTED VALUE MAXIMISATION as they decide positively on becoming self-employed. Thus, Homo oeconomicus *cannot become an entrepreneur, whereas Homo sapiens oeconomicus can.*

Based on a review of pertinent literature, we have developed a theoretical body of six propositions on entrepreneurship from the perspective of the rule-based approach. As the reasoning of HSO varies with time and place, specific empirical information is needed to develop this body into a locally valid theorem. An appropriate methodology will be outlined in PART II. The propositions will be subjected to empirical testing in our study of entrepreneurship in Japan in PART III.

References

Armour J, Cumming D (2008) Bankruptcy law and entrepreneurship. European Corporate Governance Institute, Law Working Papers, vol 105: 1–36

Audretsch DB (2004) Sustaining innovation and growth: public policy support for entrepreneurship. Ind Innov 11(3):167–191

Blind GD (2012a) Culture and economic explanation: economics in the US and Japan. By Donald Katzner. J East Asian Stud 12(1):150–153

Blind GD (2012b) Investigating entrepreneurial spirit with the rule approach: why self-employment is on the decline in Japan. Evol Inst Econ Rev 9(1):183–198

Blind GD (2016) Behavioral rules: Veblen, Nelson-Winter, Oström and beyond. In: Frantz R, Chen S-H, Dopfer K, Heukelom F, Mousavi S (eds) Routledge handbook of behavioral economics. Routledge, Milton Park, pp 139–151

Blind G, Lottanti von Mandach S (2017) Modeling the "Visitors to Rome" effect: reputation building in anglo-saxon buyout funds in Japan. MPRA working paper 7761. Munich University, Munich

Brockhaus RH (1987) Entrepreneurial folklore. J Small Bus Manag 25(3):1–6

Dennis WJ (1996) Self-employment: when nothing else is available? J Lab Res XVII(4):645–661

Dopfer K (2004) The economic agent as rule maker and rule user: Homo sapiens oeconomicus. J Evol Econ 14:177–195

Dopfer K, Potts J (2008) The general theory of economic evolution. Routledge, London

Drucker PF (2002 [1985]) Innovation and entrepreneurship: practice and principles, Ebook edn. Harper & Row, New York

Engelhardt WW (2008) Johann Heinrich von Thünen als Vordenker einer Sozialen Marktwirtschaft. Metropolis, Marburg

George G, Zahra SA (2002) Culture and its consequences for entrepreneurship. Entrep Theory Pract 26(4):5–7

Global Entrepreneurship Monitor (1999–2013) Global entrepreneurship monitor executive reports 1999–2013. London Business School and Babson College, London

Grilo I, Thurik R (2008) Determinants of entrepreneurial engagement levels in Europe and the US. Ind Corp Chang 17(6):1113–1145

Hayek FA (1948) Individualism and economic order. Routledge, London

Hofstede G (1980) Culture's consequences. International differences in work-related values. Sage, Beverly Hills

Knight FH (1964 [1921]) Risk, uncertainty and profit. Augustus M. Kelley, New York

Marshall A (1920 [1890]) Principles of economics. Macmillan, London

Obschonka M, Silbereisen RK, Cantner U, Goethner M (2015) Entrepreneurial self-identity: predictors and effects within the theory of planned behavior framework. J Bus Psychol 30 (4):773–794

Oström E, Basurto X (2011) Crafting analytical tools to study institutional change. J Inst Econ 7(3):317–343

Marx K (2004) Das Kapital – Kritik der politischen Ökonomie Dritter Band, Hamburg 1894. Akademie Verlag, Berlin

Mayer C, Schoors K et al (2005) Sources of funds and investment activities of venture capital funds: evidence from Germany, Israel, Japan and the United Kingdom. J Corp Finan 11:586–608

Meager N (1992) The fall and rise of self-employment (again): a comment on bogenhold and staber. Work Employ Soc 6:127

Metcalfe S (2004) The entrepreneur and the style of modern economics. J Evol Econ 14(2):157–175

Mises L (1998[1949]) Human action. Ludwig von Mises Institute, Auburn, AL

Schultz TW (1975) The value of the ability to deal with disequilibria. J Econ Lit 13:827–846

Schumpeter JA (1912) Theorie der wirtschaftlichen Entwicklung. Duncker & Humblot, Leipzig

Schumpeter JA (1939) Business cycles: a theoretical, historical and statistical analysis of the capitalist process. McGraw-Hill, New York and London
Shackle GLS (1979) Imagination and the nature of choice. Edinburgh University Press, Edinburgh
Shapero A, Sokol L (1982) The social dimensions of entrepreneurship. In: Kent CA, Sexton DL, Vesper KH (eds) The encyclopedia of entrepreneurship. Prentice-Hall, Englewood Cliffs, NJ, pp 72–90
Storey DJ, Johnson S (1987) Regional variations in entrepreneurship in the U.K. Scott J Polit Econ 34(2):161–173
Swett Mansfield M (1927) Why women fail in business. North Am Rev 223(883):638–644
Thünen JH v (1990) Der isolierte Staat in Beziehung auf Landwirtschaft und Nationalökonomie (1826). Akademie, Berlin
Tuttle CA (1927) The function of the entrepreneur. Am Econ Rev 17:13–25
Witt U (2000) Changing cognitive frames – changing organizational forms: an entrepreneurial theory of organizational development. Ind Corp Chang 9:733–755

Part II
The Rule-Based Approach in Empirics: A Methodological Sketch

The Dopfer and Potts rule-based approach provides the ground for the rule-based economics discussed here. Essentially, rule-based economics aims to analyse changes to the rules as part of the framework, in which economic operations take place. Rule-based analysis thus differs fundamentally from the received analysis of economic operations in an invariant framework. Dopfer and Potts contend that their approach is "ontologically and analytically consistent and complete". While this has indeed been acknowledged (e.g. Strohmaier 2010; Beinhocker 2011; Oström and Basurto 2011: 333–334), the approach has also been criticised as being operationally difficult to handle or too abstract (Runde 2009). Furthermore, after emphasising the theoretical virtues of the approach, Ostrom and Basurto note that the approach "does not provide us with enough details about the nature of rules and rule configurations operating at the meso domain to inform how changes might take place and how these changes could be measured" (2011: 334). As a matter of fact, the literature so far contains few clues about how specific hypotheses might be developed or how empirical analysis might be operationalised in detail. Accordingly, putting the rule-based approach into empirical practice in a rule-based economics requires a number of special methodological considerations.

We start below with an outline of the key premises of rule-based analysis and its foremost proponent *Homo sapiens oeconomicus* (HSO) (Dopfer 2004). Next, Chapt. 5 explains how to determine the system of factor rules (SFR) relevant for the analysis of a "response rule"—the *explanandum* of an empirical study in rule-based economics. Chapter 6 shows how the causal core of the SFR can be extracted. Owing to the fundamentally different paradigmatic orientation of rule-based economics, the data required for such an extraction is often not readily available, as an overwhelming proportion of data collection continues to focus on prices and quantities, that is, on economic operations. This challenge raises a number of practical issues. Subsequently, Chap. 7 examines the choice of techniques appropriate for an in-depth analysis of the causal core of a system of factor rules. A detailed didactic case study in Chap. 8 uses the example of the classical problem of investigating the determinants of savings to illustrate how the framework can be employed to develop an empirical research design. The example helps to clarify the distinction between a rule perspective on savings and the notion of aggregate savings: the former refers to the willingness of agents to save, and the latter addresses the outcomes of saving operations conducted by agents in applying their savings rule.

Before we can sketch our methodology for empirical research in rule-based economics, we have to consider four analytical premises, the first three of which arise directly from key characteristics of the evolutionary economic agent (Dopfer 2004) as a heterogeneous learning agent in an open environment.

First, owing to heterogeneity, individual agents apply different rules according to their individual life experience, as a result of which they have adopted a specific set of rules. At any point in time, agents can only execute operations on rules that they have adopted. The differences in individual rule sets thus give rise to differences in operations conducted.

Second, since the evolutionary economic agent is open to learning, rules applied by one specific agent have the potential to change over time. This is because agents may decide to replace a specific rule, for example, if they find one that is superior to the one currently retained. These first two postulates of heterogeneous agents that are open to learning are widely accepted in the community of evolutionary economics.

A third and less frequently recognised postulate is that an individual agent applies different rules in different situations. Modern democracies offer a helpful analogy. In a population of party supporters, (a) any member can change their mind over time, and (b) individuals may still vote differently in municipal and in state or federal elections.

Fourth, rules have populations of carriers of the rule, and the size of these populations may also change over time, which impacts on other rule populations. This implies that even when the set of existing rules remains invariant, its relative population sizes may change with significant effect.

The upshot of these four dimensions of variation is that the evolutionary explanation of the prevalence or "success" of a rule (our *explanandum*) relies on the structures and population dynamics of other rules (*explanantia*).

References

Beinhocker E (2011) Evolution as computation: integrating self-organization with generalized Darwinism. J Inst Econ 7(3):393–423

Dopfer K (2004) The economic agent as rule maker and rule user: Homo sapiens oeconomicus. J Evol Econ 14:177–195

Oström E, Basurto X (2011) Crafting analytical tools to study institutional change. J Inst Econ 7(3):317–343

Runde J (2009) Ontology and the foundations of evolutionary economic theory: on Dopfer and Potts' general theory of economic evolution. J Inst Econ 5(3):361–378

Strohmaier R (2010) The general theory of economic evolution [Book review]. Eur J Hist Econ Thought 17(2):352–356

Chapter 5
Construction of Empirical Models: The System of Factor Rules (SFR)

Abstract After outlining the key premises of the rule-based approach, we explain how to determine the system of factor rules (SFR) relevant for the analysis of a "response rule" – the *explanandum* of an empirical study in rule-based economics. Subsequent sections outline how to identify "factor rules" as potential *explanantia*, how to clear one's preliminary list of factor rules from prices and quantities, how to organise factor rules by rule class and order, how to determine the nature of their impact on the *explanandum* and how to infer on interdependencies between factor rules. Having followed these steps, an SFR should embrace all factor rules that have potentially caused change in the response rule during the investigation period.

Empirical models of economic rules need to carefully reflect the consequences of the analytical distinction between rules and operations that is at the heart of the rule-based approach. This poses a challenge to scholars accustomed to an orthodox school of economics. If we are to understand the nature of economic change, an analysis restricted to economic operations is likely to be constrained to the descriptive level. At best, it will be able to depict the nature of change, but not its origin. In contrast, rule-based economics examines the origins of economic change, distinguishing between the analyses of rules and the corresponding operations. A rule-based economics thus helps to "recognize the extent of diversity of many forms that surrounds us" and to "face the challenge of unpacking its complexity" (Oström and Basurto 2011: 318). The following sections directly draw on Blind and Pyka (2014) for outlining a methodological template for rule-based empirical inquiries.

As in any empirical study, we must first identify and select an *explanandum*. In rule-based economics, this *explanandum* is a "rule" as are routines in Nelson-Winter terminology, and habits in Veblen's tradition (for more details on these linkages, see Blind 2016). Hence, for studies of micro and meso phenomena, researchers will have to set a "response rule" rather than a response variable. This simple idea, as an empirical shift in focus, is one half of the proposed new methodology suggested here. (The other half is to shift the *explanantia* to rules, too.)

To illustrate this distinction, consider the response variables chosen in much of applied economic research, such as growth rates, employment levels, productivity, inflation rates and so on. Not only are these variables aggregate, but first and foremost, they are the results of economic operations within a given system of rules. Operations are stationary phenomena, whereas rules are evolutionary phenomena; and yet there

G.D. Blind, *The Entrepreneur in Rule-Based Economics*, Economic Complexity and Evolution, DOI 10.1007/978-3-319-62779-3_5

are static and dynamic analyses for both (Schneider 1953[1949]: 194, Blind and Pyka 2015). Operations do not represent rules themselves at all. In some instances, there are relatively close links between underlying rules and operational variables, which make the distinction even more difficult. For instance, consider the savings rate. As an aggregate it represents the average share of income put aside. The underlying rule, however, refers to the population of agents who are willing to make savings. Whether they are in a position to do so (i.e. whether their constraints allow this) is not part of the "rule story" but represents an outcome of economic operations (for further details on the distinction of rules and operations, refer to e.g., Dopfer 2004, 2012: 133). A "savings rule" can thus be primarily explained in terms of other rules and only secondarily in terms of relative prices and budget constraints.

Having selected a response rule as *explanandum*, we next identify and define the set of other rules that impact upon the *explanandum* in a second investigation stage. This explanatory set is what we call "system of factor rules": a set of rules, as defined within the framework of classes and orders of rules (Dopfer and Potts 2008). This process is outlined in five individual steps providing practical examples for each step (Sects. 5.1–5.5).

5.1 Instrumental Realism as Guiding Rail for Identifying Influencing Factors

In the first step, we identify all rules that potentially influence the population of the response rule. Empirical validity demands that we use a range of sources, such as references from previous research and discussions with rule adopters and rejecters and with scholars from neighbouring disciplines (e.g. business studies, sociology, psychology, ethnology).

In the example of the "savings rule", rule adopters and rejecters are identified not by their actual accumulation of savings but by their willingness (or not) to save. Exploring the willingness of agents helps to identify the existence of supporting or conflicting rules, for example, a hedonist rule in the case of rejecters or an investment rule in the case of adopters. Ideally, the procedure will help to establish a complete list of potential influencing factors.

5.2 Clearing One's Findings from Prices and Quantities

The second step involves clearing the list of operational entities to ensure that it exclusively consists of rules in order to secure an unbiased analysis of the rule level. Literature sources and primary research are likely to be intermingled with operational aspects such as prices and quantities. However, as we have already seen, for an understanding of economic change, we have to focus exclusively on the structure of rules. A respective validation of the list will secure a smooth establishment of the full set of factor rules. Naturally, if at a later stage the analysis of the response rule is amended with a study of operations conducted upon it, it will be necessary to revert to operational entities previously omitted, such as resource constraints.

The analysis of an investment rule, for example, obviously implies consideration of earning interest. In neoclassical economics, we would clearly focus on real interest rates. However, doing so could not be justified from a rule-based analytical perspective, because the relevant interest rate must be derived from the perception of agents. This perception corresponds to either of two conflicting 2nd order rules: NOMINAL INTEREST versus REAL INTEREST. If one imagines a slightly deflationary environment, such as in Japan (see Part III), NOMINAL INTEREST may well represent the rule prevalent in the majority of agents.

It is important to note, however, that there are occasions when operations impact on the level of rules. For instance, in Part I of this volume, we looked at cases of rule adoption caused by operational necessity (see Sect. 4.2 and Table 4.2). The interplay between the level of rules and the level of operations typically requires meticulous consideration on a case-by-case basis.

As many scholars continue to work with a theoretical imprint based on an orthodox paradigm, we suggest excluding all operational entities as a general procedure. Operational entities should only be included where they directly impact on the level of rules. This will help to increase the acuteness of analytical efforts.

5.3 Classifying Factor Rules by Class and Order

In the third step, we categorise all factor rules according to the RBA rule taxonomy (see Table 2.1). To that end, we attribute factor rules to one of the four *classes of rules* (cognitive, behavioural, social and technical rules) and to one of the three *orders of rules* (constitutional, operational and mechanism rules). This categorisation is crucial to an understanding of the nature of factor rules and how they influence the size of the response rule population.

For instance, behavioural rules influence a response rule population through mechanisms such as group pressure, customs or habits, both leading to socially conditioned action. In contrast, cognitive rules work via rationales in the minds of agents. Yet, epistemological consequences of the rule taxonomy are not limited to rule classes, but arise from the distinction of rule orders as well. Constitutional rules typically refer to all agents in an economy and hence to the entire rule population of the response rule. And 2nd order rules, such as those acquired through an educational system, often imply a substantial time lag until any consequences arise. For example, if we conceive the “savings rule” as a cognitive rule—hence, a subject rule—we gain the epistemological insight that one cannot examine any physical structure (such as for object rules) but that one has to investigate the minds of agents.

5.4 Examining How Factor Rules Impact on the Response Rule

In the fourth step, the relationship between factor rules and the response rule is determined. The individual relationships can be complementary, conflicting or neutral, reflecting the motivational forces proposed by Brandes and Weise (1999): preference, conformity or anti-conformity. Influences can be exerted either unilaterally or mutually through feedback relations. In the latter case, the object of study is obviously subject to a macro coordination process. In both studies with an exclusive meso focus (complete absence of feedback relations) and in macro coordination enquiries (feedback relations present), the term "influences" always refers to the effect on the size of the response rule population.

For instance, a hedonist behavioural rule would conflict with the "savings rule", or, in Brandes and Weise's terms, it would be characterised by anti-conformity. Consequently, a growing population of carriers of a hedonist behavioural rule would exert a negative influence on the population size of the "savings rule".

5.5 Understanding How Factor Rules Interact

In the fifth step, we check factor rules for interdependencies, often enabling us to identify cases in which a factor rule exerts only a secondary effect on the response rule. Statistics offers an apt analogy in the concepts of multicollinearity and covariates.

If, in our "savings rule" example, we believe that both the interest rule—expressed in terms of the perceived interest—and an investment cognitive rule influence the "savings rule" as our response rule, we would need to check for mutual influences between these factor rules. In this example, the interest rule arguably only exerts a secondary influence via the investment rule. Purist econometric practice would suggest excluding any secondary factors that are (near) covariates of other factors. However, if we are ultimately to develop policy recommendations, secondary influences might offer a solution. Often, neither the response rule population nor primary factor rules can be directly influenced by economic policy. However, secondary relationships, depending on their strength and the size of the respective rule population, might offer a way in.

These five steps enable the *explanantia* to be established as a system of factor rules (SFR). Possible representations of this set range from a simple tabulated list to graphical representations such as those used in network analysis. The description of the SFR is not complete in a formal sense. This is because the rule-based approach replaces the received dogma of formal closeness with empirical realism. The SFR results from the researcher's empirical estimates and efforts. It represents a locally constrained set of hypotheses subject to a timely limitation defined by the observation period.

While neoclassical theory has achieved a formally complete system at the cost of limited empirical validity, rule-based economics eschews formally complete and invariant theorising in favour of local hypotheses that—through testing—can be transformed into locally valid theorems. In essence, rule-based economics offers researchers the freedom to extract locally valid theorems without the binding constraint of a fixed formal theory but does so in exchange for their commitment to strive for greater empirical realism. Ultimately, this comes down to a choice between formal and empirical completeness.

References

Blind GD (2016) Behavioral rules: Veblen, Nelson-Winter, Oström and beyond. In: Frantz R, Chen S-H, Dopfer K, Heukelom F, Mousavi S (eds) Routledge handbook of behavioral economics. Routledge, Milton Park, pp 139–151

Blind G, Pyka A (2014) The rule approach in evolutionary economics: a methodological template for empirical research. J Evol Econ 24(5):1085–1105

Blind GD, Pyka A (2015) Erich Schneider: the admiring disciple who did not become a follower. J Evol Econ 25(1):239–252

Brandes W, Weise P (1999) Team performance as a constellation of forces: a general model. Kyklos 52(4):573–590

Dopfer K (2004) The economic agent as rule maker and rule user: Homo Sapiens Oeconomicus. J Evol Econ 14:177–195

Dopfer K (2012) The origins of meso economics. J Evol Econ 22(1):133–160

Dopfer K, Potts J (2008) The general theory of economic evolution. Routledge, London

Oström E, Basurto X (2011) Crafting analytical tools to study institutional change. J Inst Econ 7(3):317–343

Schneider E (1953[1949]) Einführung in die Wirtschaftstheorie II. J.C.B. Mohr (Paul Siebeck), Tübingen

Chapter 6
Changing and Meta-stable Sub-systems (CSS and MSSS)

Abstract The methodological considerations proposed here build on the system of factor rules (SFR) as presented earlier. Specifically, this chapter shows how the causal core of an SFR can be extracted. To that end we develop two criteria for an assessment of factor rules: (1) change in population size and (2) change in strength of influence on the response rule. These criteria suffice to identify causal influence during the observation period. Where neither of the two criteria tests positively, the corresponding factor rules can be excluded from further analysis. Importantly, these criteria allow for excluding false positives.

As an overwhelming share of contemporary data collection efforts still concentrate on prices and quantities, the data required for an SFR assessment is often not readily available. Therefore, Sect. 6.2 provides considerations and suggestions on how to obtain or substitute the data required to assess causality.

The simple methodology proposed here connects a response rule to a set of factor rules. The goal of analysis is to create a set of such factors constituting a full explanatory system of rules: all causally relevant rules are identified for the investigation period. But just as in the sense of statistical analysis we may throw anything we can think of into a regression in pursuit of significance, even when we find significance, we cannot directly infer causality from this.

An equivalent concept is applied in the methodology of rule-based analysis. Following Dopfer (2001) and Dopfer and Potts (2008), we need to identify the rule elements and also the rule connections in order to map the sub-system of factor effect and, therefore, causal explanation. To that end, Sect. 6.1 develops the criteria to check factor rules for causal influence during the observation period. For effectuating this "helpful reduction of complexity" (Blind and Pyka 2014:1092) Sect. 6.2 provides some considerations and suggestions on how to obtain the data required to assess causality.

6.1 Criteria for Extracting the Changing Core of the SFR

In order to infer the causes of economic evolution, and assuming that change in social systems always originates from change in associated entities, we need to understand which parts of the SFR have been subject to change during the

G.D. Blind, *The Entrepreneur in Rule-Based Economics*, Economic Complexity and Evolution, DOI 10.1007/978-3-319-62779-3_6

investigation period. Typically, change in the SFR will be limited to certain parts, that is, to a number of rules with their populations that is smaller than the total number of rules in the SFR. To effectuate this helpful reduction of complexity, the third investigation stage determines which rules in the SFR have been subject to change in the course of the observation period, leading to changes in the response rule population. These rules represent the changing sub-system, while all other rules form the meta-stable sub-system. The extraction of the changing sub-system requires all SFR rules to be assessed according to two criteria.

To motivate the said criteria, let us consider what forms of change can actually happen at the rule level and the consequences at the level of economic operations. First, the size of rule populations can fluctuate over time, potentially triggering most significant changes at the level of economic operations. To pursue our earlier example, let's assume that the rule population of agents having adopted the "savings rule" grows significantly. Depending on their constraints, we understand that the savings rate will potentially increase, so in this example, evolution on the rule level causes change on the operational level. It is important to note, however, that such ensuing change in operations cannot per se be considered economic evolution.

Second, evolution at the rule level occurs when new rules emerge or existing ones decline. Consider again the "savings rule" in a developing economy where savings were restricted to stockpiling until a novel rule called "trustee savings bank" emerged. While such "mutation" clearly qualifies as an evolution at the level of rules, the resulting change at the level of operations might involve a time lag owing to constraints from other rules or resources.

Third, new connections between rules can emerge over time, for example, when agents learn to recognise the significance of one rule for another. In our previous example, agents recognise that rising life expectancy creates a need for savings in order to secure consumption during old age. Conceptually, this process of recognition can be qualified as the emergence of a new cognitive rule. It is true, therefore, that the emergence of a new connection between rules equals economic evolution at the rule level. It will not always be possible to identify the underlying cognitive rule, but for most empirical purposes, it is sufficient to identify the emerging connection. In statistical analysis, this can be evidenced by the emergence of a significant correlation. Naturally, this line of thought also applies to the breaking of connections between rules as a form of change. As it implies the vanishing of a cognitive rule, this corresponds to the "forgetting of a rule", described as an "unconscious process of change" by Oström and Basurto (2011: 326, for a more detailed discussion see Blind 2016).

From the first form of change at the rule level—change in the size of rule populations—we conclude that a change in rules does not necessarily equal economic evolution. However, all forms of rule-level change yield a potential for change at the operational level of the economy. Consider, for instance, how the diffusion of a superior new technology can transform entire industries. To add one further complication to this reasoning, we state that fluctuations at operational level can also happen without a corresponding change at rule level, for example, through external shocks or changes in constraints. For example, the savings rate might increase due to some positive external income shock. There are, therefore, objects of analysis whose significance is limited to the respective rule and operational levels. As the focus of this volume is the rule level, it suffices to note that all forms of change at the rule level represent a potential for operational-level change.

Having identified three forms of rule-level change, we can now consider how to extract that part of an SFR that has caused the size of the response rule population to change during the observation period. This means identifying which part of the SFR was subject to change during the investigation period, the changing sub-system (CSS). To that end we propose to assess the rules constituting the SFR according to two criteria, corresponding to the first and second steps of the third investigation stage:

1. *Variation in population sizes of factor rules*
2. *Variation in strength of influence (of factor rules on response rule population)*

Criterion 1 refers not only to variation in population size as the first kind of change introduced above but also embraces the emergence of new and the decline of extant rules, as this equates to a change in the size of a rule population from zero to positive and vice versa. It thus represents a population view on change in individual agents as in Veblen (compare Blind 2016). Criterion 2 helps to identify the emergence of unspecified new rules that have led to a change in the strength of the connection between pre-existing rules or to changed correlations in a statistics understanding. Ideally, it will help to identify the emergence of the new rule triggering the change in the strength of the connection between pre-existing factor and response rule populations.

An example occurs in Fehr and Gächter's research on "altruistic punishment". As they set up their laboratory experiments on cooperative games and free riding, neoclassical theory was used to conjecture the complete absence of punishment if it was costly and not providing the punisher with any reward, that is, if agents were to uniformly apply Expected Value Maximisation. In their experiments, however, they witnessed a *negative* correlation between the free-riding rule and the frequency of operations on Expected Value Maximisation. This result led them to consider the existence of a cognitive rule, which they labelled Altruistic Punishment (compare Fehr and Gächter 2002).

Surveys investigating population sizes—quantifying the number of agents retaining the relevant rule, for example, through opinion polls—can be used to check on criterion 1. To investigate criterion 2, researchers should ideally make use of surveys specifically concerning these influences, such as the influence of mistrust of government pensions on the "savings rule population". Typically, however, the existence of a theoretically inferred influence will have to be evidenced by correlations between population sizes.

Rule populations of factor rules where one or both criteria have seen sizeable variation clearly represent changes. The SFR can thus be split into a changing sub-system (CSS) and a meta-stable sub-system (MSSS). Rules attributed to the MSSS do not contribute to the change in the response rule population during the investigation period. The methodology thus directs attention to the changing sub-system. It goes without saying that demographic change is an important factor to control for when investigating changes in the size of rule populations over time.

Certain information is needed to assess the factor rules against the two criteria. While retrieving suitable information is a common problem in any empirical study, these problems are even more pronounced when doing research within the evolutionary analytical framework of rule-based economics, since the collection of economic data largely focuses on economic operations. As a consequence, often only data on 1st order operational rules, i.e. those directly pertaining to resources, can easily be obtained. Using the "savings rule" example, central bank statistics on the savings rate will readily be available, possibly even a micro-census covering income and savings. Yet, if we are to determine the size of the savings rule population, i.e. the number of agents willing to save, we may have to turn to other branches of science or to the media to retrieve suitable information. Economic and societal issues have never been as closely covered by surveys and polls as in recent years, which is a promising development from the perspective of rule-based economics.

6.2 Obtaining Data for the Extraction of the CSS

This section provides guidance on how to deal with the difficulty of retrieving suitable information when doing empirical research within an evolutionary analytical framework. It reflects on the consequences of rule-based empirical research with particular reference to the distinction between the analytical levels of rules versus operations. It then considers the type of data required: primary, secondary or indicator based. Potential data sources are suggested in conclusion.

Rules in the form of patents, law, regulations or theories are not by nature observable and can only be traced in their coded form. Most technical rules take the form of patents; many social rules appear as statutes and regulations, some behavioural rules as norms or codes of conduct and certain cognitive rules as theories. While this enables the identification of many rules, it rarely suffices to establish the sizes of the respective rule populations.

Operations, in turn, also only produce physical objects when used to apply technological rules. The use of behavioural and social rules for operations may be recorded in part, for example, the use of personal bankruptcy law is documented by the number of foreclosures, but that use does not produce physical objects. Finally, operations conducted through the use of cognitive rules never produce physical objects and are only rarely documented. Table 6.1 summarises these properties.

Many scholars tend to start their analyses by reference to the visible world, which risks unintentionally restricting the analysis to operations that are observable, either as physical objects or in their coded forms. Failure to recognise both the rule dimension and non-visible operations will lead to partially invalid results in many cases. Therefore, it is useful to keep in mind that rules are never physical

Table 6.1 Manifestations of rules and operations by rule class

	Analytical level	
Rule class	Rules	Operations
Cognitive	Non-physical	Non-physical, rarely coded
Behavioural		Physical as human action, not objects; partially coded
Social		Physical as human action, not objects; partially coded
Technical		Physical products

objects and that operations may manifest themselves as (1) physically measurable items, (2) coded action or (3) internal constructs in the minds of agents where (1)–(3) depend on the rule class under scrutiny.

Ideally, researchers are in a position to design and conduct their own surveys in order to obtain primary data on rule adoption frequency, i.e. on the size of a rule population over time. Research into change at rule level will typically involve an investigation period measured in decades rather than in years. However, in a long-term investigation, the critical source of primary data runs dry with the passage of time for the simple reason that people are either unconsciously whitewashing their own past or have already passed away. However, in order to determine rule adoption frequency, i.e. the diffusion of a rule, one needs to establish the rate of rule adoption for discrete points in the past. In some cases, this kind of data might well be available from secondary sources, but if this is not the case, the time that has elapsed since the beginning of the relevant diffusion process will determine whether a history-oriented survey is possible.

As regards the frequency of operations conducted upon a rule, we are in a more fortunate position: statistics are readily available for almost all major technical rules, as well as many behavioural and social rules. There are even some domains pertaining to cognitive rules where this kind of data is also available.

Due to the different nature of analytical levels (rules vs. operations), and of classes and orders of rules, data on the frequency of rule adoption and of rule use in operations will differ substantially. Table 6.2 lists a number of possible sources of secondary data on rule adoption frequency and on the frequency of rule use as they can probably be identified for the four classes and three orders of rules. Code law and regulations are included here, because their existence and implementation schedules indicate final steps in collective diffusion processes.

Where secondary data are not available and primary data cannot be obtained, indirect measures such as indicators may be used. However, such measures should only be used where there is no alternative solution, as there is a considerable threat of misspecification, which puts data validity at risk.

In many cases, the reduced accuracy implied by the use of indicators is a necessary concession to secure the feasibility of further analytical steps (see

Table 6.2 Data sources on rule adoption and on operations by rule class and order

Rule class/ order	Rule adoption frequency (diffusion)	Frequency of rule use (operations)
Cognitive	– Opinion polls – Surveys on acceptance rates	– Specific surveys
Behavioural and social		– Qualitative research – Academic surveys
Technical	– Patent statistics	– Industrial statistics
0th order constitutional	– Code law/regulations	– Administrative action statistics
1st order operational	– Specific surveys	– Industrial statistics, national accounting, central bank statistics, etc.
2nd order mechanism	– Specific surveys	– Specific surveys

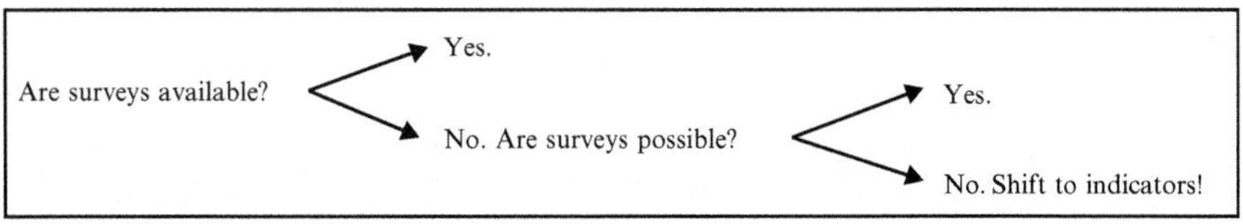

Fig. 6.1 Decision path for the selection of data sources

Chap. 7). In addition, if well chosen, indicators on the frequency of rule adoption may have considerable predictive or at least indicative capacities with regard to the properties of the frequency of operations. Figure 6.1 shows the decision path.

To increase their validity, several indicators can be pooled, with due attention to appropriate weighting and scaling. An example would be to pool indicators such as higher education curricula and government funding for applied research. The number of scientific publications, higher education curricula and media reflection rates might also offer helpful points of departure for the construction of suitable indicators (more detailed suggestions can be found in Blind 2003).

References

Blind GD (2003) Statistical methods for a dynamic analysis of meso-trajectories in evolutionary systems. M.A. thesis, St. Gallen University

Blind GD (2016) Behavioral rules: Veblen, Nelson-Winter, Oström and beyond. In: Frantz R, Chen S-H, Dopfer K, Heukelom F, Mousavi S (eds) Routledge handbook of behavioral economics. Routledge, Milton Park, pp 139–151

Blind G, Pyka A (2014) The rule approach in evolutionary economics: a methodological template for empirical research. J Evol Econ 24(5):1085–1105

Dopfer K (2001) Evolutionary economics – framework for analysis. In: Dopfer K (ed) The evolutionary foundations of economics. Kluwer Academic, Boston, pp 1–44
Dopfer K, Potts J (2008) The general theory of economic evolution. Routledge, London
Fehr E, Gächter S (2002) Altruistic punishment in humans. Nature 415(6868):137–140
Oström E, Basurto X (2011) Crafting analytical tools to study institutional change. J Inst Econ 7(3):317–343

Chapter 7
Analysis of the Changing Sub-sytem (CSS): Developing and Testing of Hypotheses

Abstract Developing and testing of hypotheses in a rule-based economic inquiry consists of four steps: specification of the CSS for the two analytical levels of rules and operations, identification of carrier subgroups, formulation of hypotheses and choice of technique for hypothesis testing.

As the choice of technique is critical to conduct valid hypothesis tests, we examine how existing techniques may be employed in rule-based inquiries. In doing so, the sections distinguish hermeneutic from statistical approaches and agent-based simulations. Guidance focuses on the merits and challenges of the said techniques as they apply to rule-based analysis and provides references to detailed accounts of the respective methods.

The last stage of the proposed methodology involves developing and testing hypotheses about the CSS. The process consists of four steps: specification of the CSS for the two analytical levels of rules and operations, identification of carrier subgroups, formulation of hypotheses and choice of technique for hypothesis testing.

We start with specifying the CSS separately for the two analytical levels: the level of rules and the level of economic operations. Although the two analytical levels are interdependent, they reside in two entirely separate worlds. Using the "savings rule" example, let's assume that the size of its population depends on the size of the population of a "providence rule" (the idea of securing consumption during old age). On the level of operations, this will translate into the savings rate depending on life expectancy.

Second, we identify subgroups of agents and their distinct rule sets. Depending on the composition of their individual sets of rules and on their operational realities (endowments), agents will be susceptible to different influences when deciding for or against the adoption of a new rule. This very much corresponds to the typologies developed for any model involving heterogeneous agents (Grebel and Pyka 2003). An analogy from marketing studies would be the segmentation of customer groups, according to how they variously adopt and retain "rules". A "providence rule", for example, might be predominantly found among junior generations, whereas a "bequeathing rule" will arguably only be found among senior generations.

Third, having identified both (1) the representations of the changing sub-system for the two analytical levels of rules and operations and (2) the nature of potential

G.D. Blind, *The Entrepreneur in Rule-Based Economics*, Economic Complexity and Evolution, DOI 10.1007/978-3-319-62779-3_7

subgroups of agents, the researcher is able to formulate more detailed hypotheses. Using this experiential knowledge, the analyst will also be able to select the most appropriate technique for hypothesis testing from among the principal choices available, a decision to be made in the subsequent final step.

Fourth, there continue to be methodological debates in the narrower sense of "methodological techniques" in the relatively young discipline of evolutionary economics. While an overview of techniques applied in evolutionary economics is readily available (Saviotti 2003), the choice of techniques has not been discussed in the context of rule-based economics, where there are some specific requirements. The following sections discuss a non-exhaustive selection of three categories of techniques: hermeneutic approaches, simulations and statistics. Naturally, the choice will be conditional upon the nature of the available data, but researchers will already have gained an overview of this during the reduction of SFR to CSS (i.e. when assessing factor rules against the two criteria). The following section critically amend Blind and Pyka (2014).

7.1 Hermeneutics

"Hermeneutics is essentially a philosophy of understanding" (Lavoie 1990a: 167). It consists of logical, reasoned efforts to interpret available information, with written text being paradigmatic of all forms of interpretation (Lavoie 1990b). Researchers reasoning in this way must include qualitative analytical tools into their methodological repertoire. Unfortunately, these techniques have acquired a reputation for unreliability due to an apparent lack of exactness. For instance, qualitative analysis is frequently pejoratively referred to as "storytelling", meaning a mere description of operations, which would be *explained* more impressively by means of inferential statistics.

However, the hermeneutic method, which we strongly endorse, serves as a remedy for two specific shortcomings frequently observed in much of recent empirical work. The first is in empirical studies where statistical analysis seemingly offers confident estimates of correlations and—where tested for endogeneity concerns—even of causality yet actually often fails to offer valuable insights as it lacks a sound antecedent analysis of the underlying rule system. In other words, statistical significance alone cannot lead to a true *understanding* of the phenomena analysed.

Here, hermeneutical reasoning has the potential to identify the rationale behind the documented statistical relationship. However, the use of hermeneutics only ex post risks unintentionally legitimating flawed statistical findings. Consider, for example, the frequent case of covariates of independent variables being mistaken for "causal factors" (compare, e.g., the critique in Blind and Lottanti von Mandach 2017a). A sound antecedent hermeneutical analysis is likely to help identify the original independent variable and relegate a faultily specified covariate to its appropriate purpose of an indicator variable in statistical analysis. Hermeneutical analysis should therefore be used preventively rather than remedially (compare, e.g. Meyer 1975: 542).

The second equally frequent shortcoming arises in studies where preconceived theories or models with proto-theoretical status are blindly used for processing empirical information (compare Blind and Lottanti von Mandach 2015, 2017b). In many such cases, storytelling is abandoned because researchers implicitly base their reasoning on a story they have been told for a long time, broadly known as "the tale of economic man". This is a comfort to the struggling student of economics, as it provides answers to the many questions that may arise from a too close inspection of economic reality. The quest for authoritative scientific discovery tends to encourage a focus on subjects, for which the "tale" provides sufficiently conclusive answers, abandoning other enquiries.

To the scholar not content with such restricted subjects, hermeneutics offers a powerful instrument for identifying alternative "tales" and novel theories. Naturally, there is no guarantee of discovery and there will be tiresome arguments with followers of established "tales", but this method offers the potential for true scientific progress.

The "lack of exactness" said to be associated with hermeneutical analysis stands in contrast to the apparent confidence associated with statistical significance in the first type of shortcoming and with the theoretical authority of a canonised "general story" in the second type of shortcoming. As we have seen, either such belief implies a potentially harmful narrowing down of the field of enquiry, although arguably this only translates into scientific damage in a minority of cases. Yet researchers striving for the best possible explanation have to start from a hermeneutic approach to their object of study. Importantly, it does not suffice to merely "confirm" the pertinence of "the tale of economic man" or of some specific theory. Many recent papers that present this type of "confirmation" lack neutrality in presuming such pertinence a priori.

In a rule context, a hermeneutic approach involves researchers' "reading" information from all available sources to identify potentially relevant factor rules when constructing the SFR of their subject matter. Thus, hermeneutic techniques represent an essential tool for rule-based economic analysis right from the first investigation stage. Current practice suggests the use of statistical methods for CSS analysis when testing hypotheses pertaining to the causes of change (see Sect. 7.2). Although it is relatively difficult to publish research obtained from testing hypotheses through hermeneutic methods, such approaches are not systematically inferior to statistical testing and indeed are often possible where data requirements for statistical testing are not met.

Yet, even where such data is available, it requires interpretation. As Berger notes in a review of Charles Taylor's *Philosophical Papers*, there is no "brute data", and "when studying human motivation and action, it is impossible to avoid the question of the meaning of situations to the agents involved in them" (Berger 1989: 211).[1]

[1]This quote is most instructive as it builds bridges to the distinction of rules (motivation) and operations (action), as well as to subgroups of agents (situations agents are involved in).

Thus, hermeneutics offers a most valuable tool for *understanding* the origins of change in an economic system, that is, for enquiring into the causes of change in a CSS. Dilthey's "hermeneutic circle" offers a close yet different analogy. The analysis has to oscillate not only between the whole of the system and its elements but also between rules and corresponding operations.

Classical references to modern hermeneutics can be found in a line from Dilthey's reading of Schleiermacher to Gadamer and Habermas (Dilthey 1900; Gadamer 1960; Habermas 1973). Earlier debates on economics as part of the social sciences also acknowledged the importance of the hermeneutic method as it aims at *understanding* (compare, e.g. the preface to Sombart and Stoltenberg 1924). With the increasing acceptance of positivism—and formal modelling—during the 1930s (Lavoie 2011: 92), hermeneutics fell out of favour. Still, it has retained an important place in major branches of the discipline, notably in institutional and evolutionary economics, where Thorstein Veblen (compare, e.g. Mirowski 1987) and Max Weber (Lachmann 1971) are important legacies. The methodological debate on its use continues (compare, e.g. Madison 1990; Addleson 2002; Di Iorio 2015).

7.2 Statistics

Statistics—particularly its multivariate resources—offers a proven way to simultaneously document influences from multiple factors on a response variable. When suitable data is available, it arguably offers the most convenient way to test the CSS model at the rule level. Regression analysis, developed over decades, offers solutions to almost every challenge. For instance, the evolution of new rules and the disappearance of existing rules can enter as dummy variables; feedback relations between populations of factor rules can be dealt with using the standard arsenal available against multicollinearity. Equally, nonconstant relationships due to changes in the strength of connection among rules can be traced by moving-window regressions, and the predictive power of a model can be tested by running it with temporal subsets of the collected data and so on. Further specific considerations for the modelling of evolutionary phenomena have already been discussed in the literature (compare, e.g. Foster and Wild 1999).

As with simulations, statistics can help to identify a faultily specified model but cannot offer deeper analytical insights except for a trial-and-error approach. However, in contrast to simulations, traditional statistical models do not dispose of a capacity to integrate the analysis of rule level and operational level; rules and operations require separate analyses. Yet, it is possible to create a joint interpretation from these separate analyses.

Working with heterogeneous data from diverse sources, compounded by the necessity to infer on nonmeasurable original variables using one or several indicator variables, may require the construction of suitable compound measures. Particularly when pooling multiple indicators, additional parameters must be carefully introduced to ensure appropriate weighting.

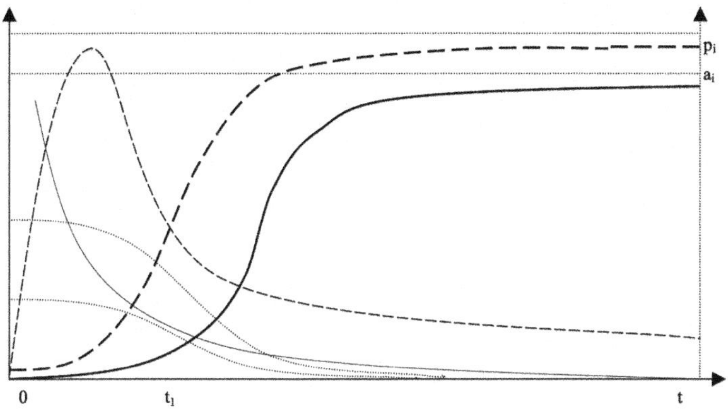

Fig. 7.1 Rethinking frequency, rule diffusion and frequency of operations. Rethinking frequency in absolute terms (*thin dashed line*), scope of adaptations (*thin line*), share of adaptations (*upper curve*) and share of rejections (*lower curve*; *dotted lines*), rule frequency/diffusion (*thick dashed line*), operation frequency (*thick dashed line*). Source: Blind 2003: 37

Where rule diffusion per se is the object of inquiry, specific procedures apply. Emerging rules typically create some "intellectual noise" which I call "rethinking frequency" (Blind 2003). Scientific publications may offer a way to track such "noise". Note that the rule will still be subject to significant modifications during this early period of diffusion (see Fig. 7.1).

The use of orthogonal regression to estimate the underlying functions is strongly recommended due to the specific slopes of these processes. High parametric functions using data on publications (for rethinking frequency), on rule diffusion and on frequency of operations enable patterns to be detected. For instance, comparing parameters, relations between parameters and time indexes for different types of rules or different time periods enables enquiry into systematic change in rule diffusion. For small samples, non-parametric test statistics may be used (for details, see Blind 2003).

7.3 Agent-Based Simulations

Agent-based simulations are one of the most powerful tools for testing complex economic interrelationships. The technique recognises that many theoretical models can hardly be captured in mathematical terms and thus enjoys considerable popularity also among orthodox economists. Recent efforts to understand macroeconomic turbulence have strongly fostered the trend towards agent-based modelling (Farmer and Foley 2009), gradually overcoming traditional hesitations (Leombruni and Richiardi 2005).

In our context, simulations can be used to test the CSS—the underlying set of hypotheses—for consistency. Misspecifications through redundant or omitted factor rules can be detected; forecasts at the rule level become feasible. The ability of simulations to model systems using probability functions offers a chance to integrate rule and operational levels of analysis.

However, even the most advanced agent-based model will ultimately only be able to serve two purposes: test for a potential model misspecification and offer a way of developing scenarios for models without discrete solutions. It cannot, however, lead to new analytical insights, except for its control function in a trial-and-error effort.

The field of simulations has produced a vast amount of literature. As a primer to the practitioner, we suggest a recent introductory volume featuring a number of useful examples (Gilbert 2008). Foster and Potts (2009) have recently provided a most helpful discussion of the potential use of simulations in combination with other techniques that specifically reflects on the context of the micro–meso–macro framework.

References

Addleson M (2002) Equilibrium versus understanding: towards the rehumanizing of economics within social theory. Routledge, London

Berger LA (1989) Economics and hermeneutics. Econ Philos 5(02):209–234

Blind GD (2003) Statistical methods for a dynamic analysis of meso-trajectories in evolutionary systems. M.A. Thesis, St. Gallen University

Blind GD, Lottanti von Mandach S (2015) Decades not lost, but won: increased employment, higher wages, and more equal opportunities in the Japanese labour market. Soc Sci Jpn J 18 (1):63–88

Blind GD, Lottanti von Mandach S (2017a) Not a coincidence: sons-in-law as successors in successful Japanese family firms. Crit Finance Rev (forthcoming)

Blind G, Lottanti von Mandach S (2017b) Secular trends in the Japanese labour market during the lost decades: a reply to Andrew Gordon. MPRA working paper 80812. University of Munich, Munich

Blind G, Pyka A (2014) The rule approach in evolutionary economics: a methodological template for empirical research. J Evol Econ 24(5):1085–1105

Di Iorio F (2015) Hayek and the hermeneutics of mind. Soc Sci Inf 54(2):177–191

Dilthey W (1900) Die Entstehung der Hermeneutik. Mohr (Paul Siebeck), Tübingen

Farmer JD, Foley D (2009) The economy needs agent-based modelling. Nature 460:685–686

Foster J, Potts J (2009) A micro-meso-macro perspective on the methodology of evolutionary economics: integrating history, simulation and econometrics. In: Canter U, Gaffard J-L, Nesta L (eds) Schumpeterian perspectives on innovation, competition and growth. Springer, Berlin, pp 53–68

Foster J, Wild P (1999) Econometric modelling in the presence of evolutionary change. Camb J Econ 23:749–770

Gadamer H-G (1960) Wahrheit und Methode [Truth and method]. Mohr, Tübingen

Gilbert NG (2008) Agent-based models. Sage, Thousand Oaks

Grebel T, Pyka A (2003) Agent-based modelling: a methodology for the analysis of qualitative development processes, vol 251. Discussion Paper Series, Institute of Economics at University of Augsburg

Habermas J (1973) Zur Logik der Sozialwissenschaften (Materials on logic in social sciences), 3rd edn. Suhrkamp, Frankfurt

Lachmann L (1971) The legacy of Max Weber. Glendessary Press, Berkeley
Lavoie D (1990a) Hermeneutics, subjectivity, and the Lester/Machlup debate: toward a more anthropological approach to empirical economics. In: Samuels WJ (ed) Economics as discourse. Springer, Dordrecht, pp 167–187
Lavoie D (1990b) Introduction. In: Economics and hermeneutics. Routledge, London, pp 1–15
Lavoie D (2011) The interpretive dimension of economics: science, hermeneutics, and praxeology. Rev Austrian Econ 24(2):91–128
Leombruni R, Richiardi M (2005) Why are economists sceptical about agent-based simulations? Physica A 335(1):103–109
Madison G (1990) Getting beyond objectivism: the philosophical hermeneutics of Gadamer and Ricoeur. In: Lavoie D (ed) Economics and hermeneutics. Routledge, London and New York, pp 32–57
Meyer W (1975) Der Nationalökonom und die Wissenschaftstheorie. Public Financ Anal (New Series) 33(3):536–545
Mirowski P (1987) The philosophical bases of institutionalist economics. J Econ Iss 21(3):1001–1038
Saviotti PP (ed) (2003) Applied evolutionary economics – new empirical methods and simulation techniques. Edward Elgar, Cheltenham
Sombart W, Stoltenberg HL (1924) Soziologie. Pan-Verlag, Berlin

Chapter 8
Rule-Based Economics in Empirical Practice: An Exemplar

Abstract We present a detailed didactical case study to illustrate how the empirical methodology presented can be employed to develop an empirical research design in rule-based economic inquiry. The case builds on the example of the classical problem of investigating the determinants of savings. The chosen example helps to clarify the distinction between a rule perspective on savings and the notion of aggregate savings: the former refers to the willingness of agents to save, and the latter addresses the outcomes of saving operations conducted by agents in applying their savings rule.

How can the proposed methodology be used effectively to create a research design for an empirical study? And in what way can the methodology enrich an analysis compared to received approaches, i.e. what is the epistemological *value added*? The following step-by-step case study illustrates our methodology (as given in Blind and Pyka 2014) using a constructed model in which the underlying case is empirically likely, but not manifest in any data. This is in the tradition of the many case studies used in management sciences that are tailored to serve illustrative and didactic purposes. Our "idealised" case study not only shows the workings of the proposed methodology but also suggests how the rule-based approach may be employed in similar cases. As we shall see, this exemplar will also have significance for the subject matter of entrepreneurship. Table 8.1 summarises the four investigation stages.

8.1 Defining the Subject Matter

In the first investigation stage of this case study, we start by defining our *explanandum*. As we are examining the savings in an economy from an evolutionary perspective, we need to understand that savings are an aggregate representing the outcome of aggregate saving operations in an economy. In turn, the latter originate from the group of agents that are willing to save, that is, from the population of agents that have adopted and currently retain a "savings rule". With this in mind, we fix the "savings rule" as the response rule (i.e. the *explanandum*) in our case study.

G.D. Blind, *The Entrepreneur in Rule-Based Economics*, Economic Complexity and Evolution, DOI 10.1007/978-3-319-62779-3_8

Table 8.1 Hypothesis building and testing in rule-based economics

Premises
(I) *Consider differences in rules adopted and applied by individual agents owing to the heterogeneity of* homo sapiens oeconomicus *(HSO)*
(II) *Consider the openness of HSO to learning necessitating historic time*
(III) *Consider the discriminatory use of rules by HSO necessitating limitations to specific contexts when conducting analyses of the operational level*
(IV) *Consider the distinction of rules vs. economic operations conducted in applying them*
Outline of procedure (synthetic scheme, detailed for meso domain)
1. *Set response rule population, investigation period and spatial delimitation*
2. *Establish full system of factor rules (SFR)*
(2.a) *Identify potential factor rules through the use of appropriate sources*
(2.b) *Check list of potential factor rules not to contain operational entities; only include the latter where these directly impact on the level of rules*
(2.c) *Classify factor rules according to the rule taxonomy*
(2.d) *Identify nature of relations between factor rules and response rule*
(2.e) *Check for interdependencies among factor rules*
3. *Split SFR into changing sub-system (CSS) and meta-stable sub-system (MSSS)*
(3.a) *Identify factor rules with significant variation in population size during sample period*
(3.b) *Determine the strengths of influences exerted by factor rules on the response rule population during the sample period; consider a potential variation in time*
4. *Conduct in-depth analysis of CSS*
(4.a) *Establish representations of the CSS separately for the analytical levels of rules and operations*
(4.b) *Identify potential subgroups of agents*
(4.c) *Establish corresponding hypotheses*
(4.d) *Test hypotheses upon choice of technique: hermeneutics, simulations and statistics*

Next, we have to decide on the time horizon and the spatial (geographical) delimitation of our investigation. While many studies make these decisions simply based on data availability, the rule-based approach has a theoretical reasoning for doing so. First, rule-based economics recognises "historic time": it argues that agents are open to learning and hence depend on their experience. Second, agents adopt different sets of rules depending on the context in which they live. Therefore, a spatial delimitation helps to capture the explanatory power soaked up in most international comparisons by region- or country-specific dummy variables. This differs fundamentally from received approaches, which continue to strive to identify "universal laws" restricted by neither time nor space.

For the purpose of our case study, we fix the spatial limitation to Japan—a country famously labelled a "special case" in international comparisons (e.g. Kaldor 1975; De Long 1988:1151; Cavelaars 2005). We choose to start the investigation in 1990, when Japan veered off its post-war high-growth path with the burst of its bubble economy.

8.2 Identify Potential Influences

The second investigation stage determines the system of factor rules (SFR), the set of rules that are relevant to the "savings rule population" as the *explanandum* in our case study. In order to determine the SFR of the "savings rule", we follow the five steps outlined in Table 8.1.

First, we need to identify potential factor rules—rules that may have influenced the response rule population during the investigation period. To determine factor rules as *explanantia*, our comprehensive approach extends the enquiry beyond the review of existing theoretical works to include insights from neighbouring disciplines (such as sociology), interviews with adopters and rejecters of the "savings rule" and a review of media coverage.

From existing empirical works on Japan (Chen et al. 2006), we infer the likely influence of tax law as factor (a). Through interviews with rule rejecters, we identify a hedonistic lifestyle (b) as one major motivation not to adopt the "savings rule", particularly among younger individuals. In another interview with a leading sociologist, we obtain an important insight regarding more senior generations. For them, the adoption of the "savings rule" reportedly often stems from the wish to bequeath significant assets to their offspring (c). We triangulate this suggestion in a discussion with a Japanese Studies scholar who confirms the particular relevance of this motive in Japanese society and by means of some semi-structured interviews with senior rule adopters (d). Finally, from standard economic works, we include the real interest rate (e). As a result, we obtain the following list of factor rules:

(a) Tax on Interest
(b) Hedonistic Lifestyle
(c) Bequests
(d) Providence
(e) Real Interest Rate

What most notably distinguishes the approach taken in our case study from a more standard research design is the explicit orientation to economic reality already being pursued at this early stage of hypothesis building. Relying on extant theoretical work is likely to have allowed only some of the five factors to be identified. Obviously, neoclassical economic literature would suggest concentrating on real interest (e). Modigliani's work on Keynesian theory (Modigliani and Brumberg 1954) might lead to considering, say, the providence rule (d). And finally, some literature may suggest considering current tax law (a) as a potential factor. However, it arguably would have been difficult to identify a hedonistic lifestyle (b) or the intention to pass on assets (c) exclusively on the basis of a review of extant literature.

In the second step (Table 8.1(2.b)), we check that our list of factor rules contains no operational entities but consists exclusively of rules, following Dopfer and Potts' definition of a rule as "a deductive procedure for operations" (2008: 104). Paying a tax is an economic operation, so Tax on Interest can be considered a rule.

HEDONISTIC LIFESTYLE also qualifies as a rule, as it implies maximising consumption, with consumption being an economic operation. Equally, BEQUESTS require the transfer of assets from one agent to one or multiple other agents, and this transfer equals an economic operation. Next, PROVIDENCE aims at securing a certain level of consumption during old age, and this requires the acquisition of corresponding options (insurance policy, state pension or—precisely—savings). As the acquisition of a financial option equally represents an economic operation, PROVIDENCE qualifies as a rule. However, reviewing REAL INTEREST RATE is a problem. An interest rate cannot be conceived of as a "deductive procedure". As a price, it is an operational entity, but not an operation itself. Hence, REAL INTEREST RATE does not qualify as a rule. Yet, we accept that the idea of gaining interest might be influenced by interest rates. Therefore, we substitute the rule of FINANCIAL INVESTMENT (which we will call e1) for REAL INTEREST RATE. The rule refers to the idea of gaining interest from investments, which—in turn—is an economic operation. Conceiving of operational entities as rules (as in the case of real interest included in our first version of the SFR) is a common mistake made by researchers with an orthodox background.

In the third step, we classify the factor rules identified in our case study according to the RBA rule taxonomy (Table 8.1(2.c)):

(a) TAX ON INTEREST: 0th order social rule
(b) HEDONISTIC LIFESTYLE: 1st order behavioural rule
(c) BEQUESTS: 1st order social rule
(d) PROVIDENCE: 1st order cognitive rule
(e1) FINANCIAL INVESTMENT: 1st order cognitive rule

From this classification, we can draw a number of conclusions regarding the nature of the factor rule populations and of the potential influences they are exerting on the response rule. For instance, potential influences of the behavioural "hedonistic lifestyle" rule and the social "bequest rule" will work via mechanisms such as group pressure leading to socially conditioned action. In turn, the cognitive rules in the above list (d and e1) become relevant through the abstract reasoning of agents.

In the fourth step (Table 8.1(2.d)), we identify the nature of relations between the factor rules and the "savings rule" as our response:

(a) The larger the group of law-abiding agents becomes, the smaller the rule population of the "savings rule" will become. Hence, the relation is conflicting.
(b) As a hedonistic lifestyle maximises consumption, there is a conflicting relation.
(c) With savings adding to the ability to bequeath, the relation is complementary.
(d) With savings as one providential measure, there is a complementary relation.
(e1) With savings as a source of equity for investment, the relation is complementary.

Finally, in the fifth step, we check the system of factor rules for interdependencies. In order to conduct a full check, we establish a corresponding matrix (Table 8.2).

For most of the combinations, we are able to exclude a systematic relationship. The conflicting relation between HEDONISTIC LIFESTYLE and BEQUESTS translates into

Table 8.2 Interdependencies within the system of factor rules (case example)

	Interest Taxation	Hedonist Lifestyle	Bequeathing	Providence	Financial Investment
Interest Taxation	–	Nonsystematic	Nonsystematic	Nonsystematic	Conflicting
Hedonist Lifestyle	–	–	Conflicting	Nonsystematic	Nonsystematic
Bequeathing	–	–	–	Nonsystematic	Complementary
Providence	–	–	–	–	Complementary

an alternative choice between one's own consumption and bequeathing "consumption opportunities" to some heir. As alternatives, both factor rules exert direct influences on the response rule.

In contrast, when looking closer at the conflicting relation identified between Tax on Interest and Financial Investment, we understand that the former only exerts *indirect* influence on the response rule via its negative impact on the latter, that is, taxing interest does reduce the attractiveness of interesting-bearing investments, but it does not directly impact on the willingness to save. Hence, we are able to exclude Tax on Interest from the system of factor rules. Yet, for the development of policy recommendations, we need to keep in mind that there is some link connecting Tax on Interest via Financial Investment to the "savings rule" as the response rule of our case study.

Finally, the complementary relationship pointing from both the bequests and the providence rule to the financial investment rule can be considered comparatively weak, as financial investments are only one way of securing assets for the two purposes of bequests and securing future consumption. On completion of this second investigation stage, we obtain a system of factor rules (SFR) comprising four of the rules noted above (b to e1).

8.3 Extracting Effective Influences

The third investigation stage identifies those factor rules within the SFR that have causally contributed to change in the "savings rule population" during the investigation period (Table 8.1(3)). This, in essence, is necessary to infer whether economic evolution has taken place during the investigation period. In two distinct steps, we check on possible sources of change: first, change in the size of the respective factor rule population and, second, change in the strength of the relationship between individual factor rules and the response rule.

We start by establishing the population sizes for factor rules (b) to (e1) of our case study by comparing annual opinion polls. It turns out that the populations of both the hedonistic lifestyle rule and the providence rule have grown significantly since the early 1990s. In contrast, the number of agents in the bequests and financial

Table 8.3 Change in population sizes and in factor–response relations (case example)

Change	HEDONIST LIFESTYLE	BEQUEATHING	PROVIDENCE	FINANCIAL INVESTMENT
In population size	Increased	–	Increased	–
In relationship to response rule	–	–	–	Increased
Part of changing sub-system?	Yes	No	Yes	Yes
Part of meta-stable sub-system?	No	Yes	No	No

interest rule populations do not show substantial variation during the investigation period.

We then investigate changes in the strength of the relationships between our factor rules and the response rule. From a series of semi-structured interviews with investment professionals, we learn that the strength of the relationship between FINANCIAL INVESTMENT and the "savings rule" has significantly increased over the past two decades. This is because more and more agents are reportedly losing confidence in real estate investments. In contrast, there is no evidence of changes in the relationship between the other factor rules and the "savings rule" (Table 8.3).

With these findings, we are able to extract the CSS from the SFR. The CSS consists of those rules for which we can confirm either of the two forms of change during the investigation period. In our case example, we are able to do so for three of the four factor rules, namely, for HEDONISTIC LIFESTYLE, PROVIDENCE and FINANCIAL INVESTMENT rules. In contrast, the bequeathing rule BEQUESTS does not contribute to variation in the "savings rule" during the investigation period. Therefore, we attribute it to the MSSS.

8.4 Evidencing Effective Influences

Finally, the fourth investigation stage consists of an in-depth analysis of the CSS in order to understand how it has influenced the "savings rule" during the investigation period. This requires four separate steps (Table 8.1(4a–d)) to be outlined as follows. Rule level (populations):

$$SR = aHL + b\mathrm{PRO} + cFI + m \tag{8.1}$$

Operational level:

$$\text{Aggregate savings} = \alpha\Sigma(\text{income}^{\text{HL}}) + \beta\Sigma(\text{income}^{\text{PRO}}) + \gamma\Sigma(\text{income}^{\text{FI}}) + \mu \tag{8.2}$$

where HL denotes HEDONIST LIFESTYLE, PRO PROVIDENCE and FI FINANCIAL INVESTMENT

The rule level (8.1) describes how factor rule populations impact on the population of the "savings rule", i.e. on the group size of economic agents that have adopted the "savings rule" and are currently retaining it. As the second modal representation of the CSS, we formulate its operational form (8.2). From the formal representation of the CSS in (8.1), the nature of the two criteria used in the previous step for its extraction becomes obvious: while the first criterion checks upon the population sizes of factor rules HEDONISTIC LIFESTYLE, PROVIDENCE and FINANCIAL INVESTMENT, the second criterion refers to the strengths of the respective relationships to the response rules *a*, *b* and *c*.

While the unit of measurement at the rule level is population size, given as the number of rule adopters, the operational level analyses aggregate savings as a monetary unit. Relating the two levels, we can see aggregate savings as the addition of all the fractions of income put aside through "savings operations" conducted by members of the three rule populations included in the CSS.

The second step searches for subgroups of agents to further sharpen the analysis of the rule level as the focus of our case study (Table 8.1(4.b)). To that end we need a criterion that comes with significant discriminatory power considering the susceptibility of agents to the influence of factor rules. In other words, we need to identify a characteristic specific to the agents in the response rule population that correlates with their responsiveness to either of the factor rules. In our case, segmentation by age achieves this objective. From public opinion polls, we know that a hedonistic lifestyle is more likely to be found among the younger generation, while concern around provision for old age typically arises within more senior age cohorts. Therefore, we distinguish a young and a senior subgroup SR^{yg} and SR^{sen}.

In the third step, we can now formulate hypotheses pertaining to the CSS of our case study, both for the "savings rule population" as a whole and for the two subgroups identified within the "savings rule population" (Table 8.1(4.c)):

1. There is a negative influence of the HL population on the SR population; i.e. a is significantly negative.

   1a. The relationship is stronger for younger age groups; i.e. $|a^{yg}|$ - $|a^{sen}|$ is significantly positive.

2. There is a positive influence of the PRO population on the SR population; i.e. b is significantly positive.

   2a. The relationship is stronger for older age groups; i.e. $b^{sen} - b^{yg}$ is significantly positive.

3. There is a positive influence of the FI population on the SR population; i.e. c is significantly positive.

   3a. The relationship is not different for SR^{sen} and SR^{yg} subgroups; i.e. $c^{sen} = c^{yg}$ cannot be rejected.

   3b. The relationship has become stronger during the investigation period; i.e. $\delta c/\delta t > 0$ for $t \in (1990, 2014)$.

where HL denotes Hedonistic Lifestyle, PRO Providence and FI Financial Investment.

This list shows that the methodology presented allows for the formulation of a rich set of hypotheses. For instance, we not only suggest the generally negative influence of a hedonistic lifestyle on the propensity to adopt and retain the "savings rule" (Hypothesis 1), but we also conjecture that this influence is more pronounced among the subgroup of younger agents than the subgroup of more senior agents (Hypothesis 1a). Correspondingly, the suggested positive influence of Providence on the population of the response rule is assumed to be stronger in senior agents than in junior agents (Hypotheses 2 and 2a). At the same rate, the suggested positive influence of the financial investment rule (FI) is arguably not different for the subgroups identified (Hypotheses 3 and 3a). However, we suppose that the strength of the relationship has increased over time (Hypothesis 3b).

As the fourth and last step in this final investigation stage of our case study (Table 8.1(4.d)), we would like to test our hypotheses, ideally by the use of standard regression statistics. To that end we need to obtain appropriate micro-data. Using data from annual government opinion polls allows us not only to infer the population sizes of the rules included in our model but also to conduct separate analyses by age group. In order to exclude the risk of a biased analysis, we correct our data for demographic change during the investigation period. This is particularly important for understanding what proportion of change at rule level—the composition of the response rule population—was merely due to population ageing. As a result, we are able to attribute the remaining share of change to an evolutionary process in the economic system.

We can extend this case study to the operational level through a change in perspective from rule and population mode to economic operation mode. To investigate the operational level of aggregate savings, we need an analysis of disposable income earned by the agents within the factor rule populations. Using socio-economic profiles of rule populations from the available micro-data, we can obtain a calibrated estimate of aggregated disposable income for the factor rule populations analysed. In order to estimate population-specific savings rates α, β and γ, we run regressions at district level in Japan using 20 years of observations. Let's assume that parameter estimates for savings rate γ_i of the FI population show a significant increase over time. This could then be interpreted as evidence for hypothesis 3b.

Distinguishing between the two levels shows why we must expect parameter values to load with significantly differing values in a statistical test of Eqs. (8.1) and (8.2). Introducing a rule perspective enables the population of agents that are willing to make savings to be determined, while the operational level incorporates the question of whether agents are in a position to do so. Comparison of results from the two levels provides valuable insights to policymakers in the form of estimates of the effect of planned policy measures on marginal savings.

8.5 Developing Policy Recommendations

Our policy recommendations consist of a threefold rule-level strategy to help the government foster aggregate savings and hence secure Japan's still solid sovereign debt rating (Blind and Lottanti 2013), which is at risk due to skyrocketing and still increasing public debt. First, we suggest lowering taxes on interest income (TAX ON INTEREST) to reduce the negative impact on the FINANCIAL INVESTMENT population. Second, we encourage the continuation of monetary policy aimed at ending deflationary tendencies, as further research points to FINANCIAL INVESTMENT depending strongly on the *perception* of interest rates—which, in turn, seems almost entirely guided by nominal interest rates (Blind 2012). Third, we briefly sketch a communication campaign aiming at instigating provisional savings among the adopters of the hedonistic lifestyle rule "to secure comfortable retirement".

***

Part II has introduced a methodological template for empirical research inspired by the rule-based approach, with a four-stage procedure for the analysis of economic change based on three premises pertaining to the economic agent—heterogeneity, openness to learning and the discriminatory use of rules for operations. The first stage determines a response rule population to distinguish change in rules from corresponding operations and to delimit the investigation spatially and temporally. The second stage proposes the identification of the most complete system of factor rules (SFR) possible, a potentially very complex model. An SFR should embrace all factor rules that have potentially caused change in the response rule during the investigation period. The third stage in turn introduces two criteria for achieving a helpful reduction of such complexity: (1) change in population size and (2) change in strength of influence on the response rule. Where neither of the two criteria tests positively, the corresponding factor rules can be excluded from further analysis. Based on the premise of heterogeneous agents, the fourth stage then shows how agent subgroups may increase explanatory power.

A touch of empirical flesh was put on the conceptual bones of our methodology with a largely fictional, yet easy-to-grasp, case study. Its purpose was to show how a rule-based theoretical frame can be linked to economic reality in an empirical study and to introduce the corresponding analytical concepts and terminology. Part *III of this volume follows the individual steps introduced here with an empirical study based on this methodology.*

References

Blind GD (2012) Investigating entrepreneurial spirit with the rule approach: why self-employment is on the decline in Japan. Evol Inst Econ Rev 9(1):183–198

Blind G, Lottanti von Mandach S (2013) Ansichtssache: Zum Zustand der japanischen Wirtschaft nach Doppelschlag und Dreifach-Katastrophe. In: Chiavacci D, Wiezcorek I (eds) Japan 2013. VSJF, Berlin, pp 131–149

Blind G, Pyka A (2014) The rule approach in evolutionary economics: a methodological template for empirical research. J Evol Econ 24(5):1085–1105
Cavelaars P (2005) Has the tradeoff between productivity gains and job growth disappeared? Kyklos 58(1):45–64
Chen K, İmrohoroğlu A et al (2006) The Japanese saving rate. Am Econ Rev 96(5):1850–1858
De Long JB (1988) Productivity growth, convergence, and welfare: comment. Am Econ Rev 78 (5):1138–1154
Dopfer K, Potts J (2008) The general theory of economic evolution. Routledge, London
Kaldor N (1975) Economic growth and the verdoorn law—a comment on Mr Rowthornz's article. Econ J 85:891–896
Modigliani F, Brumberg R (1954) Utility analysis and the aggregate consumption function: an interpretation of cross-section data. In: Kurihara KK (ed) Post-Keynesian economics. Rutgers University Press, New Brunswick

Part III
Entrepreneurship in Japan: 1992–2012

Applying the methodology developed in Part II to the case of entrepreneurship in Japan meets two objectives. First, to demonstrate how the theoretical propositions on entrepreneurship developed through the lens of the rule-based approach in Part I may guide an empirical investigation. Second, to shed light on the development of entrepreneurship in Japan between 1992 and 2012.

This Part examines the following:

1. The relationship between the rule of Individual Entrepreneurship and the operation of starting a business.
2. The factors causing and inhibiting the adoption of the rules of Individual Entrepreneurship and of Entrepreneurial Spirit.
3. The potential of 0th and 2nd order rules to inhibit or foster the use of Individual Entrepreneurship in start-up operations.

The first investigation stage requires response rules to be set (see Table 8.1, 1). In the present study, these are set to:

1. Entrepreneurial Spirit, a 2nd order cognitive rule
2. Individual Entrepreneurship, a 1st order behavioural rule

The link between the analytical levels of rules and the corresponding economic operations is established by investigating operations conducted in applying the 1st order rule of Individual Entrepreneurship. This corresponds to the frequency of business start-ups.

Entrepreneurship scholars distinguish between static and dynamic perspectives. Essentially a stock approach, the static dimension refers to the share of self-employed individuals relative to the work force, whereas the dynamic dimension relates to in- and outflows, in other words, to entry and exit rates (Wennekers et al. 2002: 29). As we are interested in entry-driven fluctuations of rule populations, we opt for the dynamic concept.

This Part is organised as follows. Chapter 9, which identifies the system of factor rules (SFR) for entrepreneurship in Japan, corresponds to the second investigation stage of the methodology outlined in Part II. Next, Chap. 10 reduces the SFR to the changing subsystem (CSS) as its causative core, that is, to the subset of factor rules that have been subject to change during the investigation period. This corresponds to the third investigation stage of our methodology. Chapter 11 identifies subgroups of agents by comparing the socioeconomic profile of the Japanese "founder force" with that of the general workforce. Specific hypotheses are then developed based on findings pertaining to subgroups of agents. Chapter 12, which corresponds to the final investigation stage, documents the testing of these hypotheses. Chapter 13 summarises findings and compares them with results from earlier studies.

Reference

Wennekers S, Uhlaner LM et al (2002) Entrepreneurship and its conditions: a macro perspective. Int J Entrep Educ 1(1):25–64

Chapter 9
Assembling the Model of Entrepreneurship in Japan: The System of Factor Rules (SFR)

Abstract We provide an exhaustive review of empirical research conducted for identifying the system of factor rules (SFR) for entrepreneurship in Japan between 1992 and 2012. It corresponds to the investigation stage of the methodology for rule-based economic analysis outlined earlier. The review covers a broad variety of sources including academic work from different disciplines as well as original research building on testimonials from rule adopters, i.e. entrepreneurs, and from rule rejecters, as well as from practitioners in finance and government. Reviewing the interrelationship between some 16 potentially relevant factor rules we achieve a first reduction of complexity by excluding factors that exert indirect influences only.

This chapter identifies what Ostrom refers to as 'rule configuration' (compare Blind 2016), i.e., all rules that potentially influence the response rules of ENTREPRENEURIAL SPIRIT and INDIVIDUAL ENTREPRENEURSHIP. Since the determinants of the frequency with which agents use INDIVIDUAL ENTREPRENEURSHIP for start-up operations are also relevant to the investigation, it might be thought that this requires three separate analyses. However, this specific set of three *explananda* is often considered an ensemble, both in most existing research[1] and in the arguments of experts and practitioners. The present study therefore conducts these inquiries jointly through the second investigation stage of our methodology (Blind and Pyka 2014), aiming to identify a triplex SFR of entrepreneurship for Japan.

9.1 Identifying Potential Factor Rules

Since our methodology calls for a diverse range of sources, we not only examine findings of previous studies but also conduct interviews with experts and with adopters and rejecters of our response rules. Interviews and fieldwork were

---

[1]Compare, e.g. Global Entrepreneurship Monitor (1999–2013) and its understanding of "entrepreneurial attitudes", "latent entrepreneurship" and "actual entrepreneurship". As noted in Part I, this closely corresponds to the rules of ENTREPRENEURIAL SPIRIT and INDIVIDUAL ENTREPRENEURSHIP and to the operation of starting a business by applying the latter.

G.D. Blind, *The Entrepreneur in Rule-Based Economics*, Economic Complexity and Evolution, DOI 10.1007/978-3-319-62779-3_9

conducted during 2008 and 2009. The 25 expert interviews involved scholars and practitioners in economics (4), sociology (3), psychology and ethnology (1 each), business studies (3), venture finance (2), experienced entrepreneurs (3), employed individuals (4) and adult individuals in higher education (4). Only those interviews which made an original contribution beyond the insights gained from literature are drawn upon here.

Many studies on self-employment and entrepreneurship in Japan examine explanatory variables originating from quite different disciplines. From the perspective of rule-based economics, this interdisciplinary tendency is a positive development. Yet such quest for more explanatory power often lacks a corresponding theoretical foundation: the clear-cut distinction of the three *explananda* identified in Part I. The literature reviewed here is thus organised not by discipline or by *explananda* but according to the methodological approach involved. Distinguishing qualitative from quantitative studies, we divide the latter into descriptive and inferential accounts. Within the last category, we make a further distinction by the type of data employed: cross-sectional versus longitudinal and micro-data versus macro data.

Qualitative Studies

Informed by the realities that entrepreneurs are facing, many *qualitative* studies meticulously investigate the local institutional environment. Similar routes of inquiry can also be found in international comparisons, such as on the (dis)similarities between Silicon Valley and Japan (Suzuki et al. 2002) or between government policies in the United States and in Japan (Aoyama 1999). We note these observations as the 0th order social rule of START-UP AID AS GOVERNMENT DUTY, which impacts positively on our response rules.

Another aspect of the institutional arrangement, PROTECTIVE BANKRUPTCY LAW, is commonly regarded a major factor to mitigate the uncertainty linked to a business start-up. It has been variously studied in general (Hughes and Burchell 2006; Armour and Cumming 2008) and also specifically for Japan (e.g. Imai and Kawagoe 2000). PROTECTIVE BANKRUPTCY LAW, a 0th order social rule, fosters entrepreneurship as it provides protection for individuals facing bankruptcy. Hence, we can note a complementary relation to our response rules.

In a review of cultural influences on entrepreneurship, George and Zahra (2002: 36) point to entrepreneurship being frequently negatively correlated with Hofstede's cultural dimension of "uncertainty avoidance" in international comparisons (e.g. Grilo and Thurik 2008). Researchers have specified this dimension for Japan as the rule of STIGMA OF FAILURE (e.g. Masuda 2010). A 2001 survey by the National Life Finance Corporation[2] provides ample evidence of the relevance of

[2]Integrated with other organizations to become Japan Finance Corporation *Nihon seisaku kin'yū kōko* in 2008, the National Life Finance Corporation *Kokumin seikatsu kin'yū kōko* (henceforth NLFC) was founded in 1949 as National Finance Corporation. It grants subsidised loans to SMEs. In 2006 outstanding loans amounted to about 60 billion euros, corresponding to 3% of the total credit volume of Japan's SMEs. As a semi-governmental institution, NLFC is under the supervision of MoF and MHLW.

this 2nd order cognitive rule. Some 80% of respondents endorsed the following statement: "our society turns its back to business failures" (NLFC 2001). Obviously, the drawbacks of business failure extend beyond pure financial risk.

Most importantly, the individual involved in a failure event understands the experience as shameful. Owing to the historical circumstances of its origin,[3] the term "culture of shame" continues to be frequently disputed. Yet it is safe to argue with Aoki that any divergence from the mean, whether positive or negative, gives rise to shame in Japan (1990). Nakamura (2008: 115) points to the earlier observation of Sakuta who reports repudiation by family members as a common reaction to failure in Japan (1967: 14). From this originates the tendency to adjust one's behaviour to the expected negative appraisal by the community to which one belongs (Hayami and Dasgupta 1996). Hence the 2nd order cognitive rule Stigma of Failure influences the decisions of agents not to embark on routes that may lead to failure, such as incurring the incalculable risk of a business start-up. Accordingly, we identify a conflicting relation to our response rules.

In a qualitative comparison of the US and Japanese entrepreneurial experiences, Daly observes that intrapreneurship in large corporations seems to be more important in Japan than in the United States (1998). With this, he implicitly alludes to the 2nd order social rule that we term the Salaryman Ideal, referring to the idealised career pattern of white collar-dependent employment in a large corporation or a government body. Obviously, there is a conflicting relation to our responses. While 2nd order Salaryman Ideal reflects the general appreciation of society, the 1st order rule of Regular Employment marks the individual preference of agents. This trade-off between dependent employment and a business start-up on the operational level has also been documented in the literature (Lee et al. 2009). Here, the satisfaction of dependently employed individuals with their job is seen as decreasing the desirability of self-employment.

Many economists have stressed the importance of interest rates for entrepreneurial activity. One of the most succinctly put renderings of this interplay is in Ludwig von Mises' *Human Action*: "A drop in the gross market rate of interest affects the entrepreneur's calculation concerning the chances of the profitability of projects considered" (1998 [1949]: 550). If reasoning with rules, however, the interest rate is only a price and thus represents an operational entity, but not a rule. In terms of rules, we note the 2nd order cognitive rule Perceived Cost of Capital as the corresponding factor rule.

Quantitative Studies: Descriptive Accounts

Arguably the largest effort in *quantitative* empirical entrepreneurship research, Global Entrepreneurship Monitor (GEM), collects most valuable data that has come to provide the basis for much of recent entrepreneurship research. GEM

[3] The term "culture of shame" originates from Benedict's 1946 volume on Japan, *The Chrysanthemum and the Sword: Patterns of Japanese Culture* (Boston: Houghton Mifflin). Mandated by the US military, the book was based almost entirely on an analysis of contemporary Japanese print media.

data has been used by researchers for evidencing the influence of business cycle fluctuations (Reynolds et al. 2002). In a rule context, business cycle fluctuations are simply prices and quantities. The underlying rule refers to the perceptions of agents that we capture through the notion of BUSINESS SENTIMENT. As a 2nd order behavioural rule, it impacts on the decisions of agents including the choice of self-employment. Depending on the circumstances of the individual agent, BUSINESS SENTIMENT may either impact positively or negatively on our responses. The line to be drawn is equivalent to the distinction between opportunity- and necessity-driven entrepreneurship (see Sect. 4.2). For instance, improving business sentiment will reduce necessity-driven business formation, while it should encourage opportunity-driven entrepreneurship.

In spite of a significant number of descriptive quantitative studies that measure differences in the characteristics of entrepreneurs across cultures (e.g. Muzyka et al. 1991; Shane et al. 1991; Thomas and Mueller 2000) and the successful cross-country cluster analysis of Mitchell et al. (2000), there is no study yet that directly compares Japanese entrepreneurs to their peers in other countries.[4] Some of the studies with an exclusive focus on entrepreneurs in Japan have produced a number of interesting insights. For instance, Ohe et al. found "Japanese entrepreneurs to have significantly higher preferences for entrepreneurial decision style, extrinsic rewards and a growth orientation" compared to corporate managers (1990). While the items covered in their survey only measure some abstract compound characteristics that are difficult to capture in concrete terms, their findings point to the relevance of the 2nd order rules of STIGMA OF FAILURE and SALARYMAN IDEAL that we have already identified.

Quantitative Studies: Inferential Accounts

Recently, a growing number of quantitative studies aspire to go beyond a descriptive approach by providing statistical inferences. Owing to data availability, most of these studies are restricted to cross-sectional comparisons, so they do not allow for a developmental perspective. Nevertheless, this type of study can provide valuable insights. For instance, a recent study on the operational effects of the STIGMA OF FAILURE rule has produced evidence of its consequences for failed entrepreneurs (Mitsuhashi and Bird 2011): access to finance proves to be significantly more restricted for failed ex-entrepreneurs.

In a four-country study of venture capital (VC) funds, Mayer et al. looked at the national characteristics of VC investments (2005). For Japan, they report that most VC funds heavily rely on so-called late-stage investments where investors are essentially not funding start-ups but expansion strategies. Their observation will help us later to assess the importance of the 1st order cognitive rule of START-UP AID AS BUSINESS, which represents the private sector equivalent of the rule of START-UP AID AS GOVERNMENT DUTY identified earlier.

---

[4]The only known attempt did not succeed in collecting a sufficiently large sample for Japan: Mitchell, R. K., B. Smith et al. (2000). "Cross-Cultural Cognitions and the Venture Creation Decision", *Academy of Management Journal* **43**(5): 974–93.

Micro-data often allow for statistically authoritative results. Genda and Kambayashi used the National Survey on Family Income and Expenditure (NSFIE) to investigate correlations between self-employment and a number of sociological factors (2002). While their choice of explanatory items was clearly guided (and obviously limited) by the data available from NSFIE, they were able to extract some characteristics linked to the likelihood of individuals becoming entrepreneurs. Similarly to Harada and Masuda (2005, 2006), they find the urban–rural divide significant, but unlike them, they use wage differences, obviously a strong covariate of the urban–rural divide, as basis for their explanation. Unfortunately, however, their research does not reflect on the compensating effect of higher purchasing power in less well-off rural areas. They also do not discuss any potential motivating factors other than monetary ones. Genda and Kambayashi's welcome attempt to compare data from two points in time (1989 and 1994) finds little evidence of change, arguably due to the relatively short time span covered. Within the socio-economic variables analysed, they identify age, gender and human capital as significantly correlated with the likelihood of becoming self-employed. These items potentially have discriminatory power for the second step of our last investigation stage (see Table 8.1), which identifies subgroups of agents.

Another recent study relying on micro-data from a retroactive panel constructs subgroups of agents by gender and education (Diamond and Schaede 2013), but discriminating by these two dimensions does not produce evidence of the push hypothesis of necessity entrepreneurship being the main driving force behind business formation in Japan. Diamond and Schaede also find that favourable job–market conditions correlate positively with business formation by highly educated women, evidence that this particular subgroup understands job–market conditions as a proxy for the potential success of an intended start-up. Their findings also confirm the observation that the average start-up funds of women founders are significantly higher than those of men (Blind 2012). Diamond and Schaede also confirm Ishida's earlier finding (2008) that becoming self-employed is strongly influenced by having a self-employed parent. This endorses our view of the 2nd order rule of ENTREPRENEURIAL SPIRIT as impacting positively on the 1st order rule of INDIVIDUAL ENTREPRENEURSHIP.

Diamond and Schaede's analysis (see their Table 3.1) also suggests that individuals quitting non-regular employment[5] are three times more likely to enter self-employment than their peers in regular employment. From rule perspective, therefore, the population of the 1st order social rule of NON-REGULAR EMPLOYMENT is subject to fluctuation through agents entering as new adopters and through agents leaving as they cease to retain the rule. Whether the size of the NON-REGULAR

[5]For Japan, we can distinguish two main categories of dependent employment: regular employees, *sei'sha'in,* and non-regular employees, *hi'sei'sha'in.* While regular employment almost imperatively implies full-time work, non-regular employment comprises the sub-categories of temporary work, *haken* (via dispatch agencies), part-time jobs, *paato,* and jobbing, *arubeito.* In public discourse, the term *furiitaa* – derived from *free* and *arbeiter* – exclusively refers to individuals in non-regular employment aged under 35.

Employment population has a positive net impact on Individual Entrepreneurship depends on a simple question: are leaving agents more likely to adopt Individual Entrepreneurship than entering agents, i.e. does retaining Non-regular Employment imply an increase in the likelihood of subsequently adopting Individual Entrepreneurship? Schaede and Diamond's findings indicate that this is actually true. As Non-regular Employment itself represents an alternative to Individual Entrepreneurship, the individual agent entering Non-regular Employment cannot adopt Individual Entrepreneurship at the same time. Yet, the larger Non-regular Employment grows, the greater the number of agents leaving the population, at least given *c.p.* conditions, e.g. stable exit rates. Therefore, we note Non-regular Employment as a potential factor increasing new entry into Individual Entrepreneurship.

These considerations deserve some discussion, as the underlying mechanisms are not necessarily obvious. What critically determines the attractiveness of self-employment relative to dependent employment is the significant differential in the social security levels implied by standard and non-standard employment (compare Blind and Lottanti 2015). While standard employment is subject to full social security coverage, non-standard employment does not come with any comparable benefits in Japan. What is more, wages in non-standard employment do not yet compensate for this in spite of a recently narrowing pay gap (Blind and Lottanti 2015, 2017a). Moreover, job security continues to be high, a societal value even respected by foreign private equity investors (Blind and Lottanti 2017b). Consequently, self-employment represents a relatively more attractive alternative to individuals in non-regular employment than to individuals in regular employment, as the transition implies no significant change in expected level of social security but promises a potentially higher income.

Conceptually, non-regular employees can be conceived as "independent temp firms" assigning themselves to a succession of jobs. It would be hard to identify significant differences between most non-regular employees and many of the about 4 million businesses without employees. On the contrary, there are strong similarities; consider, for example, a one-man taxi business and how it compares to an individual working in a call centre via a temp agency.

A renowned expert in the fields of start-up finance, Prof. Yasuyuki Hamada, points to the importance of legislation on minimum capital requirements for the incorporation of a company. On 1 April 2006, the capital requirements for establishing a joint-stock company (*kabushiki kaisha*) were lowered from 10 million yen to a symbolic 1 yen. As this is the most frequently used device for establishing legal entities, Prof. Hamada expects a significantly positive effect on new venture creation (2008). We note this as the 0th order social rule of Minimum Capital Requirements.

In an interview on recent developments in the Japanese labour market and its potential consequences for entrepreneurial activity, Prof. Ki'ichiro Yagi of Kyoto University (2008) suggests that decline in union activity favours business start-ups, as entrepreneurs encounter less difficulty in securing skilled labour. We note

ORGANISED LABOUR, the idea of collective wage bargaining, as a 0th order social rule that impacts negatively on our responses.

Discussing potential inhibitors of entrepreneurial activity in Japan, sociologist Toshio Sugiman (2008) pointed to the sustained influence of traditional class order which divided the population into a ruling class and a class of the ruled. The latter was subdivided by their respective productive functions into primary, secondary and tertiary occupations. Known as *Shinōkōshō* (士農工商) in Japan, the four Chinese characters refer to the hierarchy of a ruling military class of warriors *Shi* (士) and a class of the ruled consisting of farmers *Nō* (農), craftsmen *Kō* (工) and merchants *Shō* (商). Against this background, Prof. Sugiman argues that new business ventures outside the agricultural and manufacturing sectors continue to be regarded as minor occupations effectively inhibiting new business formation. He even suggested that suicide might represent a more honourable solution to the budget constraint implied by unemployment than commencing a commercial type of self-employment.[6] Based on these considerations, we note TRADITIONAL CLASS ORDER as a 2nd order cognitive rule that impacts negatively on the creation of new ventures.

Psychologist Dr. Naoko Nojima (2008) cited STIGMA OF FAILURE as a major inhibitor of business start-ups in Japan. Furthermore, Dr. Nojima mentioned fear of unemployment as a cause of inertia in many dependently employed individuals. As she decidedly excluded any potential of a "pre-emptive business start-up" as a cure to that anxiety, we can note that the 2nd order cognitive rule of FEAR OF UNEMPLOYMENT impacts negatively on our response rules.

Combining ample experience in corporate Japan with an academic career, Dr. Shizuo Asogawa synthesises his experiences in lecturing business studies to graduate students in Japan: "Essentially, young Japanese continue to cherish the ideal of a salaryman working at a large corporation such as Toyota, etc. Starting one's own business looks literally like fooling around to most of them" (2009). We note his observation as confirming the negative impact of the 2nd order cognitive rule SALARYMAN IDEAL on our *explananda*.

One member of a business-owning family—hence, a rule adopter—stressed the prohibitive lending policies of Japanese banks when it comes to start-up finance. To obtain start-up finance with any banking institution, the applicant has to produce either substantial collateral—mainly as real estate—or as personal guarantees from one or more solvent individuals who typically are relatives of the borrower (Asogawa 2008). This type of constraint places a heavy burden on any business founder. Consequently, we note the 1st order behavioural rule of START-UP COVENANTS as a potential factor rule impacting negatively on our responses.

A female entrepreneur active in the field of nursing services for the elderly described her personal start-up motivations primarily by comparing her current situation to the previous one in dependent employment (Tanioka 2008). While

[6]Sudden unemployment linked to economic hardship is the single most frequent reason identified for suicide among male adults in Japan.

working as contract nurse for a homecare network, she faced an unbalanced workload that directly translated into a strongly fluctuating income stream. By establishing her own homecare agency, she was able to better control her workload and regularise and even increase her income. This provides further anecdotal evidence to support Diamond and Schaede's finding on the strongly increased likelihood of individuals in non-regular employment to make the transition into self-employment.

A number of additional factors are cited among rule rejecters. One young graduate employed in the public sector points to the interplay between parental job preferences—as epitomised by the SALARYMAN IDEAL—and the Confucian value of FILIAL PIETY (*oyakōkō*), a 2nd order social rule. Individuals in the West will tend to pursue their career choices quite independently from their parents. In contrast, Confucian tradition generates a strong "parental super-ego" exerting significant influence on career choices in Japan. Our informant "would not even think of starting his own business given the preferences of his parents" (Makino 2008). The only son in his family, our informant, stated that his situation would be quite different if he had a number of brothers. In essence, we can note with Leibenstein that parental expectations towards their offspring on a per capita basis decrease with the number of siblings in a family (Leibenstein 1968). The SMALL FAMILY IDEAL represents the underlying 1st order behavioural rule that makes for changes in the intensity at which FILIAL PIETY becomes effective. The continuing relevance of confucianist values is not undebated, particularly so for larger organisational units such as in industrial relations (Lottanti von Mandach 2014). Survey data on individuals, however, indicates their continuing relevance (IStM 2013; Chapter 10).

Another rule rejecter explained that the rise of performance-based pay and career advancement (*Seika shugi*) in Japanese corporations has rendered dependent employment far more attractive to young graduates (Semba 2008). This view contrasts with the seniority principle (*Nenkō joretsu*) that has traditionally formed the key criterion for any decisions made by the human resource departments of Japanese companies. Turning his argument around, the relative attractiveness of self-employment would decrease among younger individuals, but older individuals would find self-employment a relatively more attractive choice if seniority was no longer a guarantee to high wages. Both PERFORMANCE PRINCIPLE and SENIORITY PRINCIPLE are 1st order social rules guiding the design of employee incentives. As the two rules approximately offset each other, it suffices to select one of them. We opt for PERFORMANCE PRINCIPLE as the more recent development.

In this section, we have amended the theoretical core developed in Part I with a considerable number of factor rules that potentially impact on our responses, excluding operational entities and categorising all factor rules according to the rule taxonomy (Table 2.1). This procedure also clarifies their relationships to our response rules. Table 9.1 summarises these relationships, also indicating the composition of rule populations and providing examples of operations.

Table 9.1 List of rules for establishing the rule system of entrepreneurship in Japan

Factor rule	Order, class, relation	Rule population	Operations (exemplary)
1. Minimum capital requirements	0, S, –	Law-abiding agents	Business incorporations
2. Start-up aid as government duty	0, S, +	Government	Public financial institutions, Angel tax, incubators
3. Protective bankruptcy law (PBL)	0, S, +	Law-abiding agents	Bankruptcy filings
4. Organised labour (OrL)	0, S, –	Unionised labour	Union action
5. Perceived cost of capital (PCoC)	2, C, –	Agents	Use of rule for decisions
6. Start-up covenants (bank lending)	1, B, –	Banks	Credit conditions
7. Start-up aid as a business (SUB)	1, C, +	VC community	Venture capital investments
8. Business sentiment	2, B, +/–[a]	Agents	Use of rule for guiding decisions
9. Stigma of failure (StF)	2, C, –	"	Use of rule for guiding decisions (risk aversion)
10. Traditional class order (TCO)	2, C, –	"	Use of rule for guiding decisions
11. Filial piety (FP)	2, S, –	"	"
12. Small family ideal (SFI)	1, B(–)	Individuals	Household structures
13. Salaryman ideal[b] (SI)	2, S, –	Employees	Use of rule for judgements
14. Performance principle[b]	1, S, –	Employers	Promotion and remuneration in dependent employment
15. Non-regular employment[b] (NRE)	1, S, +	Employees	Non-regular employment contracts
16. Fear of unemployment[b]	2, C, –	Employees	Use of rule for guiding decisions

[a]Sign depends on distinction between necessity- and opportunity-driven entrepreneurship
[b]Pertaining to economic alternatives to self-employment

9.2 Interdependencies Between Factor Rules

Our methodology requires an analysis of the interrelationships within the ensemble of explanatory factors as the fifth and last step of the second investigation stage. This corresponds to the efforts to avoid multicollinearity among explanatory variables in multivariate regressions. In rule-based analysis, we effect this control by reviewing associations between factor rules, which necessitates a hermeneutic approach. Importantly, this necessity does not arise from a lack of appropriate quantitative data but from the need to understand whether or not an interrelation is actually systematic. Obviously, bare correlation coefficients cannot inform such analysis. Below we discuss all rules where significant interrelationships occur. References to rule numbers in Table 9.1 are given in parentheses.

The 2nd order rules Traditional Class Order (10) and Salaryman Ideal (13) are closely related core elements of the Japanese value system. Historically, the Salaryman Ideal has evolved from the background of Traditional Class Order, which places the loyally serving warrior (士) at the top of the traditional social hierarchy. This also helps to explain the common disregard of non-regular employees who are seen as "masterless". As Traditional Class Order is found to be superseding the Salaryman Ideal, we can exclude the latter from our list of potential factor rules.

By the same token, Traditional Class Order has a negative association with the 1st order rule of Non-regular Employment (15). While losing a job in regular employment typically equals a "downgrade" into non-standard employment, individuals already retaining Non-regular Employment are naturally less likely to adopt the 2nd order rule of Fear of Unemployment (16).

The inner workings of Filial Piety (11) strongly depend on demographic change as the preferences of parents concentrate more strongly on a smaller number of offspring, representing operations on the Small Family Ideal (12). On closer inspection, we find that operations on Small Family Ideal reinforce Filial Piety and that Filial Piety in turn reinforces Traditional Class Order and Stigma of Failure (9), where offspring conform to the preferences of parents. Hence, as neither Small Family Ideal nor Filial Piety exerts a direct influence on our responses, we exclude them from the SFR. Yet, it is important to keep this hierarchical system of influences in mind for later analytical stages.

The link between Start-up Aid as Government Duty (2) and Start-up Aid as a Business (7) arguably needs less explanation, as it conceptually represents a standard crowding-out problem. In a similar vein, Start-up covenants (6) share a negative relation with Protective Bankruptcy Law (3): where bankruptcy protection is strong, banks will tend to ask for stricter covenants and vice versa.

Finally, Protective Bankruptcy Law is also linked to Stigma of Failure (9), as it seems to reflect society's need of protection against societal stigma. However, the literature on this relation in the specific case of Japan suggests that the mere act of filing for bankruptcy is associated with an extremely high level of stigma to the extent that "entrepreneurs filing for bankruptcy may experience a higher level of stigma, which is likely to deter would-be entrepreneurs from pursuing their visions" (Lee et al. 2007: 266). So, while corporations may well benefit from bankruptcy legislation, Protective Bankruptcy Law does not become effective for individual entrepreneurs. Consequently, we can eliminate Protective Bankruptcy Law from our list of potential factors.

Table 9.2 summarises the relation matrix for the list of factors as provided in Table 9.1. To that end, we first draw a matrix enabling all relations between factor rules to be reviewed. Methodologically, this represents the qualitative equivalent of correlation matrices known from statistics.

Table 9.2 Relation matrix for factor rules of entrepreneurship in Japan

	1	2	3	4	5	6	7	8	9	10	11	12	13	14	15	16
1. Minimum capital requirements		0	0	0	0	0	0	0	0	0	0	0	0	0	0	0
2. Start-up aid as government duty			0	0	0	0	–	0	0	0	0	0	–	0	0	0
3. Protective Bankruptcy Law				0	0	+	0	0	–	0	0	0	0	0	0	0
4. Organised Labour					0	0	0	0	0	0	0	0	0	0	0	0
5. Perceived cost of capital						0	0	0	0	0	0	0	0	0	0	0
6. Start-up covenants							0	0	0	0	0	0	0	0	0	0
7. Start-up aid as a business								0	0	0	0	0	0	0	0	0
8. Business sentiment									0	0	0	0	0	0	0	0
9. Stigma of failure										0	0	+	0	0	0	0
10. Traditional class order											0	+	+	0	–	0
11. Filial piety												+	+	0	–	0
12. Small family ideal													0	0	0	0
13. Salaryman ideal[a]														0	–	0
14. Performance principle[a]															0	0
15. Non-regular employment[a]																–
16. Fear of Unemployment[a]																

[a]Rules that are economic alternatives to self-employment

Based on the population approach in rules-based economics, Table 9.2 can be read as follows: if being a member of population *A* does not come with an increased (+) or decreased (−) likelihood of being a member of population *B*, the relation is marked as (0). Using this qualitative assessment of associations between factor rules, we have identified 13 cases of feedback relations for the 120 recombinations.

9.3 SFR of Entrepreneurship in Japan

With the results of the analysis of interdependencies of factor rules, we can now establish the triplex SFR for entrepreneurship in Japan. Table 9.3 provides an overview of the remaining 12 factor rules, listing the interdependencies already identified.

Table 9.3 The triplex rule system of entrepreneurship in Japan

Factor rule	Order, class, relation	Related with
1. Minimum capital requirements	0, S, –	
2. Start-up aid as government duty	0, S, +	7
4. Organised labour	0, S, –	
5. Perceived cost of capital	2, C, –	
6. Start-up covenants (bank lending)	1, B, –	
7. Start-up aid as a business	1, C, +	2
8. Business sentiment	2, B, +/–[a]	
9. Stigma of failure	2, C, –	
10. Traditional class order	2, C, –	15
14. Performance principle[b]	1, S, –	
15. Non-regular employment[b]	1, S, +	16
16. Fear of unemployment[b]	2, C, –	

[a]Sign depends on distinction between necessity- and opportunity-driven entrepreneurship
[b]Pertaining to economic alternatives to self-employment

The distinction between classes and orders of rules (see p. 25) provides important clues for subsequent analytical steps. It is important to keep in mind that operations conducted on 2nd order rules do not yield directly observable phenomena but consist of acts of cognition. For instance, where agents are judging Individual Entrepreneurship, that is, the idea of making a living from being self-employed, by referring to Traditional Class Order or Stigma of Failure, this act of cognition equals a corresponding operation. The same holds true for operations on the behavioural 2nd order rule of Business Sentiment. In contrast, operations on 1st order rules, such as the social rule of Non-regular Employment, yield directly observable operations manifested in the number of individuals newly employed in non-standard positions.

***

This chapter took us on an exploratory journey identifying factors that potentially impact on our responses during the investigation period. By relying on a broad variety of sources including academic work from different disciplines and by including testimonials from rule adopters, i.e. entrepreneurs, and from rule rejecters, as well as from practitioners in finance and government, we have conducted "sound antecedent qualitative analysis". Methodologically, we have thus applied a hermeneutic technique in a wider sense as we have opted for an interpretative analysis of texts and of oral testimonials.

Our journey has resulted in a list of as many as 16 potentially relevant factor rules. However, we were able to achieve a first reduction of complexity by reviewing their interrelationships in close analogy to the correlation matrices used for checking on multicollinearity in multivariate statistical analysis. As a result, we have found that several factors only exert secondary influences on our responses. While we have excluded these from the system of factor rules, we note them for later reference. Through their known relationships to primary factors, they may effectively serve as indicator variables where data on primary factors is not available. Also, secondary factors might prove an important vehicle for policy design, as they may offer a lever to pull where the corresponding primary factor cannot be directly targeted.

References

Aoki T (1990) Nihon Bunka-Ron [Theorizing on Japanese Culture]. *Chūō Kōronsha*, Tokyo

Aoyama Y (1999) Policy interventions for industrial network formation: contrasting historical underpinnings of the Small Business Policy in Japan and the United States. Small Bus Econ 12:217–231

Armour J, Cumming D (2008) Bankruptcy law and entrepreneurship. Law Working Papers 105, - European Corporate Governance Institute, pp 1–36

Asogawa S (2008) Dr. Asogawa on the lending practices of Japanese banks. Interview with author. Kyoto, 17 April

Asogawa S (2009) Dr. Asogawa on occupations preferences in contemporary Japan. Interview with author. Kyoto, 2 April

Blind GD (2012) Unternehmensgründer in Japan seit 1991: Evidenz zur Evolution gegensätzlicher Gründergruppen. G. Distelrath, H. Menkhaus and H. D. Ölschleger, Bonner Japanforschungen 29. Bier'sche Verlagsanstalt, Bonn, pp 19–68

Blind GD (2016) Behavioral rules: Veblen, Nelson-Winter, Oström and beyond. In: Frantz R, Chen S-H, Dopfer K, Heukelom F, Mousavi S (eds) Routledge handbook of behavioral economics. Routledge, Milton Park, pp 139–151

Blind GD, Lottanti von Mandach S (2015) Decades not lost, but won: increased employment, higher wages, and more equal opportunities in the Japanese labour market. Soc Sci Jpn J 18 (1):63–88

Blind G, Lottanti von Mandach S (2017a) Secular trends in the Japanese labour market during the lost decades: a reply to Andrew Gordon. MPRA working paper 80812. University of Munich, Munich

Blind G, Lottanti von Mandach S (2017b) When vultures bring blessings: employment growth in Japanese businesses under private equity ownership. MPRA working paper 80816. University of Munich, Munich

Blind G, Pyka A (2014) The rule approach in evolutionary economics: a methodological template for empirical research. J Evol Econ 24(5):1085–1105

Daly GG (1998) Entrepreneurship and business culture in Japan and the U.S. Jpn World Econ 10:487–494

Diamond J, Schaede U (2013) Self-employment in Japan. A microanalysis of personal profiles. Soc Sci Jpn J 16(1):1–27

Genda Y, Kambayashi R (2002) Declining self-employment in Japan. J Jpn Int Econ 16:73–91

George G, Zahra SA (2002) Culture and its consequences for entrepreneurship. Entrep Theory Pract 26(4):5–7

Grilo I, Thurik R (2008) Determinants of entrepreneurial engagement levels in Europe and the US. Ind Corp Change 17(6):1113–1145

Hamada Y (2008) Prof. Hamada on entepreneurial finance. Interview with author. Kyoto, 10 July

Harada N (2005) Potential Entrepreneurship in Japan. Small Bus Econ 25(3):293–304

Hayami Y, Dasgupta P (1996) The international economic association's roundtable conference on cultural consequences on growth and development. Yomiuri Morning Edition, Tokyo, p 13

Hughes A, Burchell B (2006) The stigma of failure: an international comparison of failure tolerance and second chancing. University of Cambridge Working Paper 334, Centre for Business Research

Imai Y, Kawagoe M (2000) Business Start-ups in Japan: problems and policies. Oxf Rev Econ Pol 16(2):114–123

Ishida T (2008) Die Entdeckung der Gesellschaft [Sociology in Japan]-Edited and translated by Wolfgang Seifert (Nihon no shakai kagaku, Tokyo Daigaku shuppansha, 1984). Suhrkamp, Frankfurt am Main

IStM (1993–2013) Kokuminsei no kenkyū. Daijūichiji nisensan'nen zenkoku chōsa [A study of the Japanese national character—the 12th nationwide survey 2008]. Research Report. Institute of Statistical Mathematics, Tokyo

Lee L, Wong PK et al (2009) Entrepreneurial intentions: the influence of organizational and individual factors. J Bus Venturing 26(1):124–136

Lee S-H, Peng MW et al (2007) Bankruptcy law and entrepreneurship development: a real options perspective. Acad Manag Rev 32(1):257–272

Leibenstein H (1968) Entrepreneurship and development. Am Econ Rev 58(2):72–83

Lottanti von Mandach S (2014) Neo-Confucianism and industrial relations in Meiji Japan. J Manage Hist 20(4):387–408. https://doi.org/10.1108/JMH-07-2013-0031

Makino K (2008) Dr. Makino on job preferences and Filial Piety. Interview with author. Kyoto, 14 May

Masuda T (2006) The determinants of latent Entrepreneurship in Japan. Small Bus Econ 26:227–240

Masuda T (2010) Entrepreneurial re-starters in Japan. Int J Entrep Small Bus 11(2):145–163

Mayer C, Schoors K et al (2005) Sources of funds and investment activities of venture capital funds: evidence from Germany, Israel, Japan and the United Kingdom. J Corp Finance 11:586–608

Mises Lv (1998[1949]) Human action. Ludwig von Mises Institute, Auburn

Mitchell RK, Smith B et al (2000) Cross-cultural cognitions and the venture creation decision. Acad Manag J 43(5):974–993

Mitsuhashi H, Bird A (2011) The stigma of failure and limited opportunities for ex-failed entrepreneurs' redemption in Japan. In: Usui C (ed) Comparative entrepreneurship initiatives: studies in China, Japan, and the USA. Palgrave Macmillan, New York, pp 222–246

Muzyka DF, Kets de Vries M et al (1991) Cross cultural aspects of entrepreneurship: a European view. In: Churchill NC, Birley S, Doutriaux J et al (eds) Frontiers of entrepreneurship research 1993. Babson College, Babson Park, pp 545–561

Nakamura, Y (2008) Bushidō-Diskurs. Die Analyse der Diskrepanz zwischen Ideal und Realität im Bushidō-Diskurs aus dem Jahr 1904. PhD Thesis, Faculty of Philosophy, University of Vienna, Vienna

NLFC (2001) 'Nidome no kaigyō' ni kan suru jittai chōsa kekka ni tsuite [Survey on Second Chancing: results]. National Life Finance Corporation, Tokyo

Nojima N (2008) Dr. Nojima on psychological aspects of entrepreneurship in Japan. Interview with author. Kyoto, 12 Sept

Ohe T, Honjo S et al (1990) Japanese entrepreneurs and corporate managers: a comparison. J Bus Venturing 6(2):135–144

Reynolds PD, Bygrave WD et al (2002) Global entrepreneurship monitor 2002 executive report. Babson College, Wellesley

Sakuta K (1967) Haji no bunka saikō [Reflection on the culture of shame]. Shikuma Shobo, Tokyo

Semba T (2008) Semba Takahiro on attractiveness of corporate careers. Interview with author. Kyoto, 13 May

Shane S, Kolvereid L et al (1991) An exploratory examination of the reasons leading to new firm formation across country and gender. J Bus Venturing 6:431–446

Sugiman T (2008) Prof. Sugiman on sociological aspects of business formation. Interview with author. Kyoto, 30 April

Suzuki K-i, Kim S-H et al (2002) Entrepreneurship in Japan and Silicon Valley: a comparative study. Technovation 22:595–606

Tanioka F (2008) Mrs. Tanioka on self-employment out of non-regular dependent employment. Interview with author. Kyoto, 4 April

Thomas AS, Mueller SL (2000) A case for comparative entrepreneurship: assessing the relevance of culture. J Int Bus Stud 31(2):287–301

Chapter 10
Reducing the Model of Entrepreneurship in Japan: Extraction of its Changing Sub-system (CSS)

Abstract Various factors grouped into the system of factor rules (SFR) are related to the level of entrepreneurship in Japan. Here, we reduce the SFR to the changing sub-system (CSS) as its causative core. The CSS embraces the subset of factor rules that have been impacting on the rule complex of entrepreneurship in Japan during the investigation period. This reduction of complexity is achieved by excluding "false positives" through systematic assessment against two criteria of change.

Upon a discussion of factor rules that are part of the economic environment in which business formation takes place, we assesse factor rules relevant to the position of business founders in society as well as the role of government in fostering self-employment and entrepreneurship. We close by discussing changes in those factor rules that represent or refer to economic alternatives to self-employment. In summary, private and public venture support and protective bankruptcy law have an insignificant influence on entrepreneurship in Japan. Similarly, there is insignificant change in labour unions, lending practices and HR management.

While all rules in the triplex SFR are reportedly influencing the responses, understanding the origins of fluctuations in the responses requires an assessment of all SFR rules against the two criteria introduced in our methodology (Chap. 6, Blind and Pyka 2014: 1093):

(a) *Variation in population sizes of factor rules*
(b) *Variation in strength of influence (of factor rules on the responses)*

This procedure helps to extract those rules in the SFR that have evolved during the investigation period and have thus caused change in the response rule. It results in a split of the SFR into the *changing sub-system* (CSS) and the *meta-stable sub-system* (MSSS).

In this chapter the rule numbers in parentheses refer to Table 9.3. First, we discuss factor rules that are part of the economic environment in which business formation takes place (Rules 5–8). Second, we assess factor rules relevant to the position of business founders in society (Rules 9 and 10). Third, we look at the role of government in fostering self-employment and entrepreneurship (Rules 1 and 2). And fourth, we discuss changes in those factor rules that represent or refer to economic alternatives to self-employment (Rules 4 and 14–16).

G.D. Blind, *The Entrepreneur in Rule-Based Economics*, Economic Complexity and Evolution, DOI 10.1007/978-3-319-62779-3_10

10.1 Economic Environment

After a discussion of the PERCEIVED COST OF CAPITAL (5), we enquire into "access to finance", an issue considered key in entrepreneurship research (Beck and Demirgüc-Kunt 2008). To that end we investigate START-UP COVENANTS (6), that is, the terms and conditions under which banks provide loans to business start-ups. Next, we illustrate the Japanese venture capital industry to assess START-UP AID AS A BUSINESS (7). And finally, we shed light on BUSINESS SENTIMENT (8) as the 2nd order rule reflecting agents' perception of business cycle movements.

Figure 10.1 provides an overview of the development of nominal interest rates and inflation and of real interest rates as the difference between the two. It shows that discount rates have been decreasing almost over the entire investigation period, implying a decreasing cost of borrowing. Typically, fully collateralised loans are charged at about two percentage points above the discount rate. Real interest rates have seen a similar development, featuring a significant decrease since 1991 with 1997, 1998 and 2006 even reaching negative figures.

As for the PERCEIVED COST OF CAPITAL (5), there are two reasons why nominal interest rates represent the principal point of reference for any agent deliberating on a business start-up. First, inflation was close to an average of zero for almost the entire investigation period. Second, and more importantly, deflation is hardly more than a vaguely familiar term to the majority of agents. This claim along with other hypotheses will be tested in the analysis in Chap. 12. Nevertheless, we can already attribute PERCEIVED COST OF CAPITAL to the CSS as we have identified significant variation in monetary policy during the investigation period (criterion 2).

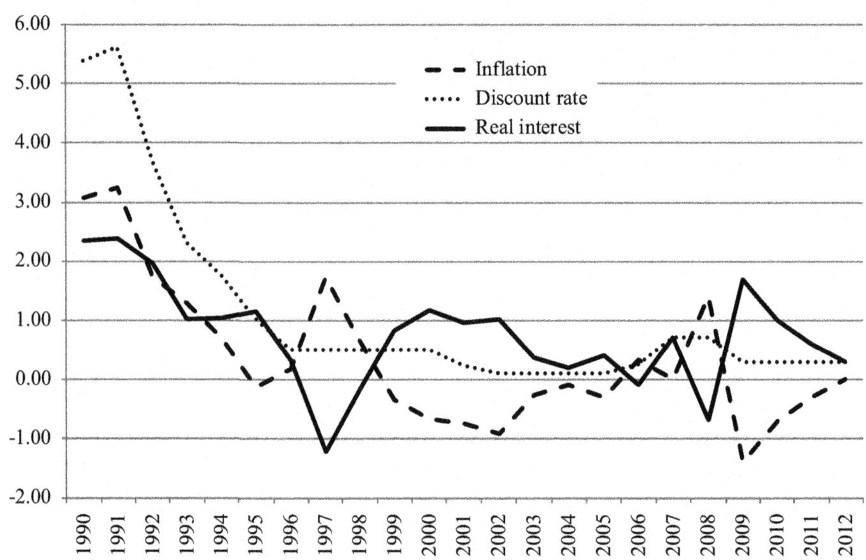

Fig. 10.1 Discount rates, inflation and real interest rates (in %), 1990–2012. Source: BoJ

While our review of monetary policy suggests that there have been positive stimuli to business formation, the actual procurement of funds continues to represent the biggest challenge to business founders in Japan. In a survey of founders of businesses started between 2001 and 2006 by the Japan Institute of Workers' Evolution (JIWE),[1] about 30% of respondents claimed to have had difficulties procuring the funds required for their start-up (JIWE 2006). These results are entirely in line with evidence gathered from business founders (Watanabe 2008), from Japanese academics (Kawai and Urata 2002; Asogawa 2008) and from representatives of the country's venture capital industry (Tagaya 2008; Takagi 2008). According to their testimonies, banks are categorically imposing full collateralisation on all types of credit to young businesses from start-up until the completion of the third year of operation. In addition to tangible collateral such as real estate and other assets, banks frequently rely on personal guarantors (Ozaki 2002). These practices reportedly go back way beyond the investigation period considered in this research (Asogawa 2008). A survey conducted by Mizuho Research (2006) finds that a mere 1.9% of SMEs choose a lender based on the conditions offered regarding collateral and guarantees. It is clear that all banks (criterion 1) are offering the same conditions including the requirement for full collateralisation for start-up loans. As this practice has remained unchanged (criterion 2) for the entire investigation period, we can attribute START-UP COVENANTS (6) to the MSSS.

Theoretically, credit supply should be balanced through the price mechanism—the interest rates charged and the individual credit risks involved. However, systemic frictions and regulatory action may cause significant distortions. Systemic frictions were at play particularly after the burst of the Japanese asset bubble in the early 1990s. In order to avoid necessary write-downs, many banks extended additional credit lines to distressed borrowers. At the same time, most banks tried to generate fresh cash flows with new credit volume (Kanaya and Woo 2000; Waldenberger 2000) and effective credit supply even increased. In a quarterly survey, the NLFC examines the assessments of Japanese SMEs pertaining to "funding difficulties" (NLFC 1987–2008). The ratio of "improving" to "worsening" increased from 40:60 in 1992 to nearly 45:55 in 1997. Obviously, these systemic frictions led to an expansion of credit supply during that period.

These practices came to an end with the 1998 banking crisis and ensuing regulatory action. On the one hand, the central bank provided large amounts of fresh liquidity to the banking system. But at the same time, banks were forced to clean up their balance sheets, which necessitated restrictions on new lending activities. While some 17% of SMEs turned to other lenders in 1998 (Bushimata and Shiro 2002), the situation was clearly less difficult for start-up financing

[1]A Tokyo-based foundation (Japanese, *Nijû'isseiki shokugyô zaidan*) was established in 1986 as Japan Institute for Women's Employment and renamed in 1993. Besides activities aimed at improving labour conditions, JIWE conducts research on various aspects of the Japanese labour market.

activities as the practice of full collateralisation allowed banks to create new business at very low risk. With the situation even improving after the turn of the millennium, we conclude that at no time during the investigation period did credit supply for start-up activities fall short of demand.

Venture capital relates to the rule of START-UP AID AS A BUSINESS (7). The pertinent literature stresses the importance of risk capital as a stimulus to economic growth (e.g. Samila and Sorenson 2011). Given the banks' insistence on full collateralisation of start-up loans, venture funding might not only offer significant profit opportunities to investors but may also represent an attractive alternative source of funds to business founders. As a 1st order rule, START-UP AID AS A BUSINESS lends itself directly to the operation of start-up finance. Accordingly, assessment of its rule population (criterion 1) requires assessment of the evolution of total funds invested.

As in most other developed economies, there are also established market structures for this type of investment in Japan. In 2007, there were more than 100 funds operating a risk capital business (VEC 2008). Figure 10.2 illustrates the development of venture capital investments since 1995 in a comparison with the United States.

Between 1995 and 2007, VC investments in the United States and Japan saw completely different trajectories. In the United States, investments multiplied to reach ten times their 1995 level by 2001. In contrast, investments in Japan increased by a mere 15% over the same period, reaching a level of only one trillion yen. This growth differential resulted in a widening gap between US and Japanese venture capital markets: US market size was five times the Japanese market in 1995 but had

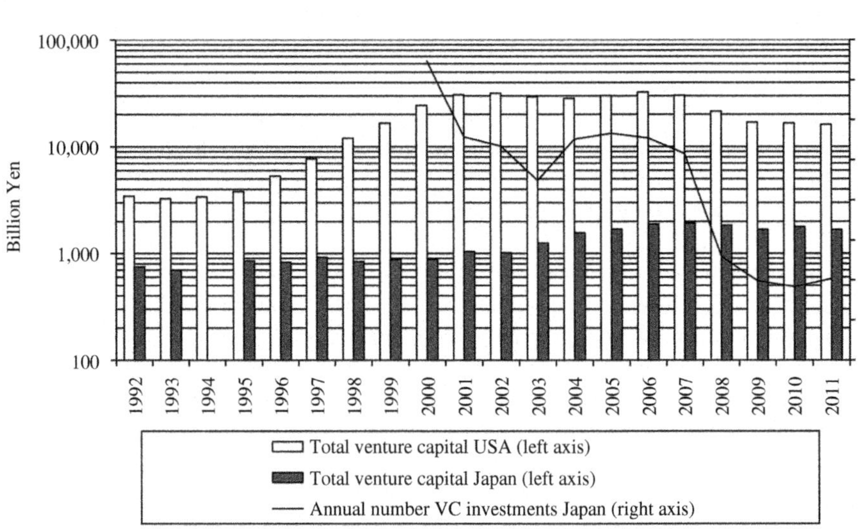

Fig. 10.2 Venture capital in Japan and in the United States, 1992–2011. Source: VEC (2002–2013) and NVCA (2013)

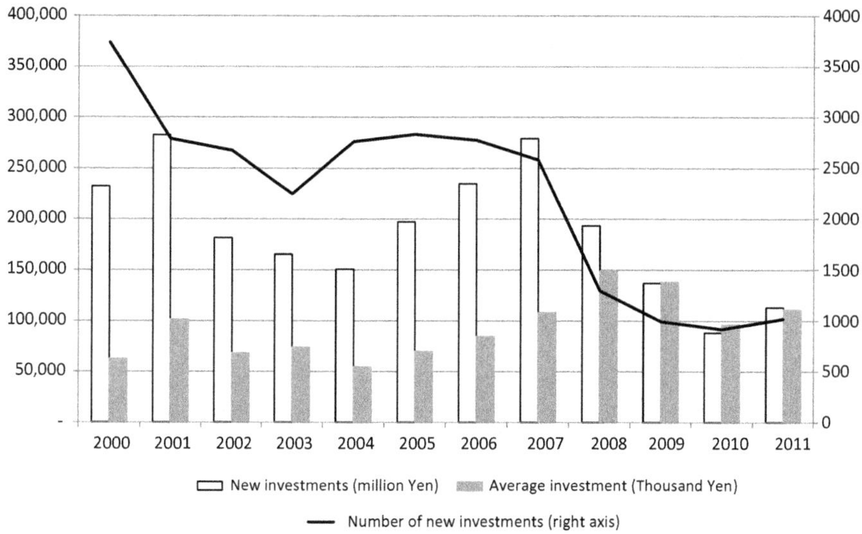

Fig. 10.3 Annual VC investments, average funds and number of targets, 2000–2011. Source: VEC (2002–2013)

surged to an impressive multiple of 30 by 2001. This ratio eventually came down to a multiple of 15 by 2007 as a result of the so-called Koizumi boom (2002–2006).

Until 1999 VEC's annual survey only included investment stocks, which effectively impedes any inferences about the annual number of new investment targets. Accordingly, Fig. 10.3 reports total and average volume as well as the annual number of new investments since 2000.

The number of annual new investment cases decreased strongly from close to 4000 cases in 2000 to a mere 1000 cases since 2009. At the same time, the average investment doubled from around 50 million yen to 100 million yen. With poorly performing equity markets, the prospects of a successful placement have strongly deteriorated. Against this background, it is hardly surprising that the implicit average capital lock-up has also strongly increased from about 4 years in 2000 to more than 10 years since 2008.

In order to assess venture capital as the manifestation of Start-up Aid as a Business (7) against our second criterion, that is, to examine the intensity between Start-up Aid as a Business and our responses, we need to compare the number of VC targets with the total number of newly founded businesses. In that way, we are able to determine how prospective business founders rate their chances of obtaining VC-backed funding. As it turns out, the approximately 3000 annual VC targets seen from 2001 to 2007 compare to a total of about 300,000 new businesses (see Fig. 11.1). Hence, the number of VC investment targets amounts to a mere 1% of annual business start-ups. While this finding already calls into question the influence of Start-up Aid as a Business on our responses, looking at this relation more closely, one realises that the actual ratio might be even significantly lower. This is

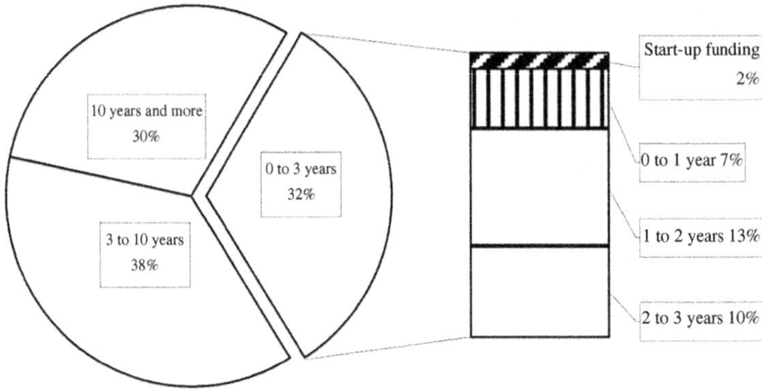

Fig. 10.4 Distribution of firm age at time of initial VC investment, 2007. Source: VEC (2008)

because many VC investments do not represent true start-up finance, but rather follow on investments in promising existing ventures. Figure 10.4 provides an overview of the ages of Japanese businesses receiving VC finance for the first time in 2007.

As noted and much deplored by Imai and Kawagoe (2000), a large share of venture capital in Japan is not employed in true start-up finance. From the 2007 yearbook of the Venture Capital Association, we can infer that a mere 2% of 2007 VC investments justify the description "start-up finance". This means that no more than 0.02% of newly founded businesses—or one in 5000 businesses—received VC capital right from their start in 2007. Even if we include businesses in their first year of operation, this figure increases to not more than 0.1%.

From the perspective of potential business founders, this means that only one in a thousand can expect to obtain VC funds upon or soon after starting their business. In this context, Ozaki's assessment, "Venture businesses are just the tip of the iceberg", remains rather euphemistic (2002). We conclude, therefore, that the intensity of the influence of Start-up Aid as a Business (criterion 2) has never been significantly different from 0 during the entire investigation period. Consequently, we do not include Start-up Aid as a Business in the CSS.

Business Sentiment (8) is one of the rules that enjoy high levels of public attention. Consequently much detailed and accurate data are readily available. For Japan, the central bank provides corresponding statistics on a quarterly basis through the *Kigyō tanki keizai kansoku chōsa*—better known both in the West and in Japan by its acronym *Tankan*. Figure 10.5 provides the results for the investigation period.

The Tankan report assesses current business conditions among a sample of approximately 10,000 companies and calculates a diffusion index (DI) as the difference between positive and negative votes. The DI calculated for large manufacturing businesses receives most media attention, with information on other categories rarely communicated to a wider public. Consequently, individual agents assessing business conditions will look to that main category. As can be

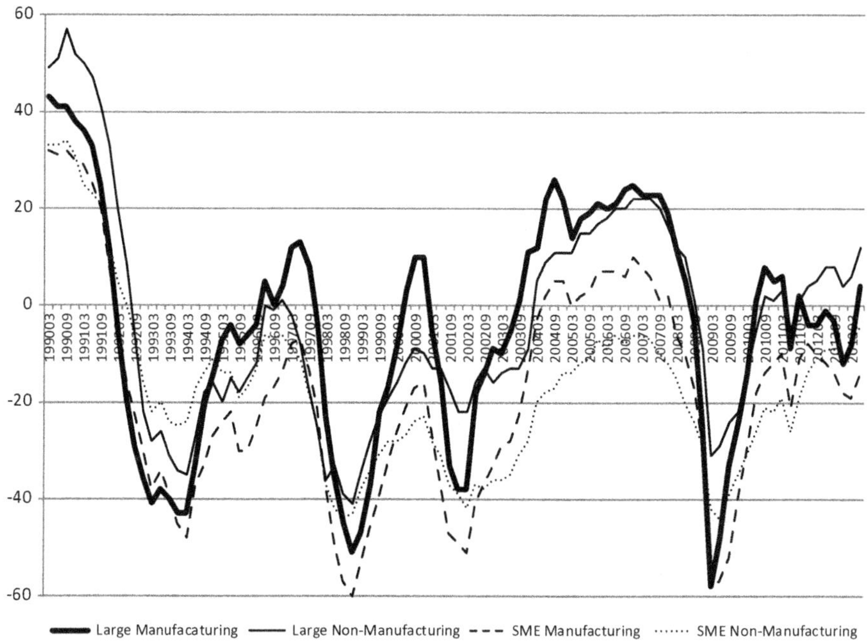

Fig. 10.5 Diffusion index of business conditions *Tankan*, 1990–2013. Source: BOJ

inferred from Fig. 10.5, Business Sentiment in Japan was subject to quite significant fluctuations during the investigation period. Accordingly, we attribute it to the CSS via criterion 2.

10.2 Business Founders as Members of Society

Stigma of Failure (9) and Traditional Class Order (10) are rules that have been firmly rooted in the Japanese value system for centuries. As 2nd order cognitive rules, they influence imagination, perception and decision making of agents. As values, they are internalised early on through the influence of parents and educators. Against this background, we can exclude significant changes in the first of our two criteria: in the absence of major societal developments, population sizes do not change significantly in just one generation. For the purposes of criterion 2 (variation in the strength of influence on our responses), we need to look into Stigma of Failure and Traditional Class Order separately.

There is no appropriate longitudinal data pertaining to Stigma of Failure. However, recent evidence points to a potentially increasing intensity of influence exerted by Stigma of Failure. In a poll conducted jointly by opinion research company *goo* and the Mitsubishi Research Institute in 2005, 47% of respondents noted a significant decline in characteristics such as "adventurous spirit" and "fearlessness of failure" among the current generations of 20–25-year-olds. Another 35% noted a moderate decline, and only the remaining 15% were neutral (MRI 2005).

Equally, data availability on Traditional Class Order precludes an accurate check of criterion 2. However, the pertinent literature strongly points to a continuing influence. According to Uematsu, the concept continued to be deeply rooted in Japanese society well into the observation period (1997: 312). While it did not imply a hierarchy within the class of the rule in ancient China, it developed into a vertical notion of class order in Japan during the Edo period (1600–1868), when professional warriors came to replace the traditional farmer–mercenaries (ibid.: 8). Traditional Class Order was officially abolished during the modernisation wave occurring after the restoration of imperial rule during the 1870s. However, this "revolution from above" only permeated society to a very limited degree (Ishida 2008: 37). Differences in the status of specific occupations continued to persist well into the post-war era. This is evidenced by an annual poll conducted by Japan's largest maker of children's satchels that asked parents about their expectations of the future career choices of their children (kuraray Co. 1992–2007). For the last two decades, occupations linked to the former warrior class either by content (e.g. sports professional) or by a notion of serving an authority (e.g. government official) have continuously received very high rankings. In contrast, self-employed occupations have received significantly less votes than the 10% share of self-employed individuals in the Japanese workforce throughout the investigation period.

In order to make sense of these findings, we need to recall two of the rules that we have excluded from the SFR (see p. 103): Filial Piety and the Small Family Ideal. Filial Piety is the 2nd order mechanism rule that enforces the effects of Stigma of Failure and Traditional Class Order through the influence exerted by parents and educators. The intensity at which Filial Piety becomes effective depends on operations conducted in applying the 1st order Small Family Ideal. Less technically, as family size declines, the obligation to pay respect to one's parents rests on ever fewer shoulders. And taking on the value system of parents represents one important way of paying respect. This mechanism is one of the relatively rare cases where operations are impacting on the level of rules. We thus include operations on Small Family Ideal back into our model.

The "Studies on the Japanese National Character" conducted every 5 years by the Institute of Statistical Mathematics confirms steady growth of the Filial Piety population. The survey includes a question on the "two most highly appreciated values". In the relevant editions of the survey in 1993, 1998, 2003 and 2008, increasing shares of respondents (69, 70, 73 and 76%) referred to filial piety (IStM 1993–2013). In order to preclude the potential bias of demographic change on sample composition, Fig. 10.6 details values for cohorts aged 30–39 and 40–49. Contrary to our concern, there is a disproportionally strong increase in the importance attached by younger generations to filial piety. This becomes particularly obvious when referring to the entire period of 45 years for which the survey is currently available.

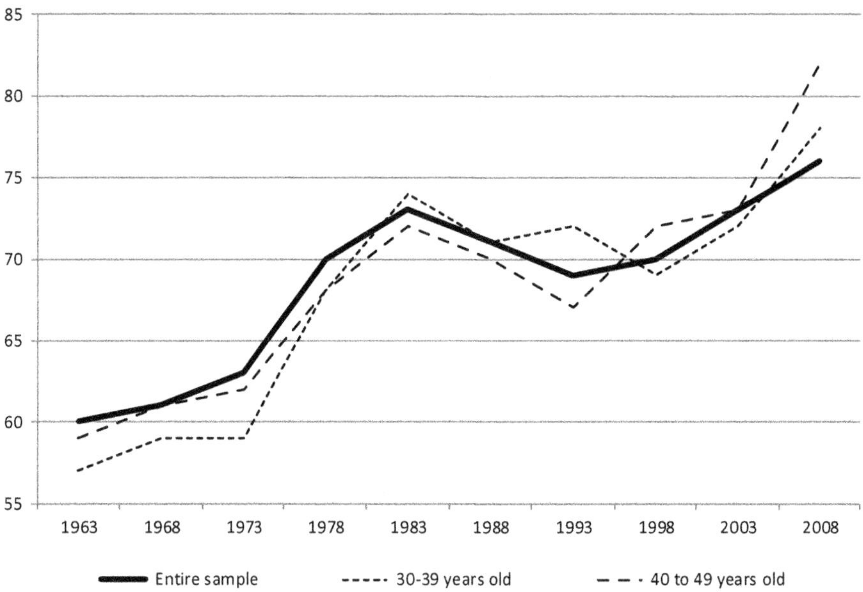

Fig. 10.6 Percentage citing FILIAL PIETY as one of their two most important values, 1963–2008. Source: IStM

While this increase might be interpreted as a change in criterion 1 (population size), we argue that in fact it is not. Every Japanese individual would be likely to name FILIAL PIETY as an important value. In that sense, the population size of FILIAL PIETY has long been at its theoretical maximum. Thus, the increasing share of respondents rating FILIAL PIETY as one of their two most important values rather represents strong evidence for change in criterion 2: the intensity with which FILIAL PIETY exerts an indirect influence on our responses via STIGMA OF FAILURE and TRADITIONAL CLASS ORDER has increased.

The rise in intensity of FILIAL PIETY appears to be due to the growing population of SMALL FAMILY IDEAL (12). As for many 1st order operational rules, data on its operations may be obtained from existing statistics. The National Family Research Committee has made available micro-data from two surveys conducted in 1999 and 2004 via the Social Science Japan Data Archive (SSJDA), from which shares of couples by number of children can be calculated. Figure 10.7 provides the results for childless couples, for one-child families and for families with two or more children. While the share of childless couples has stayed constantly below 10% during the observation period, the shares of one-child families and families with two or more children have experienced inverse development. While the share of families with two or more children declined from close to 70% to just under 40% between 1991 and 2012, the share of one-child families almost doubled from less than 30% to about 55%. As the data also includes adult children, this development

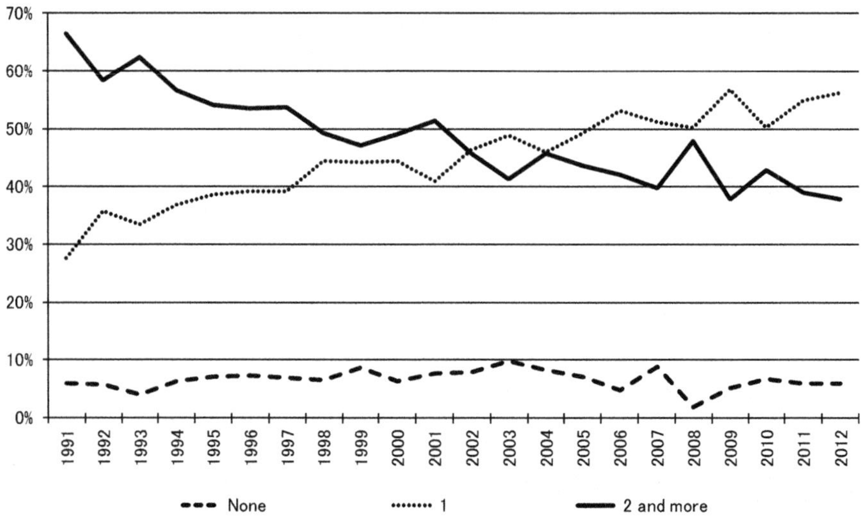

Fig. 10.7 Shares of couples by number of children, 1991–2012. Note: Figures for 2011 and 2012 have been extrapolated using annualised growth rates calculated from 1991/1992 to 2009/2010 averages. Source: National Family Research Committee (1999, 2004; author's calculations)

has to be considered both rapid and substantial, providing telling evidence for change in criterion 1.

Regarding Stigma of Failure (9) and Traditional Class Order (10), we could not trace any change in criterion 1. Turning to criterion 2, we found relatively weak evidence of an increased intensity of Stigma of Failure, but Traditional Class Order could not be traced quantitatively. Within the socio-economic system, the strength of their effect on the responses is channelled through Filial Piety, a rule that has experienced a significant increase in intensity (criterion 2) due to a strong trend towards smaller families (operations on Small Family Ideal). As a result of this trend, the duty of Filial Piety comes to rest on ever fewer children.

The relationships between Small Family Ideal, Filial Piety and our responses are only secondary and tertiary ones. Yet, as we saw in Sect. 5.5, indirect relationships between factor rules and response(s) may offer a way of testing hypotheses pertaining to factor rules, for which suitable data is not available. The mechanism linking Small Family Ideal via Filial Piety to Traditional Class Order and Stigma of Failure should therefore be kept in mind.

10.3 The Role of Government Policy

This section reviews policy measures directly influencing individuals' decisions in favour of or against self-employment: direct public financial assistance, tax schemes and a number of supply-side measures. All rules relating to government measures are classified as 0th order constitutional rules. As population size for constitutional rules (number of law-abiding agents) only changes when the reach of government changes, we cannot employ criterion 1 to effect the reduction from SFR to CSS. Therefore, we will rely on criterion 2, checking the intensity at which the relevant rules become effective in the economic system.

To determine the importance that the government attaches to the promotion of new businesses, we need to look at the structure of central government budget available for SME policies. In Japan, central government provides funds and guidelines, while regional authorities are charged with implementation. Hence, the central government budget offers an appropriate point of departure for analysing the weight attributed to the promotion of business formation compared to supportive measures for existing SMEs. Figure 10.8 illustrates the structure of the 2007 central government budget for SME measures.

It is clear from Fig. 10.8 that government efforts aimed at SMEs concentrate heavily on the preservation of economic structures over the attempt to revitalise the economy. Even if total funds used for "foundation and growth enhancement" were spent on supporting the formation of new businesses, average financial assistance to a start-up business would amount to a mere 17,000 yen (about 130 euros at 2013 exchange rates). What is more, funds for start-up and growth promotion as a share of the total SME budget amount to only 3.1%, even below the annual rate of new business start-ups (currently between 4 and 6% p.a.). Accordingly, new businesses are receiving relatively less support than existing ones, in spite of the frequent claims that help is most needed at the very beginning. Even if start-ups were to benefit from general SME financial assistance schemes in proportion to their number, their share of the budget would only increase by about one percentage point.

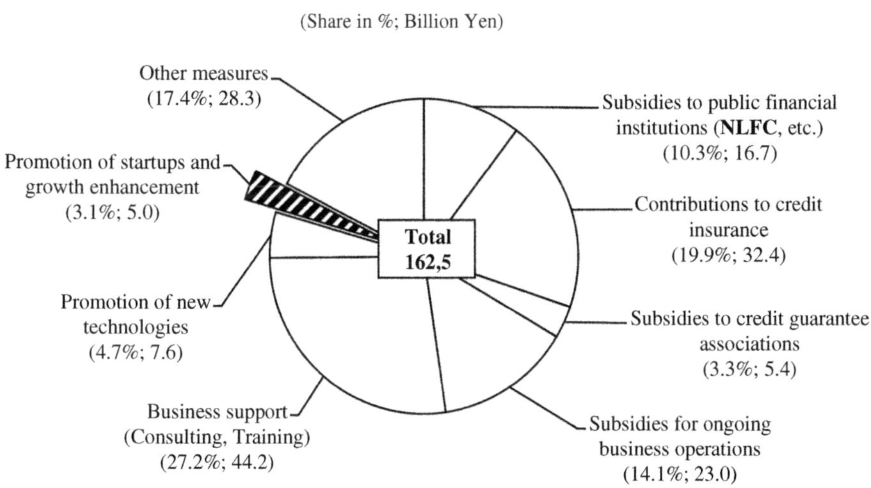

Fig. 10.8 Structure of the 2007 federal budget for SME policy, billion yen. Source: MoF (2007: 42)

Support from various government bodies in charge of regional economic development (Japan Regional Development Corporation, JRDC), investment promotion (Industrial Structure Improvement Fund, ISIF) and SME business development (Japan Small and Medium Enterprise Corporation, JASMEC) has been integrated into the Organization for Small and Medium Enterprises and Regional Innovation, Japan (SMRJ) since 2004. The SMRJ coordinates activities in the areas of SME credit insurance, subsidised loan schemes and business incubators.

Essentially a credit insurance scheme, the Japanese Credit Guarantee System *Chūshō kigyō shin'yō hoken*, is privately organised but relies on central government for reinsurance. The Japan Finance Corporation for Small and Medium Enterprises (JASMEC)[2] assumes the role of reinsurer for local credit guarantee associations.[3] Credit losses from the reinsurance business covered by central government in 2006 amounted to 100 billion yen, 0.75% of total guarantees of 13.4 trillion yen. In essence, this 0.75% acts as a direct subsidy from central government to borrowers. If an estimated 0.2–0.5% of administration expenses for small ticket loans incurred by the regional operational entities is added, total subsidies amount to about 1percentage point of total outstanding loans. As fully collateralised loans have been selling around 2.5% for more than a decade, subsidisation levels figure about 30% of borrowing cost. Bearing in mind the government's overall bias towards extending preferential support to existing businesses, it is hardly surprising that the relevant authorities do not provide a breakdown of guarantees granted to existing versus newly founded businesses. As newly founded businesses typically come with a higher risk profile, this practice has translated into a structural discrimination by way of credit refusal (Kawai and Urata 2002: 46, 50). As the situation has reportedly remained the same during the investigation period, we cannot report any change in criterion 2.

Public financial institutions are also active in the direct provision of loans. Operational responsibility for this type of support is divided between NLFC, JASMEC, and *Shōkō chūkin* bank. Total loans granted by these institutions are 9% of total outstanding SME credit (NLFC 2007: 4). Drawing on a separate fund, NLFC does not require any collateral for about 19% of its loans but charges a uniform on-top-risk premium of 1.2%. JASMEC does not provide unsecured loans at all; *Shōkō chūkin* only does so within a few special schemes but focuses on larger SMEs. Altogether these findings show that only about 1.7% of total outstanding SME loans were exempt from collateralisation requirements.

NLFC is the only public financial institution providing start-up funding. In 2007, it was involved in about 7% of total business start-ups with 21,000 loans granted (NLFC 2007: 12), even below the 9% share of government-related lending to

---

[2]Integrated into NLFC since May 2007.

[3]An introduction to the system can be found in Bushimata, T. and Y. Shiro (2002), *Chūshō kigyō kin'yū nyūmon* [Introduction to Small Business Finance], Tokyo, Toyo Keizai; p. 89 and 175. The historical background is covered in JASMEC, Ed. (2000), *Chûshôkigyô shin'yô hoken kôkôshi* [History of the Small and Medium Enterprise Credit Insurance Corporation], Tokyo, Japan Small and Medium Enterprise Corporation.

SMEs. Given this bias towards extending support to existing businesses, it is not surprising that NLFC does not disclose the share of unsecured loans granted to start-up businesses. Yet, even if all of NLFC's start-up finance was to benefit from the scheme, no more than one in ten start-ups would benefit from a non-collateralised loan. Consequently, we cannot identify significant change in this area either.

The creation of "business incubators" was one of the measures introduced with the 1998 New Business Promotion Law. Under the leadership of Japan Regional Development Corporation (JRDC; integrated into SMRJ in 2004), incubators have been established all over the country, most of them in the vicinity of universities. These centres offer both management support and subsidised office space. While about 30 centres had been inaugurated when SMRJ took over in 2004, not more than two additional centres had been added by 2011 (Harayama 2003; SMRJ 2011: 6).

In spite of the countrywide availability of this support scheme, effects on "representative founders" remain marginal due to its limited scope and focus on high-tech industries. Similar conclusions are also drawn in the literature (Masuda 2006: 238). Between 1998 and 2011, an average of only about 30 businesses a year has been founded with incubator support. It is clear from a comparison of these figures with the total number of businesses annually founded (between 200,000 and 300,000) that only about 1 in 10,000 businesses benefits from this support scheme. Accordingly, even though the measure has been newly introduced during the observation period, its intensity cannot be considered significant in terms of criterion 2.

As early as 1997, Japanese legislators reduced the taxation of gains realised by private investors in an initial public offering (IPO). The measure is known as "angel tax", "business angels" being individual private investors supporting a business start-up. The term "tax" is obviously misleading as the "angel tax" is in fact an *exemption* from the existing taxation of capital gains. In official parlance, the "angel tax" is known as "Tax regulations for the promotion of small and medium enterprises". Exemption applies to investments made within 10 years of the foundation of a business and allows for a deduction of 75%. Yet, due to the extremely low share of businesses opting for an IPO, only about 0.1% of businesses benefits from this regulation. This number is already way below the threshold of significant change in criterion 2. What is more, to have any effect on business formation, potential business founders would need to consider the option of an IPO even before starting operations.

The 1995 policy measure that has come to be known as the Creative Business Promotion Law (CBPL) refers to the legal entities of limited liability companies (*Yūgen gai'sha*) and joint-stock companies (*Kabushiki gai'sha*). The law allows a part of the funds that had previously been protected as a legal reserve to be tapped into for investment purposes aimed at developing a new business activity. Although positive effects on investment behaviour of existing businesses have been documented (Honjo and Harada 2006: 297), there is no evidence that incentives for potential business founders would be altered. This is largely because only about one in four business start-ups involves the establishment of a legal entity, that is, founders revert to other legal arrangements when funds are particularly scarce.

1 January 2006 saw the entry into force of the New Corporate Law (*Shin kaishahō*). MINIMUM CAPITAL REQUIREMENTS (1) were lowered to a symbolic 1 yen, a step that rendered the Japanese Limited Liability Company practically obsolete. Put into a wider context, this measure represents an extension of the exceptions provided by the 1995 Creative Business Promotion Law to newly founded businesses with the additional relaxation of the earlier restriction to use all thus liberated funds for investment goods.

Data from the Japanese Commercial Register (*Shōgyōtōkibo*) show a marked increase in the 2006 financial year in the number of newly registered Public Liability Companies (*kabushiki kaisha*), the Japanese PLC. Yet, this increase can be traced entirely to the conversion of existing subsidiaries and of businesses formerly registered as Limited Liability Companies to the newly "on sale" PLC.

At first sight, the possibility of risk mitigation from the founder–owner to the legal entity at close to zero cost should arguably cause an increase in newly founded businesses. However, issues around capital procurement, particularly the requirement of full collateralisation, render this potential ineffective, as Miyauchi (2001: 66) noted with reference to the LLC. On the contrary, this legislative step again brings further relief to existing businesses, which benefit from a liberation of previously tied-up capital.

What partially balances the preferential treatment of existing businesses over newly established ones are some tax advantages that can only be realised by incorporating a business. A certain accounting flexibility allows the pay of the company director(s) to be adjusted in order to minimise the sum of corporate and personal income taxes due from the owner. As this effect is at its strongest for businesses without employees, one can well expect a midterm increase in the relative attractiveness of self-employment. From this we infer a discrete one-time positive change in criterion 2 for MINIMUM CAPITAL REQUIREMENTS effective since 2006.

Administrative guidance (*Gyōsei shidō*) refers to the traditionally strong influence of government authorities on Japanese businesses. One instance of this practice is relevant for our analysis and has also been observed by the OECD. Their 2006 country report indicates that the Financial Services Agency (*Kin'yūchō*) tends to make regional banks apply lenient criteria with regard to credit conditions for SMEs (OECD 2006: 55). Against the background of the still weak capital base and the earning ratios of regional banks, the OECD has been very critical of this inverse lobbying from the government into the private sector.

It seems, however, that the FSA's pledge confirms the business logic of local banks. Again, government demands and banks' lending practices favour existing businesses over newly founded ones. As we have already seen, "lenient criteria" do not apply to newly founded businesses, with banks continuing to insist on full collateralisation. Hence, criterion 2 leads us to equally exclude any change in intensity through this instance of administrative guidance.

It is sobering to note that among government policies, only the revision of Minimum Capital Requirements in 2006 makes a significant change in intensity to our responses. All other policies that we have grouped as Start-up Aid as Government Duty (2) were equally assessed against criterion 2. However, none was found to have had a significant impact on our responses during the investigation period. Therefore, we attribute only Minimum Capital Requirements (1) to the CSS and relegate Start-up Aid as Government Duty to the MSSS.

10.4 Economic Alternatives to Self-Employment

This section analyses the set of 1st order rules identified as economic alternatives to self-employment as well as 2nd order rules pertaining to these alternatives. As we saw earlier, changes in the attractiveness of these alternatives potentially impact on the relative attractiveness of entrepreneurship. In concrete terms, the major alternatives to self-employment are unemployment and dependent employment.

Dependent employment, or simply labour, obviously represents a major research area in Japan. Although there were great many developments within dependent employment during the investigation period, in light of our response rules, we will only focus on aspects relevant to the relative attractiveness of entrepreneurship.[4]

Three 1st order social rules known as the Sacred Treasures (*Sanshu no jingi)* continue to serve as the point of departure when describing the characteristics of standard employment in Japan (Abegglen 1958). They are lifetime employment (*Shūshin koyō*), the seniority principle (*Nenkō joretsu*) for determining pay structures and career development and company unions (*Kigyōbetsu kumiai*). While the treasures have lost some of their importance since the burst of Japan's bubble economy in the early 1990s, they remain at the heart of regular employment in Japan, particularly so for lifetime employment (Blind and Lottanti von Mandach 2017a).

While we have excluded the Salaryman Ideal from the SFR, we have implicitly included the Three Sacred Treasures in our SFR. This is because Fear of Unemployment (16) and the Performance Principle (15) represent semantic inverses of lifetime employment and the seniority principle, respectively, and because Organised Labour (4) mirrors Japanese-style company unions.

In the following subsections examining Fear of Unemployment, Performance Principle and Organised Labour, the elements of the Sacred Treasures will be assessed for potential change since the early 1990s. Finally, in a separate step, we will analyse Non-regular Employment (15). This reflects the fact that the Sacred Treasures have always been the privilege of individuals in standard employment,

[4]Readers interested in more general aspects of the topic may find helpful points of departure in Blind and Lottanti von Mandach (2012, 2013, 2015) and may turn to Kiyokawa and Yamane for a rather complete guide to existing data sources (2004).

whereas non-regular employees cannot effect operations on either Organised Labour or Performance Principle.

Fear of Unemployment is a 2nd order cognitive rule. While data on this order of rules is not often available, Fear of Unemployment is a rule population that politicians are most interested in. Consequently, appropriate data is made available by the government-run Nippon Research Institute in the form of annual Consumer Sentiment Index surveys. Figure 10.9 plots their category "Anxiety about unemployment" for 1992 to 2009 and includes actual unemployment as a reference.

Figure 10.9 shows that the rule population of Fear of Unemployment fluctuated strongly during the observation period. Before we can attribute Fear of Unemployment to the CSS, however, we need to evidence that the intensity of the relationship between Fear of Unemployment and our responses is different from zero (criterion 2). To make this latter assessment, we need to determine whether agents saw self-employment as an option to mitigate the risk of unemployment in the course of the observation period.

Given the previous positive experiences during the oil crises of the 1970s and with unemployment at very low levels well into the 1990s, even individuals retaining Fear of Unemployment arguably did not think much about how to mitigate the risk of unemployment. "Finding a new job" was the most common sense option. This trust was probably shattered in 1998, when—5 years into the recession—a severe banking crisis hit the country and unemployment soared to over 4% for the first time in decades. Japan's largest newspaper *Yomiuri Shimbun* shows occurrences of the term "unemployment rate" almost tripling within that year (see Fig. 10.10).

1998 can be identified as the tipping point during the observation period when a significant number of agents retaining Fear of Unemployment consciously started to consider self-employment as a way of mitigating the risk of unemployment. In a rule-based theoretical perspective, this identification of a relevant relationship newly arising (i.e. an intensity changing from zero to non-zero) is an evidence of a learning process among agents.

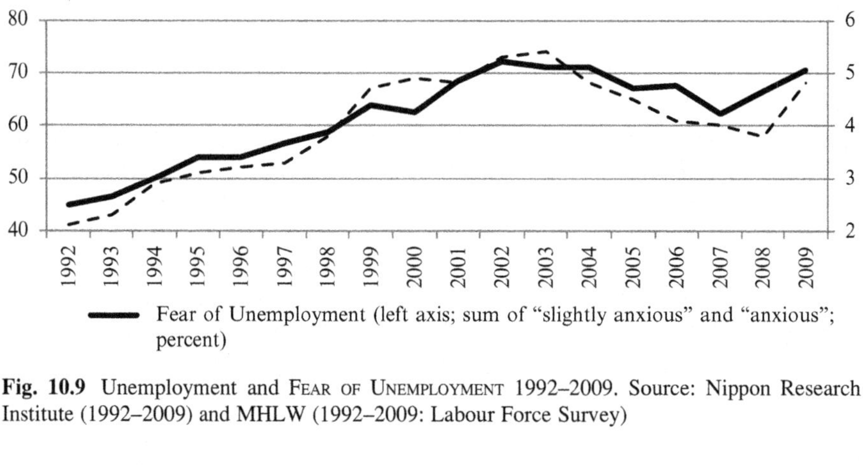

Fig. 10.9 Unemployment and Fear of Unemployment 1992–2009. Source: Nippon Research Institute (1992–2009) and MHLW (1992–2009: Labour Force Survey)

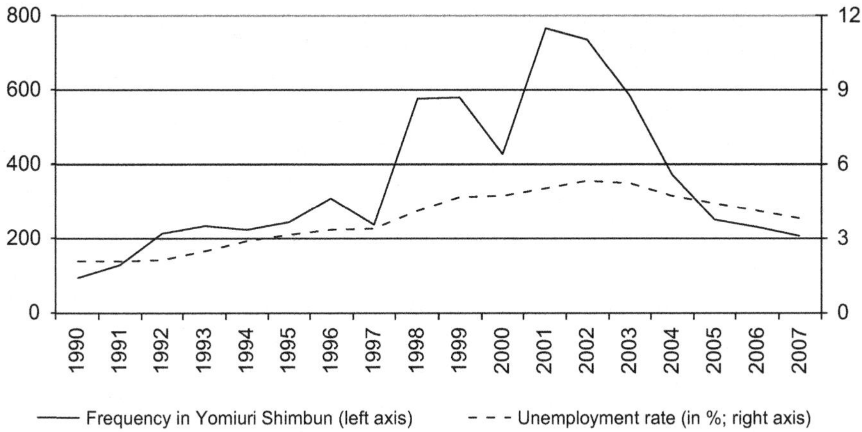

Fig. 10.10 Media attention to unemployment 1990–2007. Source: Yomiuri Shimbun Online Archives

While the assessment of Fear of Unemployment against criterion 1 has revealed a significant change in the size of its rule population, assessment against criterion 2 hints at the intensity of the relationship between Fear of Unemployment and our responses not being significantly different from zero prior to 1998. Accordingly, Fear of Unemployment can only be attributed to the CSS from 1998 onwards.

Performance-based incentive systems have been discussed in Japan with reference to a number of terms. Based on Drucker's "management by objectives" (1954), "norms" or (*Noruma*) were followed by "ability-ism" (*Nōryoku shugi*) in the 1980s and "result-ism" (*Gyōseki shugi*) in the 1990s. With *Gyōseki shugi* becoming the common reference, personal achievement (*Kojin gyōseki*), group achievement (*Bumon gyōseki*) and company achievement (*Kaisha gyōseki*) represent the constituent elements of bonus packages in Japanese corporations.

The popularity of performance-based pay peaked around the turn of the century. According to a 2001 survey by the Ministry of Labour, Health and Welfare, 65% of employers had a corresponding system in place (MHLW 2001–2009b: Table 17.13). On average, the performance-based share of total compensation amounts to about one-third with the three elements weighted approximately equally.

The following rough calculation shows that we can attribute Performance Principle to the MSSS based on an assessment against criterion 2. Let two in three dependently employed individuals be subject to a performance-based HR system. With their personal performance translating into only one-ninth of their entire salary package, the average "performance-based pay share" is only around 7.5%. Obviously, this is not significantly different from the gross margin to be expected in self-employment. Hence, we note that Performance Principle does not exert a significant influence on the relative attractiveness of self-employment during the investigation period. What is more, recent polls show that the share of businesses relying on a performance-based system is decreasing strongly; in 2007, the figure hit 45%, about 20 percentage points down from 2001.

ORGANISED LABOUR (4) deserves particular attention as it potentially impacts on our responses through two separate routes. First, strong unions pose a potential threat to self-employed individuals aspiring to become employers. Second, strong labour protection increases the relative attractiveness of dependent employment. Turning these arguments around, weak unions lessen the attractiveness of dependent employment and provide more degrees of freedom to self-employed individuals as aspiring employers.

Membership numbers may offer an initial clue to fluctuations in the population size of ORGANISED LABOUR (criterion 1). Union membership in Japan peaked in 1994 at 12.7 million but had decreased to 9.9 million by 2013 (MHLW 2013: 3, Table 9.4), a relative decline of 22%. However, absolute membership numbers do not reflect *fluctuations* in the overall labour force through demographic change. In contrast, unionisation rates as a relative measure do account for changes in the underlying base. The corresponding shares—25% of the labour force in 1994 compared to 18% in 2013—seem to point to an even stronger relative decrease of 28% in the rule population of ORGANISED LABOUR.

Yet, it is important to understand that much of this development was driven by changes in the *composition* of the overall labour force. During the last two decades, Japan has experienced a considerable rise in labour force participation rates driven by a strong increase in female non-standard employment that even overcompensated for a small loss in standard employment (Blind and Lottanti von Mandach 2012, 2015, 2017b). As eligibility for union membership in Japan is almost entirely limited to regular employees, the crude unionisation rate overstates the true extent of the decline of the ORGANISED LABOUR population. Changing the base from the overall labour force to the number of regular employees, it is possible to calculate an adjusted unionisation rate. The resulting figures of 32% for 1990 versus 27% for 2010 correspond to a significantly smaller relative decline of 16%.

To check on criterion 2, we need to distinguish between the perspectives of aspiring employers (direct effect) and dependently employed individuals (indirect effect). Government statistics show that the number of Japanese businesses with regular employees is stable at about two million (MHLW 1997–2012). With the number of business establishments decreasing from 6.5 million in 1991 to 6.0 million in 2009, the share of businesses with labour–management relations shows a slight increase (about 8%).

With respect to the indirect effect via the relative attractiveness of dependent employment, *Rengō Sōken,* a research institute funded by the Japanese Trade Union Confederation, conducts a biannual survey of attitudes towards labour unions (Rengō Sōken 2001–2013). The survey question, "how necessary are labour unions?", produced the following answers in 2013 (2003 in parentheses): "must have" 23.5% (23.7%), "rather good to have" 44.7% (48.0%), "doesn't matter" 24.7% (25.3%) and "better not to have" 7.1% (3.0%).

From the perspective of aspiring employers, the net effect of the declining unionisation rate and the increasing share of businesses with regular employees is slightly negative at about 8%. From the point of view of the relative attractiveness of dependent employment, survey results showed no significant change in criterion 2. With the magnitude of change at less than 10% for both the direct effect and the indirect effect, we may safely attribute ORGANISED LABOUR to the MSSS.

Operations based on NON-REGULAR EMPLOYMENT (15) have disadvantages in terms of job security, pay rates and social security benefits. As an alternative source of income, self-employment implies a similar level of uncertainty but promises a higher potential income. Therefore, the rule population of NON-REGULAR EMPLOYMENT will be more likely to consider self-employment.

For criterion 1, we can look at the number of individuals conducting operations on NON-REGULAR EMPLOYMENT by working as non-regular employees: During the investigation period, the number of individuals in non-regular employment has increased considerably, from 8.8 million in 1990 to 17.6 million in 2010 (Blind and Lottanti von Mandach 2012:142). The share of male non-regular employees in the workforce has even more than doubled from 8.1% in 1990 to 17.2% in 2010 (ibid.: Table 4.2). In view of the relative attractiveness of self-employment, this finding for criterion 1 points to a positive effect of NON-REGULAR EMPLOYMENT on the pool of potential entrepreneurs. With this evidence, we attribute NON-REGULAR EMPLOYMENT to the CSS.

To summarise findings from this check of factor rules against our two criteria, we find private and public venture support and protective bankruptcy law have an insignificant influence on entrepreneurship in Japan. Similarly, there is insignificant change in labour unions, lending practices and HR management. For all other rules one or other of our criteria has tested positively, indicating a need for further inquiry.

***

In this chapter we have been working on a reduction of complexity by checking factor rules for changes in population size and in strength of influence on our responses. These criteria can be likened to a multivariate regression equation, in which variables meet parameters. In our procedure population sizes correspond to variable values whereas the strengths of influence correspond to parameters.

As we are already so close to statistical methods, why should we refrain from simply using the corresponding data for testing in a regression what parameters load with significance, i.e. where strength of influence is different from 0? There are three reasons why we should not, even if appropriate data were available. First, in applying standard regression techniques to an analysis of rules without an antecedent check of potential changes in the strength of influence (parameters) over time, one might miss out on rules (variables) that are significant during parts of the investigation period, such as the indications that we have found for FEAR OF UNEMPLOYMENT. *Second, we risk missing potential discoveries if we fail to invest in understanding the quality of the object of study. And third, entrusting the researcher's duty of checking on strength of influence to algorithms might lead to the detection of "false positives" where random or misspecification happens to create a significant correlation.*

The review of potential factor rules conducted here is a prerequisite for splitting the system of factor rules (SFR) into its changing and its meta-stable sub-systems, i.e. for establishing the CSS and the MSSS, respectively. This task is the subject of Chap. 11.

References

Abegglen J (1958) The Japanese factory: aspects of its social organization. Free Press, Glencoe

Asogawa S (2008) Dr. Asogawa on the lending practices of Japanese banks. Interview with author. Kyoto, 17 April

Beck T, Demirgüc-Kunt A (2008) Access to finance: an unfinished agenda. World Bank Econ Rev 22(3):383–396

Blind GD, Lottanti von Mandach S (2012) Ansichtssache: Zum Zustand der japanischen Wirtschaft nach Doppelschlag und Dreifachkatastrophe. In: Chiavacci D, Wiezcorek I (eds) Japan 2012: Politik. Wirtschaft und Gesellschaft. Vereinigung für sozialwissenschaftliche Japanforschung, Berlin, pp 131–149

Blind GD, Lottanti von Mandach S (2013) Bescheidene Managementgehälter und sich schliessende Lohnscheren: Neue Einblicke in den japanischen Arbeitsmarkt. In: Chiavacci D, Wiezcorek I (eds) Japan 2013: Politik, Wirtschaft und Gesellschaft. Vereinigung für sozialwissenschaftliche Japanforschung, Berlin

Blind GD, Lottanti von Mandach S (2015) Decades not lost, but won: increased employment, higher wages, and more equal opportunities in the Japanese labour market. Soc Sci Jpn J 18 (1):63–88

Blind G, Lottanti von Mandach S (2017a) When vultures bring blessings: employment growth in Japanese businesses under private equity ownership. MPRA working paper 80816, University of Munich, Munich

Blind G, Lottanti von Mandach S (2017b) Secular trends in the Japanese labour market during the lost decades: a reply to Andrew Gordon. MPRA working paper 80812. University of Munich, Munich

Blind G, Pyka A (2014) The rule approach in evolutionary economics: a methodological template for empirical research. J Evol Econ 24(5):1085–1105

Bushimata T, Shiro Y (2002) Chūshō kigyō kin'yū nyūmon [Introduction to Small Business Finance]. Tōyō Keizai, Tokyo

Drucker PF (1954) The practice of management. Harper & Brothers, New York

Harayama Y (2003) Industry-University linkage in Japan. In: International conference on "New trends and challenges of science and technological innovation in a critical era", Taipei

Honjo Y, Harada N (2006) SME policy, financial structure and firm growth: evidence from Japan. Small Bus Econ 27(4–5):289–300

Imai Y, Kawagoe M (2000) Business start-ups in Japan: problems and policies. Oxf Rev Econ Policy 16(2):114–123

Ishida T (2008) Die Entdeckung der Gesellschaft [Sociology in Japan]—Edited and translated by Wolfgang Seifert (Nihon no shakai kagaku, Tōkyō Daigaku shuppansha, 1984). Suhrkamp, Frankfurt am Main

IStM (1993–2013) Kokuminsei no kenkyū. Daijūichiji nisensan'nen zenkoku chōsa [A study of the Japanese national character—the 12th nationwide survey 2008]. Research Report, Institute of Statistical Mathematics, Tokyo

JIWE (2006) Kigyō ni kan suru genjō oyobi ishiki ni kan suru ankēto [Opinion poll and status survey on start-up conditions]. Nijū'isseiki shokugyō zaidan (Japan Institute of Worker's Evolution), Tokyo

Kanaya A, Woo D (2000) The Japanese banking crisis of the 1990: sources and lessons. International Monetary Fund, Washington

Kawai H, Urata S (2002) Entry of small and medium enterprises and economic dynamism in Japan. Small Bus Econ 18(1):41–51

Kiyokawa Y, Yamane H (2004) Nihonjin no rōdōkan: ishiki chōsa ni miru sono hensen [The Japanese appreciation of work: developments as found by opinion polls]. Ōhara shakai mondai kenkyūjo zasshi 524(2004.1):14–33

kuraray Co (1992–2007) 'Shōrai tsukitai shokugyō' ankēto [Survey on desired future profession]. from http://www.kuraray.co.jp/enquete/index.html

Masuda T (2006) The determinants of latent entrepreneurship in Japan. Small Bus Econ 26 (3):227–240

MHLW (1997–2012) Koyō hoken jigyō nenpō [Employment Insurance Annual Report]. Ministry of Health, Labor and Welfare, Tokyo

MHLW (2001–2009b) Shūgyō jōken sōgō chōsa [Survey on employment conditions]. Ministry of Health, Labor and Welfare, Tokyo

MHLW (2013) Heisei 25nen rōdō kumiai kisō chōsa [The 2013 Labour Union Survey]. Ministry of Health, Labour and Welfare, Tokyo

Miyauchi Y (2001) Management theory (kei'ei ron). Tōyō Keizai Shuppansha, Tokyo

MoF (2007) Current Japanese fiscal conditions and issues to be considered. Ministry of Finance, Tokyo. Available at: http://www.mof.go.jp/english/budget/budget/fy2007/cjfc2007.pdf

MRI (2005) 'Wagakuni no monozukuri wo sasaete iru "jinzai" no kongo' dai'ikkai chōsa kekka hōkoku [First news release reporting results from the survey "Present and future of the Human Resources supporting manufacturing in our country"]. Mitsubishi Research Institute, Tokyo

National Family Research Committee (1999, 2004) Zenkoku kazoku chōsa [National Family Survey]. Japan Society of Family Sociology, Tokyo

NLFC (1987–2008) Zenkoku kigyō dōkō chōsa kekka [Results of the National Small Enterprise Trend Survey]. National Life Finance Corporation, Tokyo

NLFC (2007) Annual Report 2007. National Life Finance Corporation, Tokyo

NRI (1992–2009) Consumer Sentiment Index. Nippon Research Institute, Tokyo

NVCA (2013) 2013 Yearbook. National Venture Capital Association, Arlington

OECD (2006) OECD economic surveys: Japan. OECD, Paris

Ozaki M (2002) Jibun no kaisha wo motsu. seikō ma'nyuaru [Owning one's own company—a guide to success]. Kodansha, Tokyo

Rengō Sōken (2001–2013) Kinrôsha no shigoto to kurashi ni tsuite no ankêto [Survey on work and life of the dependently employed]. Research Institute for Advancement of Living Standards, Tokyo

Samila S, Sorenson O (2011) Venture capital, entrepreneurship, and economic growth. Rev Econ Stat 93(1):338–349

SMRJ (2011) Incubation report. Ministry of Economy, Trade and Industry, Small and Medium Enterprise Agency, Organization for Small & Medium Enterprises and Regional Innovation, Tokyo

Tagaya M (2008) Venture capital investments in Japan. Interview with author. Nippon Venture Capital, Osaka

Takagi T (2008) Venture capital investments. Interview with author. Ibis Capital Partners, Tokyo, 6 June

Uematsu T (1997) Shinōkōshō: jukyō shisō to kanryō shihai [Warriors, farmers, craftsmen and merchants: Confucianist thought and bureaucratic rule]. Dōbunkan, Tokyo
VEC (2002–2013) 2001–2012 surveys on trends in venture capital investments. Venture Enterprise Center, commissioned by METI, Tokyo
Waldenberger F (2000) Japans Finanzkrise [Japan's financial crisis]. Jpn Mag 12:12–14
Watanabe T (2008) Interview on start-up organization: emotional intelligence research. G. D. Blind, Tokyo

Chapter 11
Putting to Work the Model of Entrepreneurship in Japan

Abstract In order to optimise inferences on the changing sub-system (CSS) of entrepreneurship in Japan, we split the system of factor rules (SFR) into its changing and meta-stable parts: CSS and MSSS (changing and meta-stable sub-systems). Minimum capital requirements, perceived cost of capital, fear of unemployment, business sentiment, the rise of non-regular employment, and demographic change (via an indirect mechanism) are part of the CSS as the causative core of the SFR.

We next identify subgroups of agents by comparing the socio-economic profile of the Japanese "founder force" with that of the general workforce. We then uses susceptibility to CSS rules as the differentiating criterion for the identification of subgroups of agents, which—in turn—enables the formulation of subgroup-specific hypotheses.

To operationalise our rule-based model of entrepreneurship in Japan, we need to take stock of our findings thus far. This chapter, therefore, first specifies the split of the system of factor rules (SFR) into its changing and meta-stable parts: CSS and MSSS. A brief discussion reflecting the nature of our responses is followed by the formulation of population equations for Entrepreneurial Spirit and Individual Entrepreneurship. Correspondingly, we also specify a frequency equation for start-up operations. Next, we look at the sociodemographic characteristics of the Japanese "founder force" and its development during the investigation period. Finally, susceptibility to CSS rules is used as the differentiating criterion for the identification of subgroups of agents.

11.1 Structure of the Changing Sub-system

The testing of SFR rules against the two criteria of population size and of relationship intensity helps to effectuate this "helpful reduction of complexity" (Blind and Pyka 2014: 1092). Table 11.1, which splits the triplex SFR into its changing (CSS) and meta-stable (MSSS) parts, shows that the reduction conducted through the previous chapter has helped to exclude 6 of 12 SFR rules (compare with Table 9.3).

G.D. Blind, *The Entrepreneur in Rule-Based Economics*, Economic Complexity and Evolution, DOI 10.1007/978-3-319-62779-3_11

Table 11.1 The changing sub-system CSS of entrepreneurship in Japan

Rule order	Estimated relevance via (a) population fluctuation and (b) intensity of relation: Significant	Not significant
0th order rules	– Minimum capital requirements (1; b) (from 2006)	– Start-up aid as government duty (2; b) – Protective bankruptcy law (3; a, b) – Organised labour (4; a, b)
1st order rules	– Non-regular employment[a] (15; a, b) – Operations on Small family ideal (12; a) Indirect intensity impact via filial piety (11) on stigma of failure (9) and on traditional class order (10)	– Start-up covenants (6; a, b) – Start-up aid as business (7; b) – Performance principle[a] (14; b)
2nd order rules	– Perceived cost of capital (5; b) – Business sentiment (8; b) – Fear of unemployment[a] (16; a) (from 1998)	– Fear of unemployment[a] (16; a) (until 1997)
Rule system	System of factor rules (SFR): Changing sub-system (CSS)	Meta-stable sub-system (MSSS)

[a]Rules pertaining to economic alternatives

On the other hand, we have re-included the rules of Small Family Ideal and Filial Piety based on their function as a transmission mechanism for Stigma of Failure and Traditional Class Order. In essence, operations on the Small Family Ideal—families with fewer offspring—increase the intensity with which the relatively more conservative value system of the parental generation is transmitted to offspring generations. And Stigma of Failure and Traditional Class Order are part of the conservative value system.

In Table 11.1, the meta-stable sub-system (MSSS) contains all rules for which neither of our criteria proved positive during the investigation period. While rule-based economics denies the existence of invariant laws, it recognises that invariance may occur during limited periods of time. Therefore, attribution to the MSSS does not imply that these rules never did nor never may again cause change in our responses.

For two of the SFR rules, we have identified discrete change during the investigation period. First, the change in the 0th order rule of Minimum Capital Requirements stems from a change in legislation effective since 2006. Accordingly, in statistical analysis, we may expect to trace an effect via the intercept in a cross-sectional design, or via a dummy variable in a longitudinal design. Second, our evidence points to the emergence of a significant influence from Fear of Unemployment on our responses through a learning process that took place in early 1998. For all other rules attributed to the CSS, we have found evidence for constant change, that is, for a significant effect on our responses throughout the investigation period.

Table 11.2 CSS population and operational frequency functions

Rule level	Operational level
Pop_{ES} = f(BuS, FUe, PCoC, SFI)	N.A.
Pop_{IE} = g(BuS, ES, FUe, MCap, NRE, PCoC, SFI)	Op_{IE} = h(BuS, ES, FUe, MCap, NRE, PCoC, SFI)

where BuS = Business Sentiment, FUe= Fear of Unemployment, PCoC = Perceived Cost of Capital, SFI = Small Family Ideal, MCap = Minimum Capital Requirements, NRE = Non-regular Employment

We have referred to our CSS as a "triplex CSS" because it regroups factors impacting on three responses: on the populations of Entrepreneurial Spirit and Individual Entrepreneurship and on the frequency of start-up operations resulting from applying the latter. Conceptually, there are also operations that result from applying Entrepreneurial Spirit (see Table 4.1). However, as these operations consist of cognitive acts, corresponding statistics are not available.

At this point we can specify functional representations for each of our three responses. While all factor rules exert significant influences on the population of Individual Entrepreneurship and on the frequency of start-up operations, Minimum Capital Requirements and Non-regular Employment do not impact on the Entrepreneurial Spirit rule population. This is because as a 2nd order rule Entrepreneurial Spirit refers to the *general* appreciation of self-employment. Such general endorsement of entrepreneurship is hardly informed through concrete aspects of business formation like Minimum Capital Requirements nor by a direct comparison with economic alternatives such as Non-regular Employment. Table 11.2 provides population functions for the rule level, and a frequency function for the operational level. The population of Entrepreneurial Spirit (ES) enters these functions in two different ways: as response in its own population function Pop_{ES} and as factor rule in the population function Pop_{IE} for Individual Entrepreneurship (IE) as well as in the frequency function Op_{IE} of operations on IE. In Pop_{IE}, it impacts on the frequency with which IE is adopted; in Op_{IE} it controls the frequency with which IE is applied in start-up operations. In essence, the three functions provide a formal description of entrepreneurial attitude, latent and actual entrepreneurship.

11.2 Introducing the Japanese "Founder Force"

The heterogeneity of *Homo sapiens oeconomicus* as the agent in rule-based economics implies differences in the selection of rules among individual agents. The individual odds of adopting certain rules systematically vary with certain sociodemographic characteristics. If such a discriminating characteristic can be successfully identified, we can increase explanatory power in subsequent analyses. At the same time, this profiling will help to identify potentially important control variables.

The self-employed workforce of Japan was studied in various ways long before our investigation period (for a descriptive analysis of the situation in the 1970s, refer to Patrick and Rohlen 1987). As far as the investigation period is concerned, the literature suggests an extensive list of personal characteristics such as family background, human capital, gender and age (Bird and Mitsuhashi 2003). While these reviews provide valuable insights into the characteristics of the self-employed workforce in Japan, they are not representative of the "founder force". This is because the self-employed workforce predominantly comprises individuals who either founded their business many years ago or have inherited a family business.

This section profiles the Japanese "founder force" across a number of socio-economic dimensions and compares it to corresponding groups of the general working population. Significant differences are noted and discussed at the end of the section in order to identify the susceptibility of agents to influences from specific CSS factor rules.

Data on the structure of the founder force can be obtained from (a) the "Survey on the situation of newly founded businesses" (*Shinki kaigyō jittai chōsa*) conducted annually by the National Life Finance Corporation (NLFC 1991–2012), (b) the annual White Book of the Small and Medium Enterprise Agency (SMEA 2012)[1] and (c) the reports of the Japan Small Business Research Institute (JSBRI).[2] Takahashi (2005) provides a well-arranged overview of available statistics.

As the NLFC survey has been conducted annually since 1991, it provides a largely consistent base for the observation period. However, with its sample restricted to start-ups that have received NLFC funding, it comes with the potential drawback of a selection effect (Takahashi 2005). SMEA does not conduct its own surveys but customises data from secondary sources; its assessment of data validity and representativeness provides a helpful reference tool for researchers (SMEA 2007: 24). JSBRI's analysis is based on a representative survey at a single point in time, which precludes any intertemporal comparisons and has the further drawback of not including the sole proprietorships that make for the largest share of business start-ups (around 75%). This latter limitation also precludes an inspection of NLFC data for a potential selection effect even though Takahashi attempts to do so (2005). In this context the NLFC data represent the best available choice for profiling the "founder force" and government statistics for references to the general population.

[1]The Small and Medium Enterprise Agency (*Chūshō kigyōchō;* SMEA) is an entity within the Ministry of Economy Trade and Industry (METI). Originally founded within the former Ministry of Commerce and Industry (1925–49), it was transferred to the Ministry of International Trade and Industry (MITI, 1949–2001) in 1949. It supports legislation and provides information on SMEs, promotes economic development of SMEs and supports business founders and SME management with counselling services.

[2]Japan Small Business Research Institute (*Chūshō Kigyō Sōgō Kenkyū Kikō;* JSBRI), a Tokyo-based foundation, works on collection and analysis of data on SMEs in Japan.

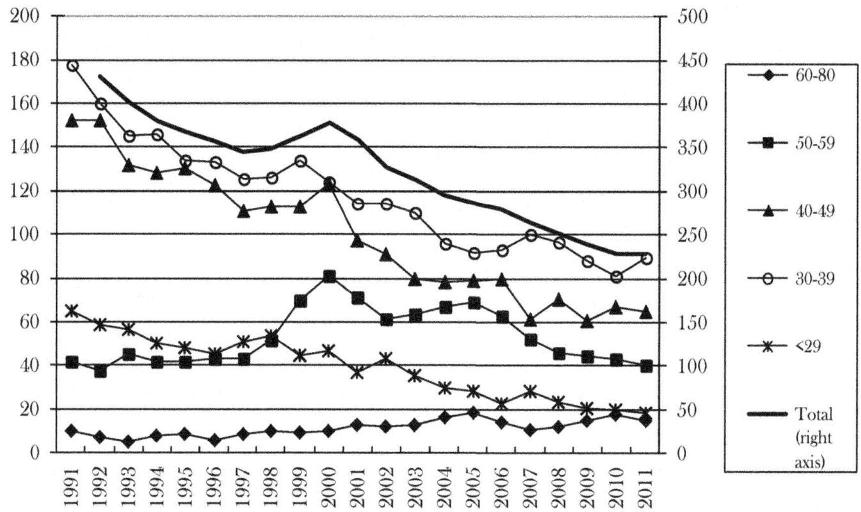

Fig. 11.1 Number of new businesses by age cohorts, 1991–2011 (thousand). Source: NLFC (1992–2012), SMEA (2012) and Establishment and Enterprise Census (METI)

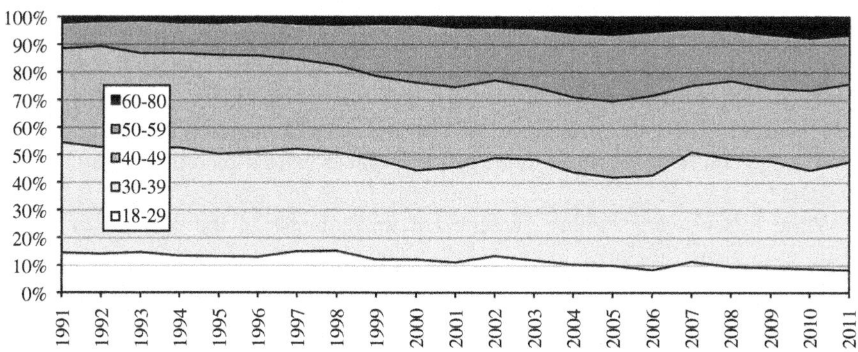

Fig. 11.2 Age profile of Japanese business founders, 1991–2011. Source: NLFC (2011)

Figure 11.1 provides an overview of the absolute development in the number of newly founded businesses for the two decades between 1991 and 2011. With the exception of the years 1997–2000, the number of newly founded business has shown a decreasing trend during the investigation period.

Senior business founders contribute a significant part of the total number of newly founded businesses: for example, in 2005 and 2006, the number of businesses founded by the 60-plus age group was almost equal to the number founded by the group aged below 30.

From Fig. 11.2, which shows the shares in the number of businesses founded by the same five age cohorts, we can infer that the share of founders in their fifties

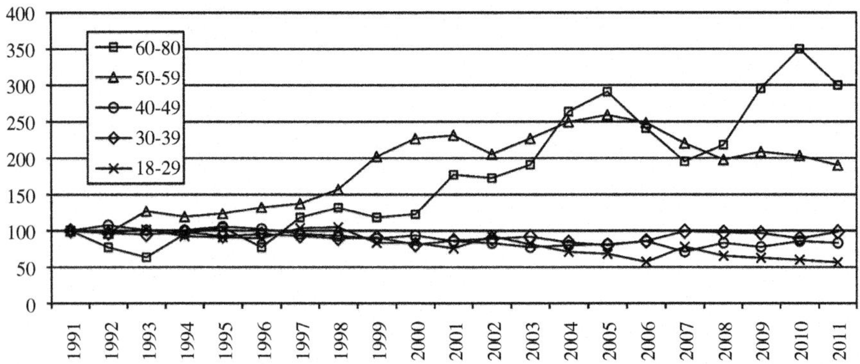

Fig. 11.3 Age profile of business founders, indexed to 1991, 1991–2011. Source: NLFC (2012)

doubled from 10 to 20% of the total, whereas the share of founders in their forties has fallen by almost 10 percentage points from 35% to 25%. Although still representing a small share of the total, founders in their sixties have more than tripled their share since 1997, reaching 8% by 2010. The average age of founders has been moderately and almost continuously increasing for the last two decades, up from 39 in 1991 to 42 in 2013.

Figure 11.3 illustrates the dynamics of this development more effectively, showing the evolution of age cohort-specific shares indexed to 1991. We can observe a disproportionally high increase for both senior citizens and individuals in their fifties. The latter peaked in 2005 at more than twice their 1991 share. The trend is even more pronounced in the case of seniors, who tripled their share in just 20 years.

While this provides telling evidence of the increase in the number of older business founders, we need to understand what share of this increase was merely due to a rising share of the corresponding age cohorts in the general population, that is, to what extent this phenomenon can be attributed to demographic change. The relevant data is taken from the 2013 Labour Force Survey (MIAC 2013). Figure 11.4 provides the relative over- and underrepresentation of age cohorts in the founder force relative to the overall labour force. This allows us not only to adjust for demographic change but also to understand which age groups are particularly active founders.

The 50–59 age group has been equally represented in the founder force and in the overall labour force for about the last decade. In contrast, the age cohorts between 30 and 50 are clearly over-represented in start-ups, while those aged below 30 and above 60 are clearly under-represented. Summing up, we can note that individuals over 50 have significantly increased their start-up activities while still being under-represented as compared to the overall workforce.

The high degree of urbanisation in Japan points to a likely concentration of business formation in a few metropolitan regions. In 2005 almost every other

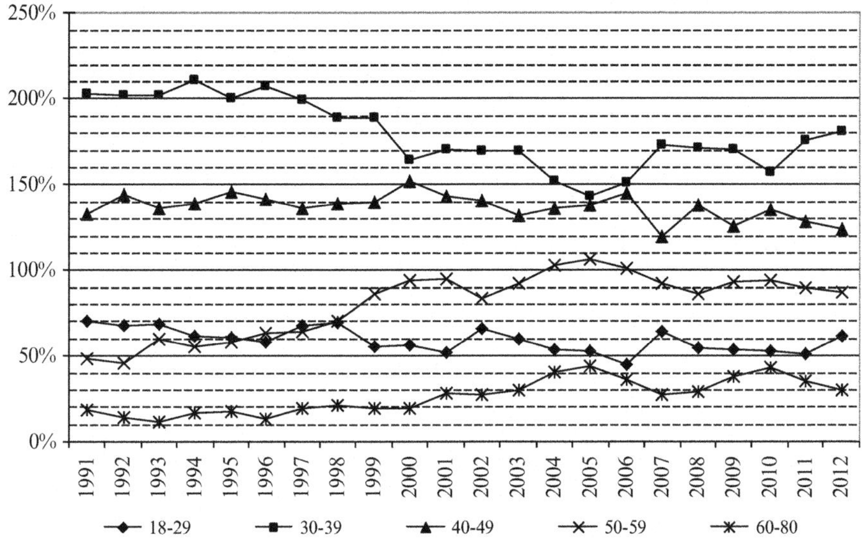

Fig. 11.4 Age profile of business founders relative to total labour force, 1991–2012. Source: NLFC (2012), MIAC (2013: Table 3.2), author's calculations

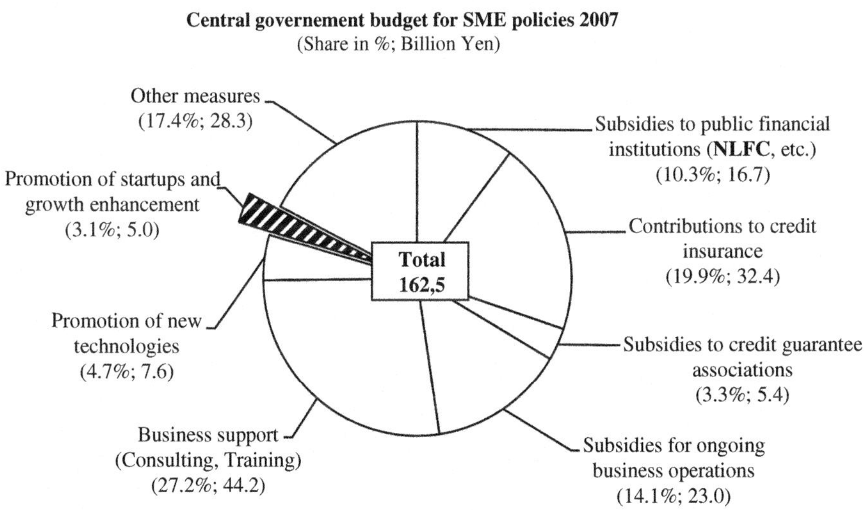

Fig. 11.5 Regional distribution of start-ups relative to GDP and population, 2005. Source: NLFC (2005), CabO (2007) and MPMHA (2008); author's calculations

business (47.2%) was founded in the *Kantō* region (Greater Tokyo and neighbouring prefectures) and a further one in five in the *Kinki* region (Osaka, Nagoya, Kobe, Kyoto). A comparison with regional GDP and population data enables the true extent of this concentration to be assessed (Fig. 11.5).

Figure 11.5 shows that the share of business start-ups in the *Kantō* region exceeds its already disproportionate share of GDP. While the *Kantō* population does not even account for a third of the national population, the region produces close to 40% of the country's GDP. With its share of business start-ups reaching almost 50%, we can assume the economic concentration process will continue into the future. Seen from the neutral perspective of a proportional relation, the *Kantō* region features about 20% more start-ups than could be expected from its share of GDP and almost 50% more start-ups than suggested by its population. Other than the *Kantō* area, only the *Kinki* region displays a higher share in business start-ups than suggested by its respective shares of GDP and of the national population. While the difference is still positive, it is less pronounced than for the *Kantō* region.

Figure 11.6, illustrating the development of the gender ratio among business founders since 1991, shows considerable variance but a generally increasing trend in the share of women founders. The increase from 12.4% in 1991 to 15.7% (or around one in six businesses) in 2012 equals a relative increase of about 27%.

However, in order to assess whether the increase is to be considered over- or under-proportional, we need to compare the gender ratio of business founders to general trends in labour participation rates for men and women. Relevant data show that female labour participation has significantly increased across all age groups since the early 1990s with a particular strong increase for the age group between 25 and 34 (Blind and Lottanti 2015, 2017). Figure 11.7 illustrates the development for all men and by age groups for women.

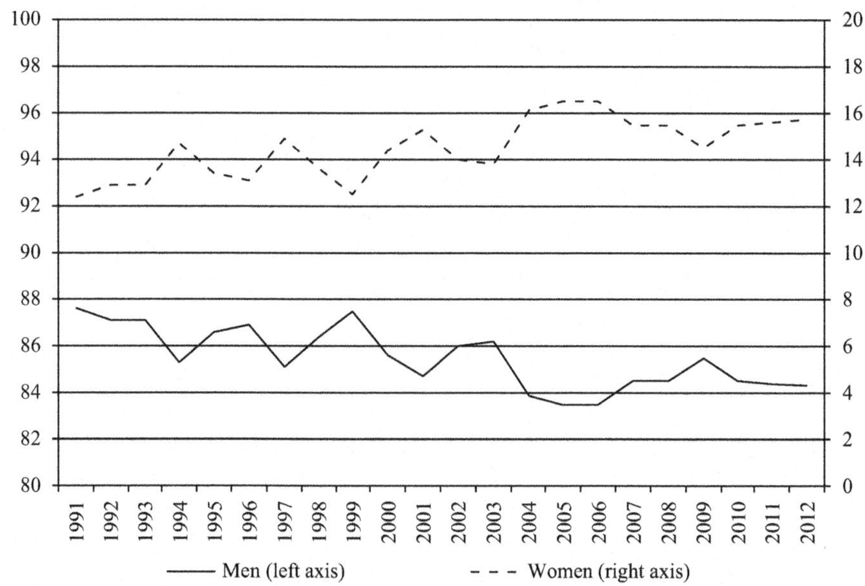

Fig. 11.6 Gender ratio among business founders, 1991–2012. Source: NLFC (1991–2012)

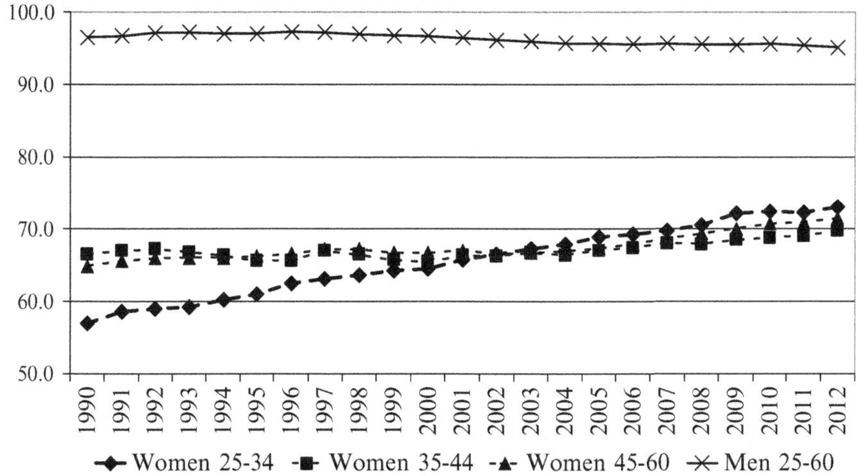

Fig. 11.7 Labour force participation rates for men and women, 1990–2012. Source: Compiled from MIAC (2013)

Overall we can note that even today almost 30% of women are not participating in the labour force in spite of the strongly increasing trend for women aged 25–34. While only 57% of women in this age group were active in the labour force in 1990, their share has increased to 73% in 2012, exceeding the share of all other age groups since 2002. In relative terms, the most pronounced increase in labour force participation for the age group 25–34 equals some 28%, slightly higher than the corresponding increase in female business founders. However, the average increase for women aged 25–60 is only 12%. This stands in stark contrast to evidence drawn from NLFC micro-data showing that the share of women founders aged over 50 increased dramatically from 13% in 1992 to 33% in 2008 (NLFC 1991–2008), which amounts to a doubling of their share even after correcting for demographic effects (Blind 2012). Consequently, we can note a disproportionate increase in the share of female business founders in general (+25%) and of women aged 50+ in particular (+100%). Interestingly, this trend is arguably independent from wage development of the spouses of married women for whom reported correlation is very low in Japan (Abe and Oishi 2007).

At first glance, the NLFC survey of the educational levels attained by business founders at the time of business start-up suggests a relatively balanced distribution. About one in three business founders has obtained a university degree, another 20% have received some specialist training in a vocational school and around another third has graduated at least from high school (Fig. 11.8). While in 1991 about 10% of business founders had only completed the 9 years' compulsory education (primary and junior high), this figure had fallen to less than 5% in 2012.

While this suggests that the educational profile of business founders is quite balanced, it is possible, using age-profile data (see Fig. 11.3) and government statistics on educational attainment available since 1950 (MEXT 2013), to

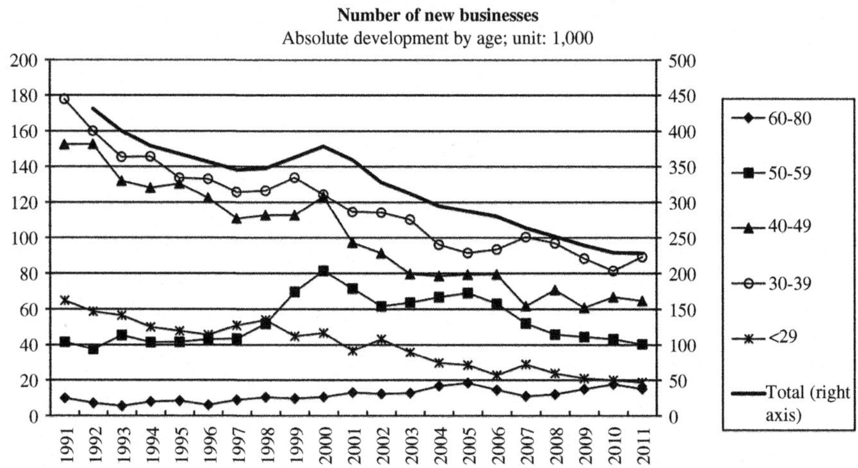

Fig. 11.8 Standard of education of founders relative to general population, 1991–2011. Source: NLFC (2012), MEXT (2013); values for 2008–2011 partially interpolated

construct a fairly exact comparison[3] between the educational profile of the founder force and a representative total population of the same age structure spanning the entire investigation period. Figure 11.8 illustrates this comparison for three educational categories—junior high school; senior high school, vocational school or similar; and college (including junior colleges)—and shows that, historically, the founder force enjoyed a slightly higher standard of education than the general population. However, this disparity is gradually disappearing. For instance, the share of business founders that had only attained junior high in 1991 was only half the respective share of the general population (10 vs. 20%) but had decreased about three percentage points by 2012. An even stronger levelling effect can be observed for graduates of senior high, vocational high and higher vocational schools, where there has been no more significant difference since about 2000. Likewise, the difference between founders with university degrees and the general population has been insignificant since about 2007.

Summing up, we find that although there was a slight educational disparity between business founders and the general population at the beginning of the investigation period, the "educational head start" has been continuously declining since the turn of the millennium and can no longer be considered significant.

Given the large proportion of founders aged 30 and over at the time of their start-up (more than 90% since 2007; see Fig. 11.2), the profile of their previous professional experience might be expected to show characteristic differences.

[3]Entry to the highest educational level attained assumed at age 20. For the share of individuals born prior to 1930 within the group aged 60 and above, we refer to the education structure as of 1950. The age profile of the founder force enters as weighting factor to the educational profile of the general population separately for every year in the investigation period.

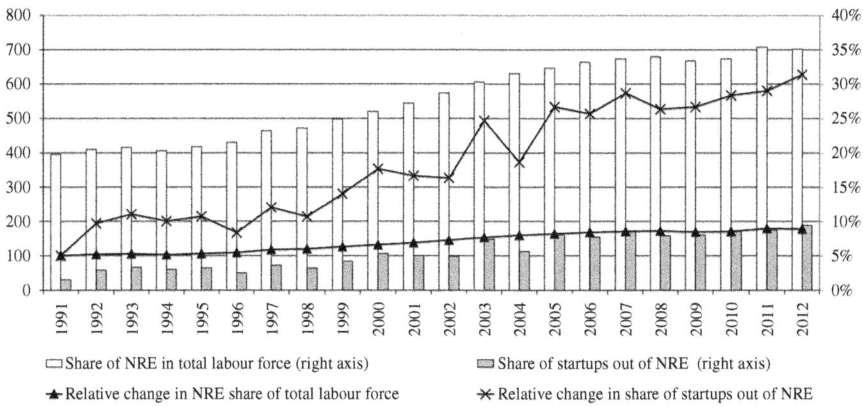

Fig. 11.9 Absolute and relative developments of non-regular employment in labour force and founder force. Source: NLFC (2012) and MHLW (2013)

Choice of occupation is of course a multi-faceted process which depends on individual circumstances at a particular time, so it is of particular interest to explore the point of departure, from which the transition into self-employment has taken place. Dependent employment is the most significant previous professional background, and within that, the distinction of regular versus non-regular employment has become the standard point of reference. Figure 11.9 indicates that less than 2% of business founders left non-regular employment for self-employment in 1991, but this figure has risen continuously, reaching almost 10% in 2012.

Like many other countries, Japan has seen a strong increase in non-standard employment during the past two decades, sparking a heated debate about increasing inequality (Tachibanaki 1998, 2006; Satō 2000; Ōtake 2005). While economic equality obviously embraces many other aspects than merely the distinction between standard and non-standard employment, the increase in the latter can be almost entirely explained by the growing labour force participation of women (Blind and Lottanti von Mandach 2013).

By indexing the shares of non-regular employment in the founder force and the overall labour force to 1991, Fig. 11.9 shows that the increase in start-ups out of non-regular employment is more than three times greater than the increase in non-regular employment in the total labour force, so we can define previous employment status as a discriminating characteristic of the founder force.

Our findings show a number of characteristics of the founder force that are significantly different from the overall labour force. First, the age profile is heavily centred on the cohorts aged between 30 and 49 throughout the investigation period, and the 50–59 age group is catching up. Second, business formation is strongly biased towards the Greater Tokyo Area and other urban areas. Third, women have strongly increased their share in business formation, outpacing the rise in female labour market participation by 25% across all age groups and by 100% in the group aged over 50. Fourth, start-ups by former non-regular employees have increased, outpacing the rise of non-regular employment in the overall labour force more than threefold.

11.3 Founder Subgroups: Differentiating Characteristics

At this point, we have to consider whether any of the four characteristics of age, spatial distribution, gender or education and professional experience differ in their susceptibility to the factor rules in our CSS. To recap, our CSS rules are Minimum Capital Requirements, Perceived Cost of Capital, Small Family Ideal, Non-regular Employment, Business Sentiment and Fear of Unemployment (Table 11.1).

The odds of adopting the first of these are obviously not influenced by any of the four subgroup characteristics identified. This is because Minimum Capital Requirements as a 0th order rule is subject to "collective adoption", as legislation is part of the rule pool of all law-abiding agents (see Table 9.1). Likewise, perceptions of the cost of capital do not depend on any of the characteristics. In a similar vein, we argue that there are no significant regional differences pertaining to the odds of adopting any of the CSS factor rules. Whereas the urban–rural divide has become less influential in the political sphere (Chiavacci 2010), it arguably still represents an important control variable in economic inquiries.

Previous employment status was found to be an important differentiating characteristic. However, as non-regular employment is a near equivalent to conducting operations on factor rule Non-regular Employment, distinguishing subgroups according to this very characteristic would imply excluding Non-regular Employment from the CSS. Yet, doing so might offer a promising approach as we expect individuals in non-regular employment to be less susceptible to Fear of Unemployment and to be more susceptible to Business Sentiment. The assumed differences for non-regular employees relate to a smaller risk in terms of Stigma of Failure and of Traditional Class Order, to unemployment representing less of a risk and to a stronger exposure to business cycles.

Female business founders represent a very specific group, and the disproportionate increase of women in the founder force deserves calls for research (with some being made, e.g. by Debroux 2006; Futagami and Helms 2009). Yet, with respect to the factor rules in our CSS, women will arguably only show differing susceptibility towards Fear of Unemployment, which on average is less of a concern to them as a significant share of female founders was either previously not working or in relatively easy-to-resume non-regular employment.

In contrast, age proves a differentiating characteristic in terms of susceptibility towards three of the six factor rules in the CSS: Small Family Ideal, Business Sentiment and Fear of Unemployment. In the course of their lives, agents will become less susceptible to influences from their family (e.g. through Small Family Ideal), unemployment becomes less of a threat as retirement approaches (Fear of

Table 11.3 Susceptibility to CSS rules by subgroup characteristics

	Subgroup characteristics			
CSS rules	Age	Gender	Region	Employment status
Minimum Capital Requirements	–	–	–	–
Small Family Ideal	Juniors +	–	–	Non-regular –
Non-regular Employment	–	–	–	*NA*
Perceived Cost of Capital	–	–	–	–
Business Sentiment	Juniors +	–	–	Non-regular +
Fear of Unemployment	Juniors +	Women –	–	Non-regular –

Unemployment), and personal networks become more important than business cycle movements (Business Sentiment). Hence, where data availability allows, distinguishing senior and junior individuals promises more explanatory power.

In addition to the characteristics derived from our profile of the Japanese founder force (see Table 11.3), we can identify further characteristics for establishing subgroups by enlarging the scope of "employment status" to also include the categories of self-employed, dependently employed and economically inactive. Being self-employed obviously implies that an agent has already adopted Individual entrepreneurship (IE) and is conducting operations based on that rule. Consequently, distinguishing a self-employed from a dependently employed subgroup will not lend itself to the analysis of Individual entrepreneurship. However, distinguishing a self-employed from a dependently employed subgroup in the analysis of Entrepreneurial Spirit is much promising as we may expect such subgroups to display significantly differing susceptibility to the factor rules of Non-regular Employment, Business Sentiment and Fear of Unemployment. In a similar vein, the consideration of an economically inactive subgroup might be helpful in separating the analysis of necessity-driven from opportunity-induced entrepreneurship in the analysis of Individual Entrepreneurship and start-up operations.

***

In Chap. 11 we have effectively split the SFR into a changing and a meta-stable sub-system. This procedure helps not only to reduce complexity prior to conducting in-depth analyses but also to avoid the accidental inclusion of "false positives", where a purely statistical analysis may find a random correlation wrongly taken for causality.

In preparation for the in-depth analysis of the changing sub-system, we have also presented a socio-economic profile of the Japanese "founder force". Many empirical studies merely provide a table of descriptive statistics, but here we have introduced a richer set of characteristics, paying particular attention to their development over the course of the investigation period. In order to understand whether such development was specific to the founder force, we included corresponding comparisons with the general population and found, notably, a disproportionate increase in the share of both older and female new business founders relative to their representation in the overall workforce. Equally, the share of founders formerly employed as non-regular employees significantly exceeds the general rise of non-regular employment. In contrast, we have not found any significant differences between Japanese business founders and the general population in terms of educational attainment.

This chapter has also discussed how the characteristics of the Japanese founder force identified may be used to determine subgroups of agents. We have done so because analyses of the CSS by subgroups yield a potential for increasing explanatory power where agents display a systematically differing susceptibility to CSS factor rules. In our review, we have found age and occupational status particularly promising characteristics. Naturally, a successful split into subgroups is contingent upon data availability and sample sizes, as will be explored in the following chapter.

References

Abe Y, Oshi A (2007) The role of married women's labor supply on family earnings distribution in Japan. J Income Distrib 16(3–4):110–127

Bird A, Mitsuhashi H (2003) Entrepreneurs and entrepreneurial processes: historical and theoretical perspectives on entrepreneurship in the Japanese contexts. Asian Perspect 27(3):125–175

Blind GD (2012) Unternehmensgründer in Japan seit 1991: Evidenz zur Evolution gegensätzlicher Gründergruppen. In: Distelrath G, Menkhaus H, Ölschleger HD (eds) Bonner Japanforschungen 29. Bier'sche Verlagsanstalt, Bonn, pp 19–68

Blind GD, Lottanti von Mandach S (2013) Bescheidene Managementgehälter und sich schliessende Lohnscheren: Neue Einblicke in den japanischen Arbeitsmarkt. In: Chiavacci D, Wiezcorek I (eds) Japan 2013: Politik, Wirtschaft und Gesellschaft. Vereinigung für sozialwissenschaftliche Japanforschung, Berlin

Blind GD, Lottanti von Mandach S (2015) Decades not lost, but won: increased employment, higher wages, and more equal opportunities in the Japanese labour market. Soc Sci Jpn J 18 (1):63–88

Blind G, Lottanti von Mandach S (2017) Secular trends in the Japanese labour market during the lost decades: a reply to Andrew Gordon. MPRA working paper 80812. University of Munich, Munich

Blind G, Pyka A (2014) The rule approach in evolutionary economics: a methodological template for empirical research. J Evol Econ 24(5):1085–1105

CabO (2007) Heisei jū'nana nendo kenmin keizai keisan [2005 Prefectural economic statistics]. Cabinet Office, Tokyo

Chiavacci D (2010) Divided society model and social cleavages in Japanese politics: no alignment by social class, but dealignment of rural-urban division. Contemporary Jpn 22(1–2):47–74

Debroux P (2006) Trends in female entrepreneurship in Japan. In: Gan X, Jaussaud J, Dzever S (eds) Economic dynamism and business strategies for firms in Asia. China Economic Publishing, Beijing, pp 326–356

Futagami S, Helms MM (2009) Emerging female entrepreneurship in Japan: a case study of Digimom workers. Thunderbird Int Bus Rev 51(1):71–85

MEXT (2013) Heisei nijūgo nendo gakkō kihon chōsa (2013 fundamental schooling survey). Ministry of Education, Culture, Sports, Science and Technology, Tokyo

MHLW (2013) The labour force survey. Ministry for Health, Labour and Welfare, Tokyo

MIAC (2013) The Labour Force Survey: 2011 annual averages. Ministry of Internal Affairs and Communications, Statistics Bureau, Tokyo

MPMHA (2008) Heisei jūnana-nen kokusei chōsa [2005 National census]. Ministry of Public Management, Home Affairs, Posts and Telecommunications, Tokyo

NLFC (1991-2012) Shinki kaigyō jittai chōsa [Fact-finding survey on newly opened businesses]. National Life Finance Corporation, Tokyo

Ōtake F (2005) Nihon no fubyōdō: kakusa shakai no gensō to mirai [Inequality in Japan - illusion and future of the disparate society]. Nikkei, Tokyo

Patrick HT, Rohlen TP (1987) Small-scale family enterprises. In: Yamamura K, Yasuba Y (eds) The political economy of Japan, Part 1: The domestic transformation. Stanford University Press, Stanford, pp 331–384

Satō T (2000) Fubyōdō shakai nihon: sayonara sōchūryū [Japan's unequal society—a farewell to the general middle class]. Chūkō, Tokyo

SMEA (2007) 2007 White paper on small and medium enterprises. Small and Medium Enterprise Agency, Ministry of Economy, Trade and Industry

SMEA (2012) 2012 White paper on small and medium enterprises. S. a. M. E. Agency, Ministry of Economy, Trade and Industry

Tachibanaki T (1998) Nihon no keizai kakusa: shotoku to shisan kara kangaeru [Japan's economic disparities—thoughts on income and assets]. Iwanami, Tokyo

Tachibanaki T (2006) Kakusa shakai: nani ga mondai nano ka [Disparate society—what is the problem about it?]. Iwanami, Tokyo

Takahashi, N. (2005) Kigyōka purofairu [Entrepreneur profiles]. In: Kutsuna K, Yasuda T (eds) Nihon no shinki kaigyō kigyō [Japan's new ventures]. Hakutō Shobō, Tokyo

Chapter 12
Evolution of Entrepreneurship in Japan: Analysis of its Changing Sub-system

Abstract We document results of hypothesis testing for the determinants of entrepreneurial attitudes, as well as for latent and actual entrepreneurship in Japan from 1992 to 2012.

For entrepreneurial attitudes we find both, the rule of Business Sentiment in the self-employed subgroup and the rule Fear of Unemployment in the dependently employed subgroup since 1998, with significant negative influence. We further identify a significant impact of smaller families via the 2nd order social rule of Filial Piety as well as a negative influence of Perceived Cost of Capital (*nominal* interest rates).

For latent entrepreneurship we evidence a push hypothesis for two subgroups: dependently employed (via business sentiment) and economically inactive (via the job-to-applicant ratio). The same finding also holds for actual entrepreneurship in the dependently employed subgroup. Filial Piety again has a negative impact on latent and actual entrepreneurship in both subgroups as evidenced from a significant negative impact of cohabitation ratios. These results are robust even after controlling for urban–rural differences and labour market structure.

This chapter formulates and tests hypotheses pertaining to subgroups in our response rule populations. In order to analyse the CSS as the evolving core of our model, an appropriate technique is required (see the methodology outline in Table 8.1). As data availability is sufficient for conducting statistical analyses, we choose this technique for its capacity to produce authoritative results (as in the case study provided in Blind and Pyka 2014). For a useful overview of statistical techniques used in empirical entrepreneurship research, see Parker (2009).

The structure of the chapter follows the hierarchical organisation within the rule complex (Ostrom's 'rule configurations', see Blind 2016:144) of entrepreneurship: after scrutinising the 2nd order rule of Entrepreneurial Spirit in a first step, we conduct a joint analysis of both Individual Entrepreneurship and of corresponding start-up operations. Both sections come with the same microstructure: discussion of available data and development of a subgroup-specific set of hypotheses and statistical testing.

G.D. Blind, *The Entrepreneur in Rule-Based Economics*, Economic Complexity and Evolution, DOI 10.1007/978-3-319-62779-3_12

12.1 The Determinants of the Rule Population of Entrepreneurial Spirit

The only international survey recording entrepreneurial spirit for Japan is Global Entrepreneurship Monitor (GEM), which includes related questions in its section on "entrepreneurial attitudes". Unfortunately, there are two drawbacks to this data. First, it does not cover our entire observation period but is only available from 2001 to 2010. Second, data for Japan is arguably subject to a systematic bias overstating the appreciation of self-employment as a career choice. This is because translators of the survey have chosen to translate the English term "own business" not with its Japanese equivalent *Ji'eigyō* but with the English borrowing *Bijinesu*. While both terms are frequently used in everyday language, any Japanese native speaker will agree that they have completely different connotations. While *Bijinesu* implies something fancy, modern and rather big, *Ji'eigyō* typically signifies a traditional, boring and small-scale activity. What is more, behavioural studies among Japanese students have shown that English terms strongly activate Western reasoning (Kuroda and Suzuki 1991: 40). Hence, the attractiveness of "doing business" in the West will be significantly reflected in positive survey responses featuring as much as 26% in 2008.

As no other data is available that directly measures Entrepreneurial Spirit in Japan, an alternative indicator suggested in our methodological sketch (see Fig. 6.1) is used. Kuraray Co., Japan's close to monopoly provider of satchel materials, conducts an annual survey of parents about the future career choices of their first-grade children (Kuraray, Co. 1992–2007). Their data available annually from 1992 to 2007 includes more than 2000 survey responses each on a nationwide scale. Moreover, the data avoids the potential drawback of translation issues, as the survey is about career choices of children, not of the respondents themselves. Although the data only covers "young parents" (individuals in their 30s), these age groups, as we have seen, account for about two in three business start-ups (see Fig. 11.2). Consequently, the attitude of parents to self-employment as a career option for their children represents an unbiased measurement of Entrepreneurial Spirit.

Analysis of the response data shows that the values for the "self-employment" category vary between 0.6 and 4.2% of respondents. Comparison of these figures with the 26% of respondents in Global Entrepreneurship Monitor voting for "founding one's own *Bijinesu*" as a desirable career option in 2008 provides ample evidence for our concerns pertaining to data validity arising from the translation issue discussed above.

The factor rule population of Business Sentiment is measured using data from the quarterly Tankan report published by the Bank of Japan. The response variable is measured every March, so we match agents' state of mind at this time by employing the most recently published data: Tankan values as of 1 January.

Data on FEAR OF UNEMPLOYMENT is available as part of the bimonthly survey conducted by the Nippon Research Institute for the calculation of their Consumer Sentiment Index (NRI 1992–2007; NRI 1992–2009). We use data drawn from the April editions between 1992 and 2007, which measure the share of respondents reporting "considerable" or "slight" anxiety about unemployment.

For data on the SMALL FAMILY IDEAL, we refer to annual data on the number of siblings in the parent generations of 6 year olds, which can be calculated for the entire sample period from the 1999 to 2004 editions of the National Family Survey. The extent of change in this dimension is most significant: 70% of individuals in their late 30s had two or more siblings in 1992; by 2007 this number was down to 40% (National Family Research Committee 1999, 2004: microdata).

Finally, as a measure of the PERCEIVED COST OF CAPITAL, we use official discount rates as published by the Bank of Japan. Again, we use data for April of each year in order to match the situation at the time of the response rule survey.

The corresponding data matrix is appended as Table 17.1 and notes the real interest for the record only, as it is not a rule but a price. The data used for the analysis of ENTREPRENEURIAL SPIRIT is a low-frequency longitudinal data set with a relatively large proportion of explanatory variables to observations, entailing a number of special provisions with regard to the selection of statistical tools.

The primary objective of this section is the explanation of *fluctuations* in the rule population of ENTREPRENEURIAL SPIRIT in Japan, but not its *absolute size*—we do not aspire to explain persistent differences in the level of appreciation of self-employment in international comparisons.[1] Yet a brief comparison of the level of 26% cited for Japan with the figures for other countries, for example, some 63% for the United States and France (GEM 2008), gives rise to some thoughts about these differences.[2]

As evidenced by Kuraray's survey, parental attitudes to occupational choices continue to strongly mirror TRADITIONAL CLASS ORDER with a clear preference for public-sector employment and a generally low esteem for the "merchant class". Since the survey's inception in the early 1990s, even the highest ever share of parents preferring self-employment for their children—4.2% in 1995—was still far below the 10% actually self-employed in the Japanese workforce. Quite obviously, self- employment does not represent the preferred occupational choice even among self-employed parents.

For the study of ENTREPRENEURIAL SPIRIT, we distinguish a subgroup SE of self-employed agents and a subgroup DE of dependently employed agents, since employment status represents the most strongly differentiating characteristic of agents pertaining to ENTREPRENEURIAL SPIRIT. Among those parents who would like their children to become self-employed in the future, we expect an important

[1]In statistical terms, the analysis inquires parameter estimates, but does not discuss the intercept.

[2]This is even more so, as our data suggests that the value of 26% may still be subject to a positive bias.

share to be entrepreneurs themselves. Close to all other parents will be dependently employed individuals.

Subgroup SE is strongly susceptible to business conditions, in other words, to the 2nd order rule of Business Sentiment. In contrast, the 2nd order rule of Fear of Unemployment is hardly a major concern to the self-employed. While not as pronounced, the opposite generally holds for subgroup DE of dependently employed individuals. Against this background, we argue that subgroup SE will show a high degree of susceptibility towards Business Sentiment, whereas subgroup DE will rather depend on Fear of Unemployment.

When it comes to Business Sentiment, we need to look more closely at subgroup SE of self-employed individuals. Although the relation to Entrepreneurial Spirit would be expected to be positive, since agents in subgroup SE with offspring as potential successors should view a rise in business sentiment as encouraging, three facts contradict this intuitive position. First, most agents in their mid-30s are probably not yet concerned about succession issues. Second, the vast majority of the self-employed in Japan do not run a business potentially in need of a successor: about two out of three businesses do not even have regular employees. And third, as we have already noted, self-employment is not the preferred choice of occupation for their children even among most self-employed parents.

In times of recession, an increasing number of agents in subgroup SE find their own situation relatively stable and pass this view onto their offspring. When business outlook improves, alternative occupational choices are considered more viable. We therefore propose the following push hypothesis:

H,i: Business Sentiment *has a negative influence on* Entrepreneurial Spirit *in subgroup SE.*

Looking at rules and not at operations, we argue that the cognitive rule of Fear of Unemployment, rather than actual unemployment, is the relevant factor driving the Entrepreneurial Spirit rule population. As we have identified subgroup DE of dependently employed individuals as particularly susceptible to factor rule Fear of Unemployment, we need to understand its interplay with Entrepreneurial Spirit as our response. For the dependently employed individuals in subgroup DE, Fear of Unemployment represents the closest proxy for the state of the economy. For them, a rise in Fear of Unemployment reduces the perceived viability of a potential opportunity-driven business start-up and vice versa. As pull hypothesis we propose the following:

H,ii: Fear of Unemployment *has a negative influence on* Entrepreneurial Spirit *in subgroup DE.*

As we have earlier hypothesised Business Sentiment as exerting a negative influence, *H,i* and *H,ii* seem to contradict each other. If there is an upswing in the economy (improving business sentiment), Entrepreneurial Spirit would decline. Yet, if Fear of Unemployment decreases in the course of an economic upswing, this would translate into an increase in the population size of Entrepreneurial Spirit. These opposing effects of business cycle fluctuations are due to the varying susceptibilities of agents to the factor rules of Business Sentiment and Fear of Unemployment.

In support of this argument, consider the two-level structure of rule-based analysis. Agents in subgroup DE might be afraid of unemployment, and this might colour their worldview, but they are still actually employed on the level of economic operations. Given their professional preferences and aspirations, they cannot imagine "necessity entrepreneurship" applying to their children. This can be formulated as follows: if self-employment was considered a desirable career choice for offspring of subgroup DE, the kind of business imagined must offer far brighter prospects than potential dependent employment. In that sense, we can conclude that rule adopters of Entrepreneurial Spirit in subgroup DE relate exclusively to opportunity-driven entrepreneurship. Hence, Fear of Unemployment serves as a signifier for the viability of opportunity-driven entrepreneurship through its role as the primary proxy for economic conditions of subgroup DE. Against this background, we propose the following composite hypothesis:

H,iia: *Both H,i and H,ii hold at the same time.*

In our assessment of factor rules against criterion 2 (the existence of a causal relationship between factor rules and responses; see Chap. 10), we have found that Business Sentiment, Perceived Cost of Capital and Small Family Ideal have been relevant factors all through the observation period and, arguably, for much longer. These factor rules represent firmly established rule populations: rules whose populations have stabilised through a diffusion process long completed, i.e. which have attained institutional status. In contrast, in our assessment of criterion 2 for Fear of Unemployment, we have found that this fear was not central to the perceptions of self-employment prior to 1998 (see Fig. 10.10). Accordingly, we propose the following hypothesis:

H,iii: Fear of Unemployment *has exerted significant influence on* Entrepreneurial Spirit *since 1998.*

Our assessment of SFR rules identified operations on the Small Family Ideal as having rule-level effects. With the average number of siblings declining, we have argued that the rule of Filial Piety is the transmission mechanism activating Stigma of Failure and Traditional Class Order. In more general terms, we assume that individuals with fewer siblings are less likely to cherish an Entrepreneurial Spirit ideal that would run counter to parental preferences. Recognising these aspects, we formulate this hypothesis:

H,iv: *Operations on* SMALL FAMILY IDEAL*—measured as the inverse of the average number of siblings—have a negative influence on* ENTREPRENEURIAL SPIRIT *in both subgroups.*

Applying the rationale of rules vs. corresponding operations in the discussion of monetary policy as an explanatory variable, we point to the distinction of the real cost of capital and the corresponding perception thereof. While in the neoclassical standard model only real interest rates are relevant, rule-based analysis looks at the PERCEIVED COST OF CAPITAL. With inflation close to zero for almost the entire observation period and deflation scarcely more than a vaguely familiar term to the majority of agents, easy-to-grasp nominal interest rates are the principal point of reference. Therefore, our hypothesis is as follows:

H,v: PERCEIVED COST OF CAPITAL *as stated in terms of the nominal interest rate has a negative influence on* ENTREPRENEURIAL SPIRIT.

A first multivariate regression of all four factor rules yields highly significant parameter estimates (1% level) for the first three factor rules: BUSINESS SENTIMENT, FEAR OF UNEMPLOYMENT and SMALL FAMILY IDEAL; and the estimate for PERCEIVED COST OF CAPITAL is close to a satisfactory level (at 89% probability).

For testing *H,iii* which suggests that FEAR OF UNEMPLOYMENT only began to exert an influence in 1998, we can compare significance levels and explanatory power of a univariate regression of FEAR OF UNEMPLOYMENT for the entire sampling period with the values obtained through the introduction of a dummy from 1998 onwards. Whilst we obtain an already significant estimate at the 90% level for the entire period with an adjusted R^2 of 18%, FEAR OF UNEMPLOYMENT shows much higher levels of significance (95%) and adjusted R^2 (0.28) after introducing the 1998 dummy. As the interaction effect is significant, we discard the main effect (marginality principle).

Rerunning the multivariate regression including the 1998 onwards dummy, we obtain highly significant parameter estimates (1% level) for all four factor rules. This result comes in spite of the small sample size and the relatively high number of four explanatory variables. Table 12.1 provides the estimation output for the fully normalised data (by means and standard deviations).

Given the large proportion of explanatory variables to observations, and the high levels of R^2 attained, multicollinearity seems a likely threat. Yet, variance inflation factors (VIF) are all far below the commonly cited conservative critical level of 5. Nevertheless, an inspection of the model's covariance matrix shows correlations >0.5 for two of the six relationships. Yet, for both of these—the correlations of FEAR OF UNEMPLOYMENT and PERCEIVED COST OF CAPITAL to SMALL FAMILY IDEAL (of 0.61 and −0.67)—one cannot identify any structural context but mere coincidence. The relevant figures are appended as Table 17.2.

Table 12.1 Estimation output for ENTREPRENEURIAL SPIRIT

	Coefficient	Std. Error	*t*-Statistic	Conf. Int. (90%)
Intercept	0.0000	0.1041	0.000	
BizSent	−0.4955	0.1111	−4.462	[−0.70,−0.30]
FUe98	−0.4440	0.1360	−3.265	[−0.69,−0.20]
PCoC	−0.5110	0.1452	−3.518	[−0.77,−0.25]
SFI	−0.6049	0.1759	−3.439	[−0.92,−0.29]
R-squared	0.8809	F-statistic		20.34
Adjusted *R*-squared	0.8376	DF		11
S.E. of regression	0.1041	Corresp. p-value		4.837e-05
Sum squared resid	0.1191	Durbin–Watson stat		1.252
S.D. dependent var	0.2581	Corresp. p-value		0.005138

Dependent variable; Entrepreneurial spirit; Method; Least squares; Sample: 1992–2007

We also apply a number of procedures to test our variable selection. Backward selection does not point to omitting any variables, neither via *Akaike* nor via the stricter *Bayesian* information criterion. BIC improvements for all four permutations of three variable models resulting from the introduction of the respective fourth variable are expectedly small but sizeable (compare Appended Table 17.3). Likewise, "leave-one-out" cross-validation does not suggest a reduced model. Moreover, when looking at univariate regressions of BUSINESS SENTIMENT, FEAR OF UNEMPLOYMENT (with and without the 1998 dummy) and SMALL FAMILY IDEAL, we find strong evidence of positive autocorrelation. In spite of parameter estimates reaching satisfactory significance levels, autocorrelation typically results from the omission of relevant variables. This further corroborates the multivariate case.

Confidence intervals for all parameter estimates confirm negative signs at the 90% level (see Table 12.1). Still, in view of both the relatively wide confidence intervals and the structure of the correlation matrix, ridge regression offers a promising alternative. Although the ridge estimator is systematically biased towards 0, not only does it allow sign stability of parameter estimates to be checked via the ridge trace, but it also compensates for multicollinearity and helps to tighten confidence intervals.

Using a modified Hoerl–Kennard estimator of 0.32, the resulting bias of parameter estimates (systematically towards 0) is negligible for BUSINESS SENTIMENT and FEAR OF UNEMPLOYMENT and still acceptable for PERCEIVED COST OF CAPITAL (6%) and SMALL FAMILY IDEAL (5%). In addition to evidence of sign stability, we find confidence intervals tightening substantially (compare Appended Table 17.4). Finally investigating the ridge trace no indications of sign instability were found (compare Blind 2012: 198).

These findings represent robust evidence in support of hypotheses *H,i* to *H,v*. Although the multivariate case already includes hypothesis *H,iia*, we test it separately through a bivariate regression of BUSINESS SENTIMENT and FEAR OF

Unemployment from 1998 onwards. The regression produces significant parameter estimates at negative signs. With this final result, we can implicitly evidence the existence of subgroups SE and DE consisting of self- and dependently employed individuals.

For the sake of completeness, we also investigate the potential influence of real interest rates to be expected from a monetarist point of view. However, we find that real interest rates do not produce significant parameter estimates, neither in a univariate regression nor in its multivariate counterpart. This strongly corroborates the validity of a core assumption in rule-based economics: that agents act based on their perceptions rather than on theoretical concepts such as the real interest rate.

12.2 The Determinants of the Rule Population of Individual Entrepreneurship and of Frequency of Start-Up Operations

Japanese government statistics include data on the number of individuals "wishing and preparing to become self-employed" in their Employment Status Survey conducted every 5 years for the 47 prefectures of Japan (MIAC 1992–2012). We obtain a sample size of $n = 235$ for the investigation period (1992–2012). Thanks to the size of the survey, the data also allows subgroups to be distinguished by employment status (dependently employed and economically inactive) and by gender. While economically inactive individuals do not show substantial differences by gender, working women and working men experience quite different working hours and pay arrangements. Therefore, we include dependently employed men only in subgroup DE, while we include both men and women, in inactive subgroup NA.

The factor rules of Minimum Capital Requirements and Perceived Cost of Capital are variables without regional variation. As a consequence, the multi-year cross-sectional design adopted here reflects these variables only in its intercept and the dummy variables for the respective survey years. The same holds for Entrepreneurial Spirit, for which no data is available at prefectural level.

MIAC's Employment Status Survey also lends itself to the calculation of an intergenerational cohabitation ratio defined as the share of the active population aged 15–64 that is co-residing as a married couple with or without children with one or more parents. This ratio qualifies as an indicator for the workings of the transmission mechanism of Filial Piety.

Data on Business Sentiment in small and medium enterprises is available at prefectural level through a quarterly survey conducted by the Organization for Small and Medium Enterprises and Regional Innovation, an agency affiliated to the Ministry of Economy, Trade and Industry (SMRJ 1992–2012). We use the

Diffusion Index (DI) calculated for the item "Development of business conditions during the last 12 months" by subtracting "improvement" versus "worsening" votes per 100 votes. In order to match the data to business conditions applying when the Employment Status Survey is conducted (30 September), we use the third-quarter results of the SMRJ surveys.

Prefectural-level data on the share of agents conducting operations on NON-REGULAR EMPLOYMENT[3]—the ratio of non-regular employees in the workforce—can be obtained from the Labour Force Survey conducted by the Ministry of Health, Labour and Welfare (MHLW 1992–2012). The latter survey also provides data on the job-to-applicant ratio that qualifies as an inverse indicator for FEAR OF UNEMPLOYMENT thanks to its strong media presence.

As we learned through the socio-economic profile of the Japanese founder force (see Chap. 11), there is a strong urban–rural divide in the geographical distribution of new businesses. In order to avoid a corresponding bias in statistical testing, we control for the urban–rural divide through a noneconomic variable: average residential land per capita. Data at prefectural level is available from the Local Tax Bureau, an agency within the Ministry of Internal Affairs and Communications (LTB 1992–2012). While data for 1992, 1997 and 2007 is directly available, values for 2002 had to be interpolated using 2000 data, and 2012 was extrapolated based on 2011 data. Table 12.2 lists variable definitions and descriptive statistics for the data used. The complete data set is given in the Appendix (Chap. 17).

We have tested data for individual survey years for normality using the well-known Kolmogorov–Smirnov procedure. As satisfactory levels of normality were reached in the majority of years for all variables (compare Appended Tables 17.5–17.10), we decided to only normalise all variables by means and standard deviations (z-transformation). This procedure allows direct comparison of the strength of influence from different factor rules.

Dependently employed agents of subgroup DE who are deliberating on the adoption of INDIVIDUAL ENTREPRENEURSHIP picture themselves as being self-employed. That is, they temporarily assume the reasoning of self-employed agents. The latter, as we have seen, rely on BUSINESS SENTIMENT to judge the current state of the economy. Given the negative impact of TRADITIONAL CLASS ORDER, we assume subgroup DE to be subject to a push hypothesis: we expect to see a negative influence of BUSINESS SENTIMENT on the responses. In the same vein, we assume that the push hypothesis holds equally for subgroup NA of non-working individuals. Accordingly, we expect to obtain evidence of this through a negative impact of the job-to-applicant ratio (as inverse indicator to FEAR OF UNEMPLOYMENT).

[3]Obviously, the number of non-regular employees does not directly correspond to the population size of NON-REGULAR EMPLOYMENT. The latter refers to the number of agents that *want* to generate income from non-regular employment, which does not necessarily coincide with the actual number of non-regular employees. Yet, given the relatively low levels of unemployment, the number of non-regular employees can be considered a sufficient proxy for the population size of NON-REGULAR EMPLOYMENT.

Table 12.2 Variable definitions and descriptive statistics for analysis of INDIVIDUAL ENTREPRENEURSHIP and of start-up operations

Variable	Definition	Mean	S.D.	Min	Max
*NIE*_DE_men	Dependently employed men aged 15–64 wishing to become self-employed as share of corresponding male population	0.0147	0.0056	0.0045	0.0317
Startup_DE_men	Dependently employed men aged 15–64 preparing to become self-employed as share of corresponding male population	0.0062	0.0026	0.0017	0.0158
*IE*_NA_all	Economically non-active individuals aged 15–64 wishing to become self-employed as share of population	0.0046	0.0018	0.0012	0.0110
Startup_NA_all	Economically non-active individuals aged 15–64 preparing to become self-employed as share of population	0.0023	0.0009	0.0006	0.0057
Cohab	Share of the population aged 15 to 64 co-residing as a couple with or without children with one or more parents	0.2695	0.1280	0.0386	0.6607
BizSent	SME assessment of change in business conditions during the last 12 months (improving less worsening votes)	(13.37)	32.28	(58.10)	37.00
NonReg_men	Share of male non-regular employment in employed male workforce	0.1304	0.0582	0.0265	0.2891
NonReg_all	Share of non-regular employment in employed workforce	0.2658	0.0770	0.1041	0.4298
JtA	Job-to-applicant ratio	1.1314	0.8030	0.2400	4.0800
Surfpercap	Residential land per capita (sqm)	97.09	29.25	30.93	166.54

It is clear that the transition from non-regular employment to self-employment is significantly more attractive than from regular employment. Therefore, we assume non-regular employment has a positive influence on our responses. As non-regular employment—particularly among men—has only become a significant phenomenon during the investigation period (compare Blind and Lottanti von Mandach 2012, 2015, 2017), we expect that the impact of non-regular employment on our responses has only developed during the investigation period.

Intergenerational cohabitation—defined as married couples with or without offspring that are co-residing with one or several parents—represents an environment where FILIAL PIETY causes a particularly strong effect of TRADITIONAL CLASS ORDER and STIGMA OF FAILURE on our responses. Therefore, the ratio of intergenerational cohabitation qualifies as an indicator for the transmission mechanism we identified earlier. We further expect this effect to be stronger for start-up operations than for the adoption of the rule of INDIVIDUAL ENTREPRENEURSHIP—the intention to become self-employed. This is because a mere wish to become self-employed may be more easily be accommodated with an adverse parental stance than the actual operation of becoming self-employed.

From these considerations, we can specify the following set of hypotheses for INDIVIDUAL ENTREPRENEURSHIP and start-up operations in subgroups DE (dependently employed) and NA (economically inactive):

H,vi: *In subgroup DE,* BUSINESS SENTIMENT *and intergenerational cohabitation exert negative influences, and non-regular employment exerts positive influence.*

H,vii: *In subgroup NA, the job-to-applicant ratio and intergenerational cohabitation exert negative influences, and non-regular employment exerts positive influence.*

H,viii: *The influence exerted by intergenerational cohabitation is stronger for start-up operations than for* INDIVIDUAL ENTREPRENEURSHIP.

H,ix: *The strength of influence exerted by non-regular employment increases during the investigation period.*

For testing hypotheses *H,vi* and *H,vii*, we pool the data available for the five editions of the survey (1992, 1997, 2002, 2007, 2012) and for the 47 prefectures of Japan, yielding a sample size of $n = 235$. In order to grasp level differences between different editions of the survey (i.e. those originating from differences in PERCEIVED COST OF CAPITAL, ENTREPRENEURIAL SPIRIT and the discrete change in MINIMUM CAPITAL REQUIREMENTS of 2006), we introduce dummy variables for 1992, 1997, 2002 and 2007. Due to the use of normalised data, the intercept represents level differences relative to 2012. Table 12.3 provides parameter estimates for both subgroups.

Parameter estimates for all factor rules, the dummy variables and the control variable load with satisfactory significance levels (all 5% or better) in both subgroups. The signs of the estimates turn out as expected (positive for non-regular employment and negative for the other factor rules and the control variable),

Table 12.3 Parameter estimates for INDIVIDUAL ENTREPRENEURSHIP by agent subgroup

	Subgroup DE	Confidence interval (90%)		Subgroup NA	Confidence interval 90%	
Intercept	−1.225***	−1.596	−0.853	−0.867***	−1.165	−0.568
BizSent	−0.338**	−0.579	−0.097	0.321**	0.058	0.583
Cohab	−0.101**	−0.176	−0.027	−0.316***	−0.395	−0.236
NonRegmale	0.328***	0.142	0.515	−0.231***	−0.338	−0.124
Surfpercap	−0.119***	−0.186	−0.053	−0.201***	−0.328	−0.075
Dum92	2.371***	1.714	3.028	1.216***	0.536	1.896
Dum97	2.174***	1.558	2.79	0.827***	0.360	1.295
Dum02	0.808**	0.252	1.364	1.979***	1.673	2.285
Dum07	0.770***	0.596	0.945	0.310**	0.097	0.523

Significance codes: *** 1%, ** 5%, * 10%

Table 12.4 Parameter estimates for Individual Entrepreneurship in non-working individuals, 1992, 1997 versus 2002–2012

	1992, 1997	Confidence interval (90%)		2002–2012	Confidence interval 90%	
Intercept	−0.042	−0.418	0.333	−0.756***	0.113	−0.943
Surfpercap	−0.463***	−0.608	−0.317	−0.271***	0.060	−0.370
Nonregall	−0.110	−0.444	0.223	0.194**	0.089	0.047
JpA	−0.332**	−0.565	−0.100	−0.129**	0.065	−0.236
Cohab	−0.297**	−0.513	−0.082	−0.241***	0.077	−0.369
Dum97	0.084	−0.633	0.801			
Dum02				1.881***	0.222	1.513
Dum07				0.386***	0.133	0.165

corroborating *H,vi* and *H,vii* for the rule population of Individual Entrepreneurship. Appended Tables 17.11 and 17.12 provide detailed estimates for the two subgroups. Given the relatively high levels of R^2 attained, multicollinearity is a likely threat. Yet, variance inflation factors are all far below the critical threshold for both models (see Table 17.13, which also provides correlation matrices).

To verify whether the influence of non-regular employment on Individual Entrepreneurship has only developed during the investigation period (*H,ix*), we split the sample into an earlier part (1992 and 1997) and a later part (2002, 2007 and 2012). Table 12.4 provides parameter estimates results in subgroup NA for both subsamples.

Non-regular employment (NonRegall) is not found to load significantly in the earlier subsample (1992 and 1997) but does so in the later subsample (2002, 2007 and 2012). With all other factor rules and the control variable producing significant estimates in both subsamples, we have evidence to support *H,ix* for Individual Entrepreneurship in subgroup NA (see Appended Tables 17.14 and 17.15). Again, multicollinearity was not a concern (see Table 17.13). For subgroup DE, however, running the same procedure did not produce supporting evidence for *H,ix*.

Next we turn to the determinants of start-up operations as they result from applying the rule of Individual Entrepreneurship. Table 12.5 provides the estimation output for dependently employed men (subgroup DE) and for economically inactive individuals (subgroup NA), respectively. Detailed regression outputs are provided in Appended Tables 17.16 and 17.17.

The models explaining start-up operations result in significant parameter estimates for all factor rules, three of the four dummy variables and the control variable in subgroup DE of dependently employed men. As the signs of the estimates again turn out as expected, we have evidence to corroborate *H,vi*. For subgroup NA, however, Fear of Unemployment represented by its inverse indicator, job-to-applicant ratio (JpA), did not load with a significant parameter estimate. This means that we have found only partial evidence for *H,vii*.

Finally, we use the two subsets of our data (split into an earlier part and a later part, as above) to test whether the influence of non-regular employment on start-up operations has also only developed during the investigation period (*H,ix*).

Table 12.5 Regression output for actual entrepreneurship by agent subgroup

	Subgroup DE	Confidence interval (90%)		Subgroup NA	Confidence interval (90%)	
Intercept	−0.897***	−1.370	−0.424	−1.067***	−1.427	−0.707
BizSent	−0.455**	−0.763	−0.148			
Cohab	−0.155***	−0.250	−0.060	−0.311***	−0.440	−0.181
NonRegmale	0.310**	0.072	0.547			
Nonregall				0.570***	0.254	0.887
Surfpercap	−0.169***	−0.254	−0.084	−0.310***	−0.406	−0.214
JpA				−0.042	−0.195	0.111
Dum92	1.800***	0.963	2.637	1.640***	0.820	2.460
Dum97	1.696***	0.912	2.480	1.391***	0.827	1.954
Dum02	0.195	−0.514	0.903	1.800***	1.431	2.169
Dum07	0.793***	0.570	1.015	0.503***	0.247	0.759

Table 12.6 Parameter estimates for actual entrepreneurship in non-working individuals 1992 and 1997 versus 2002–2012

	1992, 1997	Confidence interval (90%)		2002–2012	Confidence interval 90%	
Intercept	−0.108	−0.519	0.302	−0.767***	−0.996	−0.539
Surfpercap	−0.401***	−0.560	−0.242	−0.274***	−0.395	−0.154
Nonregall	0.080	−0.285	0.445	0.300***	0.120	0.480
JpA	−0.041	−0.296	0.213	−0.099	−0.229	0.032
Cohab	−0.330**	−0.566	−0.094	−0.329***	−0.485	−0.174
Dum97	0.217	−0.567	1.001			
Dum02				1.719***	1.271	2.167
Dum07				0.583***	0.314	0.852

Table 12.6 provides the estimation results in subgroup NA for the two subsets. As with INDIVIDUAL ENTREPRENEURSHIP, the model does not produce conclusive evidence for subgroup DE.

As in the case of INDIVIDUAL ENTREPRENEURSHIP, the model of start-up operations for subgroup NA also produces evidence in support of *H,ix*: while non-regular employment does not load significantly in the earlier subsample (1992 and 1997), it does so in the later subsample (2002, 2007 and 2012). This mirrors *H,ix*, where we have argued that agents did not consider self-employment an alternative to unemployment until the turn of the millennium. Detailed regression output can be found in Appended Tables 17.18 and 17.19.

We have furthermore argued that the impact of TRADITIONAL CLASS ORDER and STIGMA OF FAILURE via the transmission mechanism of FILIAL PIETY should be stronger for actual than for latent entrepreneurship (*H,viii*). If we compare the corresponding parameter estimates (variabe Cohab) obtained from the models of

INDIVIDUAL ENTREPRENEURSHIP and start-up operations, we can observe that the estimates for actual entrepreneurship *do* load about 30 to 50% stronger.

- In subgroup DE, the estimates are −0.101 on the rule level versus −0.155 on the operational level (see Appended Tables 17.11 and 17.16).
- In subgroup NA, the estimates are −0.231 on the rule level versus −0.311 on the operational level (see Appended Tables 17.12 and 17.17).

While this points to the validity of *H,viii*, confidence intervals for the parameter estimates overlap in both cases. Therefore, we have to technically reject *H,viii* at this point.

***

What meaning do our findings have in a wider perspective? And how should we interpret these in relation to the theoretical propositions derived in Part I? We discuss these questions in the following chapter, meanwhile deriving some insights from reviewing how we have built and tested hypotheses in the course of this chapter.

Through our in-depth analysis of the changing sub-system, we were able to evidence a number of insightful hypotheses shedding light on the factors determining the size dimension of latent and actual entrepreneurship in Japan. Again, antecedent analyses—the reduction of the SFR to its evolving core and the identification of appropriate agent subgroups—have enabled a sound and efficient in-depth analysis. The analysis was sound in the sense not only of not missing out any relevant factors but also of avoiding the accidental inclusion of "false positives". And it was efficient in that it was not necessary to test a variety of differently specified models in order to identify "the most relevant" one.

Significantly, distinguishing subgroups of agents has enabled their heterogeneity, according to their personal circumstances, to be recorded. For instance, we were able to document that push and pull factors with opposing influences are effective simultaneously for self- and for dependently employed individuals. Also, engaging in qualitative argument has again proved beneficial, enabling us to exclude data distorted by a poorly translated questionnaire. Similarly, putting data on the population of ENTREPRENEURIAL SPIRIT *in perspective to the share of self-employed in the workforce was essential for formulating a corresponding push hypothesis.*

References

Blind GD (2012) Investigating entrepreneurial spirit with the rule approach: why self-employment is on the decline in Japan. Evol Inst Econ Rev 9(1):183–198

Blind GD (2016) Behavioral rules: Veblen, Nelson-Winter, Oström and beyond. In: Frantz R, Chen S-H, Dopfer K, Heukelom F, Mousavi S (eds) Routledge handbook of behavioral economics. Routledge, Milton Park, pp 139–151

Blind GD, Lottanti von Mandach S (2012) Ansichtssache: Zum Zustand der japanischen Wirtschaft nach Doppelschlag und Dreifachkatastrophe. In: Chiavacci D, Wiezcorek I (eds) Japan 2012: Politik, Wirtschaft und Gesellschaft. Berlin, Vereinigung für sozialwissenschaftliche Japanforschung, pp 131–149

Blind GD, Lottanti von Mandach S (2015) Decades not lost, but won: increased employment, higher wages, and more equal opportunities in the Japanese labour market. Soc Sci Jpn J 18 (1):63–88

Blind G, Lottanti von Mandach S (2017) Secular trends in the Japanese labour market during the lost decades: a reply to Andrew Gordon. MPRA working paper 80812. University of Munich, Munich

Blind G, Pyka A (2014) The rule approach in evolutionary economics: a methodological template for empirical research. J Evol Econ 24(5):1085–1105

GEM (2008) GEM 2008 global report. Global Entrepreneurship Research Association, London Business School, London

Kuroda Y, Suzuki T (1991) A comparative analysis of the Arab culture: Arabic, English and Japanese languages and values. Behaviormetrika 18(30):35–53

LTB (1992–2012) *Kotei shisan no kakakura no gaiyô chôsho* [Summary report on real estate value and other aspects]. Ministry of Internal Affairs Communications, Local Tax Bureau, Tokyo

MHLW (1992–2012) *Rōdōryoku chōsa* [The labour force survey]. Ministry for Health, Labour and Welfare, Tokyo

MIAC (1992–2012) *Shūgyō kōsō kihon chōsa* [The employment status survey]. Ministry of Internal Affairs and Communications, Tokyo

National Family Research Committee (1999, 2004) *Zenkoku kazoku chōsa* [National family survey]. Japan Society of Family Sociology, Tokyo

NRI (1992–2009) Consumer sentiment index. Nippon Research Institute, Tokyo

Parker SC (2009) The economics of entrepreneurship. Cambridge University Press, Cambridge

SMRJ (1992–2012) *Chūshō kigyō keikyō chōsa* [Business conditions in smaller enterprises]. Ministry of Economy, Trade and Industry, Small and Medium Enterprise Agency, Organization for Small & Medium Enterprises and Regional Innovation, Tokyo

Chapter 13
Entrepreneurship in Japan: Interpretation of Findings

Abstract We present an overview of findings on entrepreneurial attitudes, latent and actual entrepreneurship in Japan between 1992 and 2012. Drawing on micro-data from the Japanese edition of Global Entrepreneurship Monitor we further triangulate the results pertaining to the relevance of cultural factors. Importantly, age shows a negative correlation to the perceived status of entrepreneurs and to fear of failure, which corroborates the finding that Fear of Failure and Traditional Class Order are reinforced through the transmission mechanism of Filial Piety.

A direct comparison to two earlier studies on the same dependent variables evidences the superior explanatory power originating from the integrated empirical design of a rule-based inquiry. By amending our earlier theoretical propositions with evidence specific to Japan and to the observation period we achieve inductive closure.

Building on our methodological template (Part II; Blind and Pyka 2014) we have worked on the detection of potential influencing factors (Chap. 9), the extraction of factors effectively exerting influence during the investigation period (Chap. 10), and the identification of agent subgroups (Chap. 11). Based on these efforts we have been able to formulate and test a number of hypotheses for the "rule configurations" (Oström and Basurto 2011, Blind 2016) of our responses (Chap. 12). At this point, we take stock of the evidence and offer a discussion of the results in the light of previous research and of the theoretical propositions from Part I.

13.1 Understanding Entrepreneurial Spirit in Japan

Our analysis of Entrepreneurial Spirit (previous chapter and Blind 2012) represents the first attempt at identifying the determinants of this rule population as a broad measure of "entrepreneurial attitudes" in Japan. In spite of the limited availability of appropriate data, we have succeeded in providing evidence on significant differences in the relevant rule sets of two subgroups: dependently employed and self-employed individuals. Dependently employed agents were found to refer to an idealised image of "opportunity entrepreneurship" for their general appreciation of self-employment, evidence of the pull hypothesis (*H,ii*): as their Fear of Unemployment declines in an

G.D. Blind, *The Entrepreneur in Rule-Based Economics*, Economic Complexity and Evolution, DOI 10.1007/978-3-319-62779-3_13

economic upswing, members of subgroup DE of dependently employed individuals become more likely to adopt Entrepreneurial Spirit.

We found contrasting results for subgroup SE of self-employed agents whose "entrepreneurial attitudes" strongly reflect their personal situation. Contrary to the idealised image of entrepreneurship dominant among dependently employed individuals, most self-employed agents refer to their own experience as "necessity-driven entrepreneurs" when asked to voice their appreciation of self-employment. Based on these considerations, we have formulated a push hypothesis for subgroup SE (*H,i*), which was supported by our analysis: deteriorating Business Sentiment motivates members of subgroup SE to increasingly adopt Entrepreneurial Spirit.

Furthermore, and most significantly, we were able to provide evidence on demographic change causing negative effects on Entrepreneurial Spirit in the specific cultural context of Japan (and East Asia). With the continuing growth of the rule population of the Small Family Ideal, birth rates are continuing to decline. This, in turn, causes the transmission mechanism of Filial Piety (*H,iv*) to become stronger and stronger as the expectations of parents concentrate on a lower average number of offspring. Through this mechanism, the impact of conservative values such as Traditional Class Order and Stigma of Failure on younger generations is growing stronger. Our study has been able to isolate this mechanism and to produce strong evidence for this causal relationship, which we can term a "side-effect" of demographic change.

Finally, we were able to trace a significant negative influence of Perceived Cost of Capital on the population size of Entrepreneurial Spirit (*H,v*). Interestingly, it became obvious from statistical testing that the perception of agents during the observation period was informed not by real interest rates but by nominal interest rates. This result is particularly revealing, as our findings supplement conceptual challenges to the Lucas critique (Chen 2005) with an empirical one. It seems that money illusion is close to perfect when inflation rates are oscillating around zero as in the case of Japan during the investigation period (7 deflationary, 9 inflationary years included in the sample). In rule terms, *Homo oeconomicus japonicus* is simply not following a real interest rule in his perception of the cost of capital.

As there have been no other studies of the determinants of entrepreneurial spirit in Japan, we lack a point of reference for matching our findings on the rule of Entrepreneurial Spirit. For the results evidencing (1) a negative influence of Perceived Cost of Capital, (2) the pull hypothesis for the dependently employed, and (3) a push hypothesis for the self-employed, the absence of a point of reference is not a serious issue, as similar findings are known from entrepreneurship research on other countries. However, this does not extend to the influence exerted by Traditional Class Order and Fear of Failure on Entrepreneurial Spirit, as it happens via the transmission mechanism of Filial Piety.

For triangulating our findings pertaining to this most particular relationship, we examine the correlation structure within the most recent micro-data available from the Japanese edition of Global Entrepreneurship Monitor (GEM 2010). This can be used to evidence age-specific differentials pertaining to Traditional Class Order and Fear of Failure—rules transmitted via the mechanism of Filial Piety from parents to offspring. Age shows a significantly negative correlation of 9% to the survey item coded as: "In my country, those successful at starting a business have a high level of status and respect". With this, we have effectively evidenced an intergenerational differential in TRADITIONAL CLASS ORDER. Moreover, FEAR OF FAILURE is also age dependent. While those approaching or already in retirement are naturally less concerned about potential business failure due to their pension entitlement, the age bracket of 18–54 features a highly significant positive correlation of 5.5% between age and FEAR OF FAILURE. These two correlations drawn from Global Entrepreneurship Monitor country data for Japan corroborate our finding that FEAR OF FAILURE and TRADITIONAL CLASS ORDER are reinforced through the transmission mechanism of FILIAL PIETY.

13.2 Understanding Latent Entrepreneurship and Start-Up Operations in Japan

Guided by the strong general preference for dependent employment (see the discussion of TRADITIONAL CLASS ORDER in Sects. 9.1 and 10.2), we have formulated push hypotheses for both latent and actual entrepreneurship. In subgroup DE of dependently employed agents, we found evidence of this in a negative relationship with BUSINESS SENTIMENT: in the event of an economic upswing, maintaining one's preferred employment status becomes a more viable prospect. Consequently, the population of INDIVIDUAL ENTREPRENEURSHIP declines, and the number of start-up operations decreases (*H,vi*). Turning this argument around, a decline in BUSINESS SENTIMENT pushes dependently employed individuals to consider alternatives to their current status. Correspondingly, their chances of adopting INDIVIDUAL ENTREPRENEURSHIP increase, as does the likelihood of applying that rule in a start-up operation.

We were also able to evidence a corresponding push hypothesis for subgroup NA of economically inactive agents: as the job-to-applicant ratio worsens, the chance of adopting the rule of INDIVIDUAL ENTREPRENEURSHIP increases (*H,vii*). However, we were not able to trace a significant relationship for start-up operations. One possible interpretation for this is that a process of self-selection occurs whereby significant numbers of economically inactive carriers of INDIVIDUAL ENTREPRENEURSHIP have adopted that rule only after concluding an unsuccessful job search. Whether or not they subsequently apply INDIVIDUAL ENTREPRENEURSHIP in a start-up operation would then depend on other factors.

As with ENTREPRENEURIAL SPIRIT, the transmission mechanism of FILIAL PIETY channels a negative impact of TRADITIONAL CLASS ORDER and STIGMA OF FAILURE on both latent and actual entrepreneurship. The effect is significant for both subgroups (DE and NA): the higher the share of individuals in intergenerational cohabitation, the smaller the rule population of INDIVIDUAL ENTREPRENEURSHIP becomes and the fewer start-up operations can be observed (*H,vi* and *H,vii*).

For start-up operations, absolute values of parameter estimates figure about 35–50% higher than the values for INDIVIDUAL ENTREPRENEURSHIP. While this indicates that the transmission mechanism may have a stronger effect for actual than for latent entrepreneurship—validating hypothesis *H,viii*—90% confidence intervals for the parameter estimates are overlapping, and we have to technically reject it. Still, conceptually, it makes complete sense that FILIAL PIETY moderates start-up *behaviour* more than it impacts on the mere *idea* (rule) of becoming self-employed.

Finally, we have found that significance in both subgroups for latent and actual entrepreneurship positively depends on the share of non-regular employees in the dependently employed workforce (*H,vi* and *H,vii*). Where non-regular employment serves as the current or potential alternative to self-employment, it has a similar risk profile but promises more chances. With this finding, we are able to confirm the sizeable existence of "improvement-driven entrepreneurship" (GEM 2007) for the case of Japan.

Building on the observation that the rise in non-regular employment is a relatively recent phenomenon (Blind and Lottanti von Mandach 2015, 2017) we have furthermore assumed that a majority of agents did not consider self-employment as a potential alternative to non-regular employment at the beginning of the observation period (*H,ix*). Through splitting the sample into an earlier (1992 and 1997) and a later part (2002, 2007 and 2012) and by running separate regressions, we were able to evidence that non-regular employment has started to exert significant positive influence on latent and on actual entrepreneurship only since the early 2000s in subgroup NA of economically inactive individuals. For subgroup DE, however, this procedure did not yield any conclusive evidence.

Comparing our results for ENTREPRENEURIAL SPIRIT with the findings on INDIVIDUAL ENTREPRENEURSHIP and corresponding start-up operations, we find two common determinants: first, BUSINESS SENTIMENT entering negatively as a push factor; and second, the negative influence of TRADITIONAL CLASS ORDER and FEAR OF FAILURE via the transmission mechanism of FILIAL PIETY.

In contrast, FEAR OF UNEMPLOYMENT exerts seemingly contradictory influences: while it weakens the propensity to adopt ENTREPRENEURIAL SPIRIT in dependently employed individuals, it reinforces the adoption of INDIVIDUAL ENTREPRENEURSHIP in non-working individuals. To disentangle this apparent contradiction, it helps to recall the differences (a) between the 2nd order rule of ENTREPRENEURIAL SPIRIT and the 1st order rule of INDIVIDUAL ENTREPRENEURSHIP and (b) between the individual circumstances, under which dependently employed and non-working individuals deliberate on the adoption of these rules.

Since dependently employed individuals consider the adoption of ENTREPRENEURIAL SPIRIT from a *general* perspective (such as when contemplating the future of their children), implicitly they will only consider opportunity-driven entrepreneurship. From their perspective, increasing FEAR OF UNEMPLOYMENT indicates a decline in the viability of opportunity-driven entrepreneurship.

In contrast, when non-working individuals are contemplating to adopt INDIVIDUAL ENTREPRENEURSHIP, agents are reflecting their personal circumstances. Naturally, non-working individuals—most of whom are essentially unemployed—experience unemployment not as an abstract economic indicator but as part of their personal life. We have referred to their case as "true necessity entrepreneurship" (see Table 4.2).

To render this argument less abstract, imagine an unemployed father for whom self-employment merely represents the best available choice given his level of education and the state of the local economy. While preferring self-employment as a way out for himself, he is likely to endorse a "safe" alternative for his children, such as diligent study aimed at securing public-service employment. From this we understand how ENTREPRENEURIAL SPIRIT may follow a pull logic, while push factors may be dominating the adoption of INDIVIDUAL ENTREPRENEURSHIP.

For further triangulation of our findings on latent and actual entrepreneurship, we can refer to two earlier studies (Harada 2005; Masuda 2006). Both used data from the same government survey to measure their responses. While Harada uses data sets from four editions of the survey (1982, 1987, 1992, 1997) to build a pooled panel of prefectures, Masuda executes a cross-sectional analysis using data from the 1997 survey. In their studies, the two authors find the unemployment rate bears a stronger relationship to latent entrepreneurship than to GDP-related measures such as cash earnings and expected profits. Therefore, they argue in favour of a push hypothesis of necessitated entrepreneurship.

While both authors effectively evidence the push hypothesis for Japan by confirming a positive relationship with the unemployment rate, their studies contribute few additional insights (Harada) or even produce faulty conclusions (Masuda). The integrated design of our study—particularly the antecedent causality check implied by the reduction from SFR to CSS and the distinction of agent subgroups—helped to avoid serious misjudgements. Moreover, we were able to identify and evidence a number of new phenomena such as the relationship between non-regular employment and "improvement-driven entrepreneurship" and the growing influence of traditional values via the transmission mechanism of FILIAL PIETY.

13.3 Theoretical Propositions on Entrepreneurship in Empirical Perspective

The empirical part of this research represents a macro coordination analysis of causal relationships between populations of rules. We have extended the analysis to also include start-up operations on the 1st order rule of INDIVIDUAL ENTREPRENEURSHIP. We did not, however, investigate the propagator role of entrepreneurs in the diffusion of specific rules—which would have implied a meso analysis. Consequently, our empirical findings can shed additional light only on those propositions relevant to theoretical aspects of entrepreneurship as a rule, but not to those relating to the propagator role of the entrepreneur in a rule-based economy.

Proposition 1 states that opportunity-driven business start-ups carry risks that cannot be insured. Although we were not able to evidence the pull hypothesis for the rule of Individual Entrepreneurship for Japan, we can amend *Proposition 1* to also include improvement-driven entrepreneurship. This is because we have found strong evidence of the prevalence of improvement-driven entrepreneurship in Japan (the increasing share of agents commencing a business out of non-regular employment). As improvement-driven entrepreneurship equally implies the incurring of risks that cannot be insured in the absence of a necessity to do so, we amend *Proposition 1* to:

Proposition 1a:
Opportunity- and improvement-driven start-up of a business by an individual agent corresponds to an operation conducted in applying the previously adopted rule of Individual entrepreneurship *(IE) and implies the taking of significant risks that cannot be insured.*

Proposition 2 contrasts the opportunity-driven adoption of the rule of Individual Entrepreneurship with its necessity-driven counterpart, where the latter denotes the situation of an agent falling short of an alternative source of income. With the job-to-applicant ratio reducing the inclination to adopt Individual Entrepreneurship in non-working individuals, we can evidence an instance of operational entities causing change at rule level: budget constraints causing the adoption of Individual Entrepreneurship as postulated by *Proposition 2*.

Proposition 3 describes the likelihood of adopting the rules of Entrepreneurial spirit and of Individual Entrepreneurship as depending on 2nd order rules. With our finding that the transmission mechanism of Filial Piety channels the influence of the 2nd order cognitive rules of Traditional Class Order and Stigma of Failure, we can empirically corroborate the claims of *Proposition 3*.

Proposition 4 claims rational choice (the rule of Expected Value Maximisation) is only potentially prevalent in necessity-driven entrepreneurs. Against the background of our evidence on necessity-driven (push hypothesis) and improvement-driven entrepreneurship, we can refine it into:

Proposition 4a:
The rule of expected value maximisation may only be prevalent in new entrepreneurs whose capital requirements (i.e. "value at risk") do not exceed

1. *The cumulative loss of income implied by continuing unemployment times the chances of not finding dependent employment for economically inactive individuals or:*
2. *The income differential to inferior employment conditions plus the risk of failure times current income from dependent employment times expected time horizon until failure or cessation of operations for individuals in non-regular employment.*

It is evident from this that the prevalence of Expected Value Maximisation is most unlikely both in necessity-driven and in improvement-driven entrepreneurs, as both the chances of finding employment and the risk of failure will be most difficult to calculate in the vast majority of cases.

Proposition 5 denotes the potential impairment of the rate of conversion from latent to actual entrepreneurship through impeding 0th and 2nd order rules. Our findings include evidence on the relevance of both types of inhibiting factor rules. On the one hand, we have found the 0th order rule of MINIMUM CAPITAL REQUIREMENTS an important supply-side aspect, the suspension of which in 2006 has encouraged a growing number of business incorporations. On the other hand, the 2nd order rules of TRADITIONAL CLASS ORDER and FEAR OF FAILURE have been found significant inhibitors of start-up operations, i.e. for the conversion of latent into actual entrepreneurship.

Finally, *Proposition 6* designates "the bringing of new rules to the market" as a definition of the distinction between equilibrium-disturbing and equilibrium-creating entrepreneurs. As our study did not involve the mapping of a newly emerging rule, we cannot add empirical flesh to the theoretical bones of *Proposition 6*. Thus studies on the diffusion process of specific rules are a desirable area for future research (see Chap. 14).

The results from our analysis of the case of Japan also corroborate our arguments on "the limits to generality as imposed by localism" (see Sect. 4.4), where we contend that locally specific theorems need to be built on the theoretical torso provided by the six propositions. As we have seen from our results on Japan, *Homo oeconomicus*, or rather *Homo sapiens oeconomicus* (Dopfer 2004), reasons differently at different points in time and in different environments. For instance, only in the course of the investigation period have agents come to consider non-regular employment an alternative source of income when deliberating on the potential adoption of INDIVIDUAL ENTREPRENEURSHIP. And obviously, the transmission mechanism of FILIAL PIETY is highly locally specific. It is these limitations to specific theorising in time and space that prove the need to empirically inform one's theoretical reasoning. Where researchers rely solely on the application of universalist theory, solid analytical results are unlikely to result.

References

Blind GD (2012) Investigating entrepreneurial spirit with the rule approach: why self-employment is on the decline in Japan. Evol Inst Econ Rev 9(1):183–198

Blind GD (2016) Behavioral rules: Veblen, Nelson-Winter, Oström and beyond. In: Frantz R, Chen S-H, Dopfer K, Heukelom F, Mousavi S (eds) Routledge handbook of behavioral economics. Routledge, Milton Park, pp 139–151

Blind GD, Lottanti von Mandach S (2015) Decades not lost, but won: increased employment, higher wages, and more equal opportunities in the Japanese labour market. Soc Sci Jpn J 18 (1):63–88

Blind G, Lottanti von Mandach S (2017) Secular trends in the Japanese labour market during the lost decades: a reply to Andrew Gordon. MPRA working paper 80812. University of Munich, Munich

Blind G, Pyka A (2014) The rule approach in evolutionary economics: a methodological template for empirical research. J Evol Econ 24(5):1085–1105

Chen P (2005) A biological perspective of macro dynamics and division of labor: persistent cycles, disruptive technology, and the trade-off between stability and complexity. In: Dopfer K (ed) The evolutionary foundations of economics. Cambridge University Press, Cambridge
Dopfer K (2004) The economic agent as rule maker and rule user: Homo sapiens oeconomicus. J Evol Econ 14:177–195
GEM (2007) GEM 2007 Global Report. Global Entrepreneurship Research Association, London Business School, London
GEM (2010) Adult population survey: micro data for Japan. Global Entrepreneurship Monitor. http://www.gemconsortium.org/docs/download/3132. Accessed 28 Mar 2014
Harada N (2005) Potential entrepreneurship in Japan. Small Bus Econ 25(3):293–304
Masuda T (2006) The determinants of latent entrepreneurship in Japan. Small Bus Econ 26:227–240
Oström E, Basurto X (2011) Crafting analytical tools to study institutional change. J Inst Econ 7 (3):317–343

Part IV Conclusion

This study has produced a number of important results. It has clarified the function of the entrepreneur in a rule-based economy and has set out the theoretical difference between the function of the entrepreneur and the rule of Individual Entrepreneurship (Part I). Using the methodology proposed in Part II, it has then embarked on an empirical journey analysing latent and actual entrepreneurship in Japan since 1992 in Part III.

We start this conclusion with brief summaries of the findings of the first three parts (Chap. 14). These summaries serve three specific purposes. First, to lay the foundations for a future research agenda. Second, to formulate effective policy recommendations aimed at countering the issues identified in Part III (Chap. 15). Third, recalling key elements of the methodology introduced in Part II, we assess the experience of applying the methodologicy in empirical research (Chap. 16).

Chapter 14
The Entrepreneur in Rule-Based Economics: Summary of Findings and Research Outlook

Abstract Summarising major findings on the theory of entrepreneurs and entrepreneurship in rule-based economics, on empirical methodology and on the study of entrepreneurship in Japan between 1992 and 2012, we sketch an agenda for future research.

Starting from the empirical case, two theoretically derived forms of entrepreneurship, namely, "time-lagged opportunity entrepreneurship" and "necessity-induced opportunity entrepreneurship", may be explored in future inquiries. Similarly, the effect of demographic change on latent and actual entrepreneurship encourages empirical tests for other economies.

In this research we have combined three purposes: the development of a theoretical approach to entrepreneurship (Part I), the provision of methodological guidance aimed at enabling rule-based analysis in empirical investigations (Part II, Blind and Pyka 2014) and an analysis of entrepreneurship in Japan from 1992 to 2012 showcasing rule-based economics and its methodology in applied research (Part III, Blind 2012b).

14.1 Entrepreneurship as a Rule and the Entrepreneur as a Propagator of Rules

The entrepreneur is a largely absent figure in most economic textbooks, where he gives way to more prominent figures, such as the Walrasian auctioneer, or some benevolent dictator bestowing Pareto improvements on his populace. In order to bring the entrepreneur back into economic theory, we have reverted to instrumental realism, that is, we have based theoretical reasoning on considerations pertaining to the entrepreneur as part of an economy that can be observed. For guidance, we initially asked three essential questions: what is an entrepreneur, what do they do and who becomes one?

To answer the first question, we have gone back to the definition most widely used in empirical research: "Anyone who starts a business" (Brockhaus 1987). This is because the distinction between equilibrium-creating and equilibrium-disturbing

G.D. Blind, *The Entrepreneur in Rule-Based Economics*, Economic Complexity and Evolution, DOI 10.1007/978-3-319-62779-3_14

entrepreneurs is an entirely empirical one: The "Kirzner–Schumpeter divide" (compare, e.g. Grebel et al. 2003) can only be resolved ex post through a case-by-case analysis. What is more, both types of entrepreneurs *do* start businesses, and the potential for entrepreneurship of both types directly depends on the number of individuals that are *willing* to start a business: on the size of the INDIVIDUAL ENTREPRENEURSHIP population. It is also important to recognise that both types of entrepreneur play an indispensable role in economic evolution: while the Schumpeter type disturbs evolutionary equilibrium, the levelling out of this very disturbance by Kirzner-type "second movers" creates new "generic uncertainty", which in turn triggers the search for new novelty by other Schumpeter-type entrepreneurs.

The second question—pertaining to what the entrepreneur actually *does*—can be answered using the meso analytical level of the rule-based approach. The concept of meso provides the theoretical frame for analysing the diffusion of a novel rule from one agent into a population of agents. In the course of this trajectory, the entrepreneur assumes two decisive functions: first, to convince investors to provide the funds required for the commercial launch of the corresponding innovation and, second, to instil in market participants a willingness to pay for access to the innovation. From a rule perspective, markets provide the mechanism that determines the frequency with which rules are applied in operations. Proceeds from this brokering of rule access, referred to as "generic profits" (Dopfer and Potts 2008: 36), are split between the entrepreneur and the investor. As more and more agents acquire access to the novel rule in the course of the diffusion process, generic profits decrease. This causes the Schumpeterian entrepreneur to search for new novelty.

The three terms "inventor", "entrepreneur" and "investor" have been developed in the context of the study of technological innovations. While they are also used in the rule-based approach, the inclusion of cognitive, social and behavioural rules (compare Dopfer and Potts 2008: 6–10) calls for a generalised terminology designating the three functions. The example of behavioural rules demonstrates this need: entrepreneurs and investors will only assume their roles in the diffusion of rules for which corresponding operations yield marketable products or services. As similar considerations apply to social and cognitive rules, the terms "originator", "propagator" and "supporter" (Blind 2003) designate the generalised functions of inventor, entrepreneur and investor, respectively (see Table 3.1).

This exposition illustrates how these generalised functions help to unfold a broad social science view of cultural evolution. In the author's view, the line demarcating the discipline of economics cannot simply be located along the marketability of operations resulting from the application of a rule: it has to be empirically informed. Rules for which corresponding operations yield direct or indirect influences on economic variables qualify as the subject matter of a rule-based economics.

In his propagator capacity, the entrepreneur thus forms the analytical link between the level of rules and the level of operations. Brokering the access to a novel rule by marketing the corresponding operations, he causes a new rule population to emerge. Once generic profits are depleted, he embarks on a search for further novelty. Yet, the entrepreneur represents merely one of the figures that may assume the role of rule propagator. For capturing the whole spectrum of economically relevant phenomena, propagators other than the entrepreneur need to be incorporated in rule-based analysis.

Our third question—as to how an agent eventually *becomes* an entrepreneur—implies a shift in perspective. Reverting to the empirically inspired definition of entrepreneurship as the act of becoming self-employed (see, e.g. GEM 1999–2013), we develop a rule-based reading of the related concepts of (1) "latent" and "actual entrepreneurship" (Storey and Johnson 1987), (2) "necessity" and "opportunity" as motivations for start-up and (3) the societal appreciation of entrepreneurial activity referred to as "entrepreneurial attitudes".

From the individual agent's perspective, the rule of INDIVIDUAL ENTREPRENEURSHIP translates into the following instruction: "To generate income, become self-employed". Empirical entrepreneurship research refers to this rule by the term "latent entrepreneurship". Applying the rule of INDIVIDUAL ENTREPRENEURSHIP through start-up operations equals "actual entrepreneurship". More recently, empirical studies have also investigated "entrepreneurial attitudes and perceptions" (Global Entrepreneurship Monitor 1999–2013). From the perspective of rule-based economics, these attitudes and perceptions correspond to 2nd order rules and impact on the frequency with which agents adopt the 1st order rule of INDIVIDUAL ENTREPRENEURSHIP. For simplicity's sake, we have summarised these "attitudes and perceptions" into the 2nd order rule of ENTREPRENEURIAL SPIRIT, which refers to the general appreciation of self-employment in a society.

Systematic reasoning about the corresponding rule configurations (Oström and Basurto 2011, Blind 2016) allows refining the distinction between "necessitated entrepreneurship" and "opportunity-driven entrepreneurship". In addition to these received categories, we have identified two additional patterns of entrepreneurship formation: "time-lagged opportunity entrepreneurship" and "necessity-induced opportunity entrepreneurship". In both patterns, the respective agent has already adopted ENTREPRENEURIAL SPIRIT and, in other words, entertains a positive general view of self-employment. In the case of "time-lagged opportunity entrepreneurship", constitutional 0th order rules such as trade regulations impede the transition from "latent" to "actual' entrepreneurship until these rules become obsolete (e.g. through legislative action). In the case of "necessity-induced opportunity entrepreneurship", 2nd order rules retained by the agent inhibit either the adoption of INDIVIDUAL ENTREPRENEURSHIP or the conduct of corresponding start-up operations. As necessity eventually arises (e.g. through the loss of dependent employment), the inhibiting 2nd order rule is no longer retained. By capturing such "micro-institutional change", rule-based theorising thus helps to capture additional forms of the "entrepreneurial process". The complexity implied by these additional patterns in the sequence of adoption of the rules relevant for the genesis of the entrepreneur arguably explains many of the difficulties encountered in empirical studies.

We have used the rule-based theorising to clarify the distinction between the function of the entrepreneur in a rule-based economy on the one hand and entrepreneurship as a rule of occupational choice on the other. While the former serves as a theoretical building block of rule-based economics, the latter represents one of the many possible subjects of a rule-inspired empirical inquiry. With this distinction in mind, it has been possible to frame elements of a theoretical approach to both the role of the entrepreneur in an evolving economy and the entrepreneurial process referring to the *making* of an entrepreneur. Whether a specific entrepreneur assumes a propagator function through the brokering of access to a new rule, or whether he follows a "second-mover strategy" in business studies parlance, can only be assessed in an ex post case-by-case analysis.

14.2 A Manual for Rule-Based Empirical Research

Trying a truly "fresh start" (Part II, Blind and Pyka 2014), we set off by clarifying the nature of an evolutionary agent. Incorporating important legacies from Veblen, Nelson-Winter, and Oström (Blind 2016) we note three characteristics for our agent. First, *homo sapiens oeconomicus* represents a heterogeneous agent, where the heterogeneity of agents refers to the set of rules they have adopted previously. Second, their "rule choices" are context dependent. Third, agents are able to acquire new rules or to give up on previously retained rules. As this is seen to occur in "historical time", all rule-inspired empirical inquiry necessarily has to consider a time dimension.

As we are to inquire economic evolution, it is important to understand what is seen to evolve in the rule-based approach. Dopfer and Potts distinguish rules from operations, where operations are always conducted by applying rules. Consequently, only a change on the rule level can cause the economy to evolve.

Accordingly, our four-stage methodology starts by defining a response rule population, a specific investigation period (owing to historic time) and a spatial delimitation (owing to the susceptibility of agents to different socio-economic environments). For capturing the entire entrepreneurial process as the object of our empirical inquiry, this meant setting as dependent variable the rule complex of Entrepreneurial Spirit and Individual Entrepreneurship including corresponding start-up operations.

In the second stage, we establish the full system of factor rules (SFR) as the ensemble of rules potentially influencing the size of the response rule population. For identifying these rules, we suggest to connect extant theoretical work in economics to that of other disciplines and to include insights derived from interviews of experts and of rule adopters and rejecters. We then suggest classifying rules in the SFR according to the RBA rule taxonomy (Table 2.1) as this will often prove helpful for the subsequent analysis of associations between factor rules. Through this precaution it becomes possible to exclude factor rules, which only exert indirect influence on the responses.

The third stage commits to the extraction of those rules in the SFR that effectively have caused change in the response rule populations. For conducting this ex ante significance test, we propose to assess all rules in the SFR against two criteria: (a) change in the size of the respective rule populations and (b) change in the strength of influence on the response rule population. Rules, for which either or both criteria are different from zero, qualify as part of the changing sub-system (CSS), i.e. as part of the causal core of the model. We assign all remaining factor rules to the meta-stable sub-system (MSSS).

Finally, in the fourth stage, we develop and test hypotheses pertaining to causal relationships between CSS factor rules and the responses. For doing so, we suggest distinguishing subgroups of agents in the response rule population. These can be identified by assessing their level of susceptibility to changes in CSS factor rules. While distinguishing subgroups represents an implicit acknowledgement of agent heterogeneity, doing so comes with a chance of obtaining results with comparatively more explanatory power.

14.3 Entrepreneurial Spirit, Individual Entrepreneurship and Start-Up Operations in Japan: 1992–2012

What is the conclusion with regard to the prevalence of Entrepreneurial Spirit in *Homo sapiens japonicus* since 1992? As the size of this rule population corresponds to the general appreciation of self-employment, we have measured Entrepreneurial Spirit as the population of individuals who find self-employment the most desirable future occupational choice for their offspring, evidencing four factor rules that impact on this rule population.

First, the increased relevance of Filial Piety—caused by a secular demographic trend through operations on the Small Family Ideal—channels a negative influence, the 2nd order rules of Stigma of Failure and Traditional Class Order on the propensity to incur the risk of self-employment. Second, a rise in Perceived Cost of Capital expectedly also leads to a decrease in the size of the rule population of Entrepreneurial Spirit. We also find that the perception of the cost of capital mainly relates to nominal interest rates.

Third and fourth, for the two major subgroups in the Entrepreneurial Spirit rule population—dependently employed and self-employed individuals—we identify opposing influencing factors. In dependently employed individuals, Fear of Unemployment reduces belief in the viability of opportunity entrepreneurship as an alternative to dependent employment. In contrast, self-employed individuals are naturally hardly concerned about unemployment. Their key point of reference is Business Sentiment. In a recession an increasing number of self-employed individuals find their own situation relatively stable and endorse this view to their offspring. However, as the business outlook improves, they tend to revert to what they see as generally preferred occupational choices, that is, dependent employment. Accordingly, Fear of Unemployment *and* Business Sentiment impact negatively on different agent subgroups in the Entrepreneurial Spirit response rule population.

Inquiring into the determinants of latent and actual entrepreneurship—the INDIVIDUAL ENTREPRENEURSHIP population and the number of start-up operations—we have formulated and successfully evidenced push hypotheses both for latent and for actual entrepreneurship. In dependently employed men, we have found BUSINESS SENTIMENT impacts negatively on the INDIVIDUAL ENTREPRENEURSHIP population, as well as on the number of start-up operations. Similarly, in non-working individuals FEAR OF (continued) UNEMPLOYMENT impacts positively on the size of the INDIVIDUAL ENTREPRENEURSHIP rule population as well as on the frequency of business start-ups.

As with ENTREPRENEURIAL SPIRIT, significant influences prove to be FEAR OF FAILURE and TRADITIONAL CLASS ORDER. While the size of their rule populations has been stable during the investigation period, we have seen that FILIAL PIETY works as a transmission mechanism through which the intensity of the negative impact of these rules on latent and actual entrepreneurship has increased. These findings are equally true of the two subgroups of dependently employed men and non-working individuals. A higher share of intergenerational cohabitation is associated with a significantly smaller INDIVIDUAL ENTREPRENEURSHIP population size and with a reduced frequency of start-up operations. Despite some corresponding indications, we could not find statistically robust evidence that the transmission mechanism has a stronger effect on actual than latent entrepreneurship.

For the very first time, evidence was also found of significant improvement-driven entrepreneurship in Japan: non-regular employees are more likely to become latent and actual entrepreneurship. Further, we found that this is a relatively recent development: self-employment was not a preferred alternative to non-regular employment in the 1990s, when these kinds of jobs were still largely confined to retired people, part-time homemakers and those in education (Blind and Lottanti von Mandach 2015). Separate regressions on partitions of the data (1992 and 1997

Table 14.1 Overview on evidence found by response variable and by agent subgroup

	ENTREPRENEURIAL SPIRIT		INDIVIDUAL ENTREPRENEURSHIP		Start-up operations	
Hypotheses	SE	DE	NA	DE	NA	DE
Negative influence of *fear of unemployment* (Pull hypothesis)		√				
Negative influence of *business sentiment* (Push hypothesis)	√			√		√
Positive influence of *fear of unemployment* (Push hypothesis)			√		√	
Negative influence of *traditional class order* via *Filial piety*	√	√	√	√	√	√
Negative influence of *perceived cost of capital*	√	√				
Positive influence of *non-regular employment* (Improvement entrepreneurship)			√	√	√	√
Influence of *non-regular employment* developing during investigation period			√	x	√	x

Note: *SE* Self-employed, *DE* Dependently employed, *NA* Economically inactive versus 2002, 2007 and 2012) have provided evidence in the subgroup of non-working individuals. Table 14.1 summarises the hypotheses formulated and evidence found for the three responses of Entrepreneurial Spirit, Individual Entrepreneurship and start-up operations.

Finally, we have made a telling observation from the regression analysis of the relative population size of Individual Entrepreneurship for the more sizeable subgroup of dependently employed men. The parameter estimates of the dummy variables and of the intercept in its function as the 2012 dummy decrease with every single issue of the survey (see Table 17.11). This means that the Individual Entrepreneurship population as a proportion of the corresponding adult population has been on the decrease ever since 1992. This suggests that there may be other factors systematically and negatively influencing latent entrepreneurship in Japan, which we have not been able to identify.

14.4 Research Outlook

Studies applying research designs from overseas to economic phenomena in Japan provide strong evidence in support of localist approaches in economics, as we saw in Part III. Yet a change from generalist to localist approaches seems unlikely to occur at present:

> It seems awkward that a misfit of Western economic models apparently hardly ever bothers contemporary Japanese economists. [. . .] arguably, this is due to the strong orientation that textbooks and economic scholarship in Japan have taken from the US paradigm. Within their thus "homogenized-from-the-outside" scientific community, Japanese economists perceive few indications that the learned Western models might not be entirely appropriate. If contrasted with the neighboring discipline of business studies that has developed an entire canon of "Japanese-style management," scholars of economics still have to work on a "Japanese-style economics"
>
> (Blind 2012a).

Admittedly, received patterns of economic explanation do not typically produce completely flawed results even when applied without appropriate adaptation. However, failing to follow a localist approach incurs a significant risk at worst of drawing faulty conclusions and at best of missing important points. By the same token, unreflected experimenting with culturalist reasoning comes with a major risk of drawing wrong conclusions (compare the cases discussed in Lottanti von Mandach 2014 and Blind and Lottanti von Mandach 2013,2017). Following the research methodology presented in Part II effectively helps to mitigate both sides of this risk token.

In this context, the "side-effect of demographic change" identified in this study whereby Filial Piety is the local transmission mechanism that channels the impact of Traditional Class Order and Stigma of Failure on entrepreneurial outcomes can be considered an important contribution to the construction of a "cultural economics" (Dopfer 2011). These results are not only relevant for Japan but also for other economies in East Asia that share a Confucian imprint. Researchers might be interested in seeking evidence of this transmission mechanism in South Korea, an economy where the pace of demographic change is second only to Japan.

The data available for this study did not allow to make statistical inferences about the relationship between "entrepreneurial attitudes" and "latent entrepreneurship". Fortunately, micro-data for Japan from the Global Entrepreneurship Monitor surveys between 2001 and 2010 became publicly available in 2014. The survey design offers promising possibilities for a joint investigation, based on a single integrated data set of the rule complex of ENTREPRENEURIAL SPIRIT (2nd order rule), INDIVIDUAL ENTREPRENEURSHIP (1st order rule) and start-up operations. Specifically, this data set promises further empirical insights into two additional forms of the entrepreneurial process: "time-lagged opportunity entrepreneurship" and "necessity-induced opportunity entrepreneurship" (see Table 4.2). What is more, the availability of micro-data covering a broad variety of socio-economic factors is likely to enable a more detailed segmentation of agent subgroups. Unfortunately, however, the limited time frame of the data still restricts the potential for analysing dynamic phenomena such as the learning processes investigated in this research.

A canon of empirical studies on trajectories of technological rules and the role of the propagator–entrepreneur has developed, over the past three decades, beginning with Dosi (1982) (compare, e.g. Prencipe 1997; Geels 2002; Walsh 2004). From these studies, a rich methodological repertoire is available for the study of various diffusion patterns (compare, e.g. Jimenez and Carbonell 2006). A promising endeavour would be to apply this type of study to social, cognitive and behavioural rules joining the some early empirical investigations in rule-based economics (Blind 2012a; Grebel 2013; Wäckerle 2013). An extension to other rule classes would also create opportunities to obtain further insights into the different types of propagators (see Table 2.1).

The findings of this study and the associated prospects for further research represent a strong case for truly interdisciplinary research. In the rule-based approach, the economic researcher has at their disposal not only a realistic version of an agent as a heterogeneous individual capable of learning but also an analytical device that can be used to study complex interdisciplinary phenomena.

References

Blind GD (2003) Statistical methods for a dynamic analysis of meso-trajectories in evolutionary systems. M.A. Thesis, St. Gallen University

Blind GD (2012a) Culture and economic explanation: economics in the US and Japan. By Donald Katzner. J East Asian Stud 12(1):150–153

Blind GD (2012b) Investigating entrepreneurial spirit with the rule approach: why self-employment is on the decline in Japan. Evol Inst Econ Rev 9(1):183–198

Blind GD (2016) Behavioral rules: Veblen, Nelson-Winter, Oström and beyond. In: Frantz R, Chen S-H, Dopfer K, Heukelom F, Mousavi S (eds) Routledge handbook of behavioral economics. Routledge, Milton Park, pp 139–151

Blind G, Lottanti von Mandach S (2013) Bescheidene Managementgehälter und sich schliessende Lohnscheren: Neue Einblicke in den japanischen Arbeitsmarkt. In: Chiavacci D, Wieczorek I (eds) Japan 2013. VSJF, Berlin, pp 203–228

Blind GD, Lottanti von Mandach S (2015) Decades not lost, but won: increased employment, higher wages, and more equal opportunities in the Japanese labour market. Soc Sci Jpn J 18 (1):63–88

Blind GD, Lottanti von Mandach S (2017) Not a coincidence: sons-in-law as successors in successful Japanese family firms. Crit Financ Rev (forthcoming)

Blind G, Pyka A (2014) The rule approach in evolutionary economics: a methodological template for empirical research. J Evol Econ 24(5):1085–1105

Brockhaus RH (1987) Entrepreneurial folklore. J Small Bus Manag 25(3):1–6

Dopfer K (2011) Economics in a cultural key: complexity and evolution revisited. In: Davis JB, Hands DW (eds) The Elgar companion to recent economic methodology. Edward Elgar, Cheltenham, pp 319–340

Dopfer K, Potts J (2008) The general theory of economic evolution. Routledge, London

Dosi G (1982) Technological paradigms and technological trajectories. Res Policy 11(3):147–162

Geels FW (2002) Technological transitions as evolutionary reconfiguration processes: a multi-level perspective and a case-study. Res Policy 31(8):1257–1274

Global Entrepreneurship Monitor (1999–2013) Global entrepreneurship monitor executive reports 1999–2013. London Business School and Babson College, London

Grebel T, Pyka A et al (2003) An evolutionary approach to the theory of entrepreneurship. Ind Innov 10(4):493–514

Grebel T (2013) On the tradeoff between similarity and diversity in the creation of novelty in basic science. Struct Chang Econ Dyn 27:66–78

Jimenez JC, Carbonell F (2006) Local linear approximation of jump diffusion processes. J Appl Probab 43:185–194

Oström E, Basurto X (2011) Crafting analytical tools to study institutional change. J Inst Econ 7 (3):317–343

Prencipe A (1997) Technological competencies and product's evolutionary dynamics a case study from the aero-engine industry. Res Policy 25(8):1261–1276

Storey DJ, Johnson S (1987) Regional variations in entrepreneurship in the U.K. Scott J Polit Econ 34(2):161–173

Walsh ST (2004) Roadmapping a disruptive technology: a case study: the emerging microsystems and top-down nanosystems industry. Technol Forecast Soc Chang 71(1–2):161–185

Wäckerle M (2013) On the bottom-up foundations of the banking-macro nexus. Econom: Open Access Open Assess E J 7(2013–40):1

von Mandach SL (2014) Neo-confucianism and industrial relations in Meiji Japan. J Manag Hist 20(4):387–408

Chapter 15
Policy Design in Rule-Based Economics: Implications for Entrepreneurship in Japan

Abstract This chapter sketches the development of policies in rule-based economics. Importantly, focusing on interventions at the rule level enables to achieve more long-term, and more sustainable improvements than traditional policy which continues to target mainly the operational level. As is shown with concrete examples, rule-based policy comes with a trade-off between the potential of self-sustainability and immediacy.

Policy targeting 2nd order rules has the highest potential for self-sustainability but comes with important time lags, whereas policy measures targeting 1st order rules have smaller potential for sustainability but come with smaller time lags. At the other extreme of this trade-off, operational policy has no potential for self-sustainability but comes with almost immediate effect. We exemplify these considerations by sketching policy measures aimed at fostering entrepreneurial activity in Japan.

Even if the lack of positively motivated "opportunity entrepreneurs" may be partially compensated for by manager–entrepreneurs in Japanese corporations ('Intrapreneurship'), our evidence on the negative transmission mechanism associated with Filial Piety suggests further decline in Entrepreneurial Spirit and Individual Entrepreneurship for decades to come (Chapter 13, Blind 2012a). This poses a serious threat to the capacity to bring innovation to the market and thus to the already dim growth prospects of Japan. This is because the potential for the propagator-type entrepreneur decreases in proportion to the pool of individuals willing to become self-employed. This latter pool fluctuates around 2% of the Japanese population, compared to about 5% for Germany and 10% for the United States (Isobe 2003). Untapped entrepreneurial potential remains substantial among women and senior individuals (Blind 2012b).

As regards policy recommendations, rule-based economics suggests focusing on interventions at rule level in order to achieve more long-term, sustainable improvements. The following sections outline policy recommendations for interventions targeting the rules of Entrepreneurial Spirit and Individual Entrepreneurship, as well as some measures directly aimed at increasing the number of start-up operations.

G.D. Blind, *The Entrepreneur in Rule-Based Economics*, Economic Complexity and Evolution, DOI 10.1007/978-3-319-62779-3_15

15.1 Fostering Entrepreneurial Spirit

True opportunity-driven entrepreneurship, as we have seen, requires the prior adoption of the rule of Entrepreneurial Spirit (see Table 4.2). But the effect of Entrepreneurial Spirit is more than just a prerequisite for opportunity-driven entrepreneurship in an individual agent. It also impacts on the collective likelihood of adopting Individual Entrepreneurship. This is because *homo sapiens oeconomicus* as a social being considers his or her environment when deliberating on the potential adoption of a new rule, a fact also recognised in the most recent Japanese literature (Takahashi et al. 2013). Hence, policies aimed at fostering Entrepreneurial Spirit will have a twofold impact on what can be considered the "pipeline of entrepreneurs". Any policy failing to address this issue cannot be considered an evolutionary efficient policy.

As becomes evident from international comparison (GEM 2001–2013), key elements of Entrepreneurial Spirit are exceptionally weak in Japan. Of the 24 industrialised economies surveyed, Japan ranks lowest for "entrepreneurship as a good career choice", fourth lowest for "high status of successful entrepreneurs" and second highest for "fear of failure" (GEM 2013). This is in line with our results on the rules of Traditional Class Order and Fear of Failure: less than half of self-employed parents recommend their own occupational choice to their offspring. The "side-effect of population ageing" that we have identified further reinforces this trend. Japanese authorities urgently need to work on breaking this vicious circle.

Tackling these issues requires policy measures aimed at changing the image of self-employment in Japan. Accepting Veblen's notion that such rules are in large part "handed down from the past" (1899: 191, Blind 2016: 141) such effort need to concentrate on agents' early lives. This may be achieved through various measures: legislating against the discrimination of failed entrepreneurs in the labour market, reviewing the content of state-run media or making much needed changes to secondary-school curricula and teaching methods.

For instance, while current curricula include an introduction to Traditional Class Order, they do not cover its negative consequences such as the delayed economic development of Japan during the rule of the shogunate, which considered the rising merchant class a rival, but not an ally. Technical mastery and craftsmanship as symbols of the former *kō* class continue to be praised and cherished. The Ministry of Education, Culture, Sports, Science and Technology regularly designates "living national treasures", but the curricula of the same ministry include little about the entrepreneurial figures that have built Japan into a modern economic powerhouse. Where textbooks do introduce figures such as Matsushita Kōnosuke, who single-handedly grew his start-up company into a global player (Panasonic), they fail to convey the central message that "everyone has the potential to achieve this".

In both schools and homes, Japanese educators continue to overwhelmingly rely on "teaching the right way" rather than helping students "find the right way". Trial and error as the most prominent algorithm for "finding a possible way" does not form part of the didactic repertoire of Japanese schools or parents. Making this an integral part of public education would help young people to understand failure as merely the "error part" in a creative improvement process. A change in mindset of this kind through 2nd order policy would not only help to curb the negative influence of FEAR OF FAILURE on ENTREPRENEURIAL SPIRIT but would equally be effective in increasing the pool of latent entrepreneurs and reducing the loss in conversion to actual entrepreneurship—albeit with a considerable time lag.

These issues and policies illustrate both the potential power and the significant time lags that are typically linked to policy measures targeting 2nd order rules. Obviously, the timespan between the introduction of 2nd order rule policy and the first sign of effects will typically amount to a multiple of standard election periods. From this we might infer that effective 2nd order rule policy is rather unlikely to come about in a democratic system. Yet long-term orientation is one of the strong characteristics of organisational thinking in Japan (Hofstede and Bond 1988), as the successful track record of post-war Japanese industrial policy shows (Audretsch and Yamawaki 1988; Okuno-Fujiwara 1991), so there is fertile ground for the development of effective 2nd order policy measures. Once a change in society's mindset is achieved with the institutionalisation of new rules, there is potential to reach a meta-stable state, in which the intended outcomes create self-sustaining intergenerational effects.

15.2 Increasing Levels of Latent Entrepreneurship

Unlike 2nd order rule policy, measures aimed at 1st order operational rules typically take effect much more quickly, although their effects are significantly less sustainable. While they may bring about permanent change in the composition of rules retained by individual agents, there is only limited potential that policy outcomes will eventually develop a self-sustaining capacity. We can illustrate this with reference to the 2nd order rule policies described in the previous section, such as curriculum changes. Whereas 2nd order rule policy has the potential to establish self-sustaining change in general society, agents who have become carriers of INDIVIDUAL ENTREPRENEURSHIP as result of a 1st order rule policy will only be able to influence their personal environment, thus limiting the potential for replication effects. Nevertheless, 1st order rule policy may help to address pressing issues such as those Japan is currently facing with the substantial decrease in the number of potential business founders. Obviously, the time lags to be expected for effects from 2nd order rule policy call for additional and immediate 1st order policy measures.

A correlation analysis of 2010 GEM micro data for Japan shows that network effects are fundamental for a successful diffusion of the INDIVIDUAL ENTREPRENEURSHIP rule: the Pearson correlation between the items "knows a person who started a business in the past 2 years" and "expects to start up in the next 3 years" amounts to as much as 0.243 and is highly significant (1% level). This means that knowing someone who successfully started their business recently comes with a 24%

increased likelihood of being a carrier of Individual Entrepreneurship. Critics might object that we cannot exclude an endogeneity problem when guessing from correlations on causation. Admittedly, adopting Individual Entrepreneurship may encourage the agents to try and get in touch with experienced business founders. But if we consider the typical process of making acquaintances in Japan, the former is more likely than the latter.

Consequently, policy measures aimed at enabling networking activities for newly self-employed individuals would significantly boost diffusion of Individual Entrepreneurship. Japanese authorities' strong tendency towards centralisation frequently leads to local disinterest if not outright opposition towards initiatives originating from central government, so initiatives should be offered from within local communities. "Meet an entrepreneur" events in schools, universities and community centres might prove effective. Local authorities have been quite creative in developing "community building" activities (*machizukuri*), many of which have targeted a revitalization of commercial activity, and the involvement of organisations such as local Chambers of Commerce may help to secure effective implementation.

Our study suggests that measures specifically aimed at encouraging non-regular employees to consider self-employment as an alternative source of income would increase the Individual Entrepreneurship population. However, such fostering of "improvement-driven entrepreneurship" would require a radical shift in the Japanese policymakers' thinking. So far, the rise of non-regular employment observed during the last two decades unfortunately has only been discussed as a development threatening the public pension system, societal cohesion and even birth rates (Blind and Lottanti von Mandach 2015, 2017). It is yet to be seen as a potential starting point for new businesses and an ensuing growth dynamic.

This applies to an even greater extent to non-working individuals, particularly those that are currently unemployed. Note that the Japanese equivalent of "unemployed person", *Shitsugyōsha*, literally translates into "someone who has lost their job". It does not simply describe someone who is looking for a job but carries an implicit connotation of having carelessly lost something. Accordingly, the efforts of some Western European countries—including the UK and Germany—to encourage unemployed individuals to consider creating their own employment, in other words, to become self-employed, seem still impossible for Japanese policy makers to imagine.

The next step, of course, is to design campaigns to attract non-regular employees and unemployed individuals into self-employment. For instance, business plan contests are a proven way of fostering the intention to become self-employed. While this instrument is well established in many Western economies and often targets individuals very early on (e.g., in high school), Japan conducted its first ever national business plan contest as recently as early 2015. Organised by the Small and Medium Enterprise Agency, a section of the famous Ministry of Economy, Trade and Industry, the event exclusively targeted adult individuals who had previously attended one of the 290 ministry-licensed start-up courses.

While this move per se represents a positive development, the nature of the three winning projects (METI 2015) gives rise to serious concerns about the contest itself and the officially licensed classes: the winning project boasts a fast-food product based on whale meat, the runner-up project intends to create a café offering "not only cake and coffee, but also a space for communication" and the special price for regional entrepreneurship goes to a lady planning to offer a "make your own pizza" experience using only local ingredients. Even when taking into account the particular characteristics of Japan's dual economy and the strong lead of intrapreneurs in propagating technological rules, many may consider these results somewhat disappointing. First and foremost, they raise considerable doubts about the contents of the officially licensed start-up courses. Again, "teaching the right way" strongly outweighs any attempt to encourage the pursuit of more original business ideas.

15.3 Enabling More Actual Entrepreneurship

Policy measures aimed at operational level have the potential to be almost instantly effective. By contrast, the corresponding effects are limited to the time frame during which the measures are actually applied. In stark contrast to rule policy, the effects of purely operational interventions are not potentially self-sustaining.

From our causality check on the SFR (see Sect. 10.3), we know that public start-up assistance in Japan has to be considered marginal. What is more, a stunning 97% of the government budget available for SME policies goes into measures aimed at supporting established businesses. Against this background, a strategic shift away from a focus on the preservation of economic structures and towards the decisive support of a more dynamic development, or, in Schneider's terminology, from a stationary to an evolutionary focus (1953 [1949]: 194, Blind and Pyka 2015: 247) has to be considered essential.

Specifically, the risk-adjusted SME loans recently introduced by some public institutions (see p. 122) should be expanded. So far, significant numbers of carriers of Individual Entrepreneurship who prefer to limit their personal insolvency risk or are simply short of appropriate collateral have been prevented from starting a business by the uniform provision of cheap yet fully collateralised loans. On one hand, such policy would help to avoid negative selection effects for the public credit insurance currently implied by their policy of charging uniform interest rates. On the other hand, risk-adjusted lending would turn those potential entrepreneurs into actual business founders willing to use a larger share of their profits to remunerate lenders in exchange for an uncollateralised loan.

As we have seen from our earlier descriptive analysis of the Japanese "founder force", business start-ups by former non-regular employees still only represent a small fraction of 10% of total start-ups, though this has increased from less than 2% in 1992. A number of considerations suggest that this development will continue even if the share of non-regular employment in the overall workforce stabilises at current levels. This is obvious from a comparison of the age profile of non-regular employees with that of business founders. Non-regular employment used to be principally represented by women re-entering the labour market after raising a family and by retirees. By 2002, this picture had entirely changed. Whereas non-regular employment still was at only 20% among the 55- to 60-year-olds, as many as 50% of employees below 35 were in non-regular employment (Tachibanaki 2006:196). If the average age of Japanese business founders (42 in 2013) is taken into account, we can see that the potential of start-ups from non-regular employment has just started to materialise.

In terms of concrete measures, training and education are promising routes for turning latent into actual entrepreneurs in the case of Japan. Another correlation analysis of 2010 GEM micro data shows that individuals who believe they "have the required knowledge/skills to start a business" are some 37% more likely to "expect start-up during the next 3 years". While these figures probably contain some statistical bias in that the survey item "have the required knowledge" partially measures the latent variable of "self-confidence", the positive effects of educational opportunities such as start-up classes are indisputable.

Given the strong evidence supporting the push hypothesis for Japan, extending similar opportunities to non-working individuals is likely to prove an effective way to increase conversion rates from latent to actual entrepreneurship. Japanese policymakers remain rather sceptical about encouraging unemployed individuals to start their own business. Yet, with Japanese academics demanding similar measures (compare Masuda 2006), policymakers will eventually be brought to consider these opportunities for intervention. Online registration for unemployed individuals enables post-participation start-up rates to be monitored closely. This, in turn, helps to refine both candidate profiling and course design.

The share of new businesses founded by women has greatly increased since the early 1990s, outpacing the increase in women's general labour market participation. Since this has occurred despite the rising care burden of an ageing population and poor progress in childcare provision, there is significant potential even for small-scale measures. For instance, while common practice in many countries (e.g., Switzerland), childcare costs are currently not tax deductible. An equivalent special provision for self-employed female individuals would help to advance the conversion from latent to actual entrepreneurship by several years, and its introduction could also provide a significant one-off stimulus.

References

Audretsch DB, Yamawaki H (1988) R&D rivalry, industrial policy, and U.S.-Japanese trade. Rev Econ Stat 70:438–447

Blind GD (2012a) Investigating entrepreneurial spirit with the rule approach: why self-employment is on the decline in Japan. Evol Inst Econ Rev 9(1):183–198

Blind G (2012b) Unternehmensgründer in Japan seit 1992. Evidenz zur Evolution gegensätzlicher Gründergruppen. Bonn Japanstudien 29:19–68

Blind GD (2016) Behavioral rules: Veblen, Nelson-Winter, Oström and beyond. In: Frantz R, Chen S-H, Dopfer K, Heukelom F, Mousavi S (eds) Routledge handbook of behavioral economics. Routledge, Milton Park, pp 139–151

Blind GD, Lottanti von Mandach S (2015) Decades not lost, but won: increased employment, higher wages, and more equal opportunities in the Japanese labour market. Soc Sci Jpn J 18 (1):63–88

Blind G, Lottanti von Mandach S (2017) Secular trends in the Japanese labour market during the lost decades: a reply to Andrew Gordon. MPRA working paper 80812. University of Munich, Munich

Blind GD, Pyka A (2015) Erich Schneider: the admiring disciple who did not become a follower. J Evol Econ 25(1):239–252

GEM (2001–2013) GEM Global Report. Global Entrepreneurship Research Association, London Business School, London

Hofstede G, Bond MH (1988) The Confucius connection: from cultural roots to economic growth. Organ Dyn 16(4):5–21

Isobe T (2003) Sekai kara mita Nihon no benchā katsudō [Japan's venture activities from a global]. Ryūtsū kagaku kenkyū 3(1):145–159

Masuda T (2006) The determinants of latent entrepreneurship in Japan. Small Bus Econ 26:227–240

METI (2015) Dai 1kai zenkoku sōgyō suku-ru senshuken jisshi hōkoku [Press release for 1st national business plan contest]. Small and Medium Enterprise Agency, Ministry of Economy, Trade and Industry, Tokyo

Okuno-Fujiwara M (1991) Industrial policy in Japan: a political economy view. In: Krugman P (ed) Trade with Japan: has the door opened wider? University of Chicago Press, Chicago, pp 271–296

Schneider E (1953[1949]) Einführung in die Wirtschaftstheorie II. 2nd edn. JCB Mohr (Paul Siebeck), Tübingen

Tachibanaki T (2006) Kakusa shakai: nani ga mondai nano ka [Disparate society – what is the problem about it?]. Iwanami, Tokyo

Takahashi N, Isobe T et al (2013) Kigyō katsudō ni ei'kyō o ataeru yō'in no kokusai hikaku bunseki [International comparison on factors influencing business formation]. RIETI Discussion Paper Series 13(J-15)

Veblen T (1899) The theory of the leisure class. Macmillan, New York

Chapter 16
Rule-Based Economics in Empirical Practice: Effective Tool for Theory Building

Abstract We assess the benefits and challenges that rule-based economics implies for theory building and empirical research. Benchmarking empirical results drawn from an original study presented earlier against evidence from inquiries relying on more traditional approaches it can be shown that rule-based analysis implies four important advantages: (1) the distinction of rules from operations enables a more clear-cut analysis and helps to exclude false positives, (2) the distinction of sub-groups of agents allows conducting more profound analysis, (3) the transdisciplinary nature of rule-based economics enables the testing of a more complete set of influencing factors, and (4) the evolutionary perspective secures the inclusion of dynamic phenomena.

At the same time, rule-based economics implies a number of challenges such as intricacies linked to the distinction of rules from operations, data availability issues and a considerably larger workload. In spite of these challenges, rule-based economics offers potential for superior research outcomes if the methodological guidance is duly followed.

Rule-based reasoning cannot be effectively applied without an understanding of the difference between the primary objectives of orthodox and evolutionary analysis. Rule-based economics enables analysis of both: the framework (evolutionary analysis) and the economic operations that take place within (orthodox analysis). It does so by mapping the development of human knowledge from idea to rule (micro), rule diffusion and the emergence of institutions (meso) up to its interdependent development (macro). In the terminology of rule-based economics, the empirical research conducted in this study represents a macro coordination analysis.

Echoing the quest by Oström and Basurto (2011) for methodological specification of the rule-based approach (Dopfer and Potts 2008), we have proposed an outline of how the theory might be specified operationally and enriched empirically, and the resulting methodology (Part II, Blind and Pyka 2014) has been applied to operationalise the theoretical reading of entrepreneurship proposed in Part I. The localist approach to the study of entrepreneurship in Japan, as indicated in rule-based economics and postulated beyond (Katzner 2008, Blind 2012b), required the collection, review and interpretation of data from a wide variety of sources.

G.D. Blind, *The Entrepreneur in Rule-Based Economics*, Economic Complexity and Evolution, DOI 10.1007/978-3-319-62779-3_16

This chapter reviews the results obtained and compares our findings with other research on the same subject. The benefits and challenges of rule-based economic in general, and the proposed methodology in particular, are considered. In conclusion we assess our experience against the three claims made earlier regarding the superiority of rule-based empirical research and our methodological approach.

16.1 Benchmarking Rule-Based Economics Against Traditional Approaches

By comparing results obtained from our research with findings from two studies using the same data but relying on more traditional designs (Harada 2005; Masuda 2006), we can identify four areas where the rule-based methodology was decisive in producing superior research outcomes.

First, the distinction of rules from corresponding operations was instrumental in clarifying the nature of the subject matter right from the very outset. In contrast to Harada (2005), our research succeeded in consistently conceiving of latent entrepreneurship as a rule and of actual entrepreneurship as corresponding operations. Obviously, a clear-cut definition of the subject matter of each is key to the subsequent construction of an explanatory model.

In the same vein, the ex ante causality checks advised by our methodology have led to statistical testing only of those factors for which a causal relationship can be confirmed in antecedent stages of analysis. For instance, our check of the potential influence of venture capital on business formation has helped to exclude it from further consideration. As Masuda's study (2006) did not include an equivalent check, it incorrectly introduced a corresponding dummy variable into its regression.[1]

Furthermore, the distinction provided critical guidance for the selection of factor rules. For instance, with Entrepreneurial Spirit as a cognitive rule entering the model as the dependent variable, all explanatory variables were approached via their rule properties, and not via the properties of corresponding operations. This meant choosing Business Sentiment over GDP growth, Perceived Cost of Capital over real interest rates and Fear of Unemployment over actual unemployment. The importance of rules in the decision making of agents has become particularly evident from the successful choice of nominal interest rates as the indicator for Perceived Cost of Capital (Chap. 13, Blind 2012a).

Second, agent heterogeneity in rule-based economics enables different sets of explanatory factors to be modelled for subgroups of agents where their heterogeneity refers to differences in susceptibility to factor rules. Our research has

[1]Also failing to include a suitable control variable for the urban-rural divide, the respective dummy eventually produced significant parameter estimates as it accidentally proved a strong covariate of the missing control.

therefore succeeded in producing more solid evidence for the push hypothesis of latent entrepreneurship than Masuda did (2006).[2]

To add another example from our study, the identification of subgroups was instrumental in the successful formulation and simultaneous estimation of a push and a pull hypothesis in the analysis of ENTREPRENEURIAL SPIRIT. Whereas dependently employed individuals are very much concerned over their job security, their self-employed counterparts derive most of their economic worldview from an appraisal of the business cycle. This line of thought was only possible thanks to the heterogeneous characteristic of *Homo sapiens oeconomicus* as the agent in rule-based economics.

Third, the openness of rule-based economics allows a wide set of potential factors to be included in the explanatory model, reaching far beyond the horizons of orthodox analysis. For instance, TRADITIONAL CLASS ORDER or FEAR OF FAILURE, two 2nd order cognitive rules found to negatively impact on entrepreneurship in Japan, pertain to areas of study such as social history or cultural studies. Similarly, the identification of the transmission mechanism of FILIAL PIETY is conventionally considered with social psychology. In contrast to the wide search encouraged in a rule-based economics, the studies of Harada and Masuda narrow their search space along two dimensions—limitation to the discipline of economics and consideration of operations only—thereby restricting their variable selection to those considered in received economic approaches, namely, to variables representing economic operations.

Fourth, our research has shown how a rule-based economics, by recognising the process quality of knowledge (trajectories), enables the consistent modelling of dynamic phenomena in studies with longitudinal designs. For example, it was essential to consider learning processes when modelling the casual relationship between non-regular employment and our responses. Similarly, it was important to anticipate such processes when identifying potential influencing factors prior to developing our hypothesis that FEAR OF UNEMPLOYMENT significantly influences ENTREPRENEURIAL SPIRIT only as a result of a particular critical event. In contrast, Harada (2005) did not consider this possibility in spite of having access to four surveys dating between 1982 and 1997.

16.2 Rule-Based Economics: Challenges of an Evolving Framework

As a relatively recent theoretical framework, working with rule-based economics implies some specific challenges which should be reviewed in our assessment of its relevance for empirical research. The fundamental differences between rule-based

[2]As Masuda had to rely on a rather weak argument based on difference in significance levels for his parameter estimates, his evidence has to be considered much less robust.

and received approaches to the modelling and testing of economic phenomena present the first challenge. While even the fundamental recognition of the important distinction between rule and operations as in Schneider (1953[1949], Blind and Pyka 2015) cannot be taken for granted, such distinction becomes particularly intricate in empirical inquiries. This is even so for 1st order rules, which directly lend themselves to corresponding operations such as the distinction of the rule of NON-REGULAR EMPLOYMENT from the operation of working as a non-regular employee. Yet, as we have seen from the separate analyses of INDIVIDUAL ENTREPRENEURSHIP and start-up operations, such distinction is both critical and possible. Discussions with fellow researchers reveal that such challenges are particularly pronounced during early stages of rule-based empirical work. Failing to overcome these challenges leads to a considerable risk of producing ill-specified models.

However, for scholars who have not been subjected to orthodox economics training, the distinction of rules from operations or the recognition of heterogeneous agents represents much less of a challenge. This is true both of students in the early stages of economics education and of scholars from neighbouring disciplines. As a simple analysis of citations reveals, a significant share of publications citing the foundational core of the rule-based approach (Dopfer 2004; Dopfer et al. 2004; Dopfer and Potts 2008) originates from disciplines other than economics (e.g., geography, history, business studies, psychology or education studies). This observation supports several of our claims for a rule-based economics: its analytical performance is superior to received approaches, its applicability extends beyond the boundaries of economics to include phenomena of social change in general and its diffusion into "general-purpose economics" is essentially a matter of time.

A second challenge for theoretical and empirical studies in rule-based economics is the limited availability of suitable time series data on rule diffusion. This is because most available surveys concentrate on economic operations, hardly ever covering the underlying rules. For instance, for our analysis of latent and actual entrepreneurship, data on TRADITIONAL CLASS ORDER and on FILIAL PIETY were not available at Japanese prefecture level. Fortunately, we were able to overcome this challenge with recourse to appropriate indicators.

There are, however, two reasons for expecting this challenge to largely disappear in the medium term. First, the amount of available data has been increasing exponentially ever since the beginning of the "digital age". Such "big data" not only tends to cover operations but also increasingly extends to rules. For instance, group membership in social networks may be effectively used for measuring rule diffusion. Second, gradual recognition of the benefits of an analysis of rules will generate support from official data-collecting bodies. While it may still be some time before such recognition diffuses into a sufficiently large population, once this threshold is reached, major progress can be expected in a relatively short time.

Third, our proposed methodology involves a significantly larger workload than more traditional approaches. Two requirements determine this: the broad interdisciplinary scope of the initial identification of factor rules and the detailed checks during the reduction to the causal core of the model.

Difficulties in obtaining suitable data for the study of entrepreneurship in Japan have compounded with the large scope of the investigation. For instance, our extensive review of potential factor rules produced as many as 16 allegedly relevant factors, all of which required assessment against our two criteria of change: population size and strength of influence on our responses. Obviously, relying exclusively on insights from extant research for hypothesis building would have greatly reduced the time required. Economists typically turn to *efficiency* as their guiding criterion. This, however, has potentially detrimental consequences for the selection of subjects and methods: where these choices become a simple function of expected returns in terms of publications, progress will be limited to incremental innovation.

As we saw when we matched our results to those from some earlier research on the same subject, the investment in time and effort was strongly rewarded with results superior to those obtained by traditional approaches. Thus, rule-based analysis has proved a most *effective* way of conceiving of evolutionary change in an economic system.

True fundamental research implies inquiry in spite of uncertainty about expected outcomes and about the value of such potential results. Such conditions are entirely common in much of natural science, where considerable resources may be invested to investigate subjects the results of which are unpredictable. As the discipline of economics has traditionally found a good deal of its inspiration in natural science, we hope that the rule-based analysis will increasingly be used to research the "black holes" of economics.

While Ostrom once argued that "no one can legislate a language for a scientific community" (1986: 5), the Dopfer and Potts rule-based approach offers the heterodox community a common terminology for accommodating the theoretical body of Veblen, Ostrom and Nelson–Winter (compare Blind 2016: 151). At the same time, the approach represents what Ostrom had asked for: an analytical framework, rather than a theory. Combined with an appropriate empirical methodology as presented in the second part of this volume, it promises to become an influential device in the adjustment process of some prevailing "preconceptions", which—as Veblen holds—happens "only tardily and concessively" (1925: 49).

16.3 Living Up to Expectations: The Rule-Based Approach in Empirical Research

It is true that our methodology is grossly at odds with the search for universal economic laws and negates any attempt at working with "single-rule systems" (Blind 2016:139). Instead, it offers a set of coherent and empirically meaningful ways of explaining diversity and change of knowledge, which governs economic operations in a society. Having assessed the benefits and challenges of working with our methodology, we are now able to evaluate our three earlier claims. Put simply, these are:

1. That building models tailored to the rule level of the economy would help to increase explanatory power in empirical studies
2. That researchers can construct more consistent models if they acknowledge the heterogeneity of agents and their openness to learning, in accordance with instrumental realism (Dopfer 2004)
3. That the approach would allow us to integrate theoretical insights from various disciplines into a consistent whole

Regarding the first claim, we find that the proposed methodology *does* allow for analyses with increased explanatory power. The broad scope of the initial identification of the system of factor rules (SFR, Ostrom's "rule configurations") and the ex ante causality checks help us neither to miss relevant explanatory variables nor to include "false positives". For example, the methodology helped to include relevant factors such as FILIAL PIETY. Equally, the ex ante causality checks helped to exclude the "false positives" of venture capital or educational attainment.

Importantly, the very distinction of rules and operations implies more explanatory power as it helps to investigate a subject in a more complete analysis. Although it might seem obvious to investigate not only the number of newly founded businesses but also the underlying rules in the case of entrepreneurship research, this does not correspond to any standard practice in received economic reasoning (as a matter of fact, empirical entrepreneurship research largely developed from within a community of business scholars). The "savings rule" (see Chap. 8) as well as a "Free Trade Rule" (Chiavacci, Blind et al 2012, Blind and Ziltener 2014) are two examples of subjects where operations (aggregate savings, international trade flows) are much studied, but the development of the carrier populations is hardly ever investigated. Extending the reach of analysis from operations to underlying rules may not only translate into "increased explanatory power" in a narrower (statistical) sense, but it has also considerable potential for increasing the *quality* of an analysis of operations.

Moreover, analysing agent subgroups individually naturally allows for more explanatory depth: examples include the separate analyses of dependently and self-employed individuals in regard to ENTREPRENEURIAL SPIRIT and distinguishing the subgroups of dependently employed and non-working individuals in regard to INDIVIDUAL ENTREPRENEURSHIP and start-up operations.

Turning to our second claim: our methodology allows for the construction of more consistent models by replacing *Homo oeconomicus* with Dopfer's *Homo sapiens oeconomicus*, "*sapiens*" referring to the capacity of agents to "learn". Accepting that this attribute also applies to economic agents implies that longitudinal models must be designed in such a way as to account for a potential change in the composition of rules carried by agents, that is, for a change in actor mindset. Our research provides two examples of learning processes leading to a change in the set of relevant factor rules. First, carriers of NON-REGULAR EMPLOYMENT have learned to consider INDIVIDUAL ENTREPRENEURSHIP as a potential alternative only in the course of the investigation period. Second, it was only several years after the burst of Japan's bubble economy that the 1998 employment crisis made self-employed individuals susceptible to Fear of Unemployment for the retention of Entrepreneurial Spirit.

It is important to note that recognising the potential for change in the mindset of agents implies not only a chance to construct more consistent models but also the need to check for changes in the intensity of the influence of factor rules on the response rule. There is also an "intellectual temptation" that uses learning processes to fabricate ex post explanations of disruptive statistical evidence. Importantly, this kind of risk is not specific to research inspired by the rule-based approach, but is common to any type of inquiry.

However, where ex ante checks provide indications for learning processes—as with both instances identified in our study—this risk is arguably largely mitigated. This can be illustrated in probabilistic terms by comparing the ex ante checks devised by our methodology to the case of ex post efforts to make sense of findings from longitudinal studies. In the first case, risk refers to the coincidence of two independent events: the erroneous identification of a change in intensity of influence coinciding with random statistical significance. In the second case, in contrast, risk refers to the conditional probability of an erroneous identification of a change in intensity of influence given that the event of finding random statistical evidence has already occurred. Where researchers take the precaution of conducting ex ante checks as prescribed by our methodology, the implied risk reduces to the first type of coinciding independent events.

Finally, we can also confirm our third claim, namely, that the openness of the proposed methodology enables insights from different disciplines and schools of thought to be integrated. This is more than a mere option available to the researcher willing to cross-disciplinary boundaries; our methodology (Blind and Pyka 2014) actively calls for boundary-crossing investigation. This is because an investigation of rules from all classes is required to ensure that all potentially relevant factor rules are included in an analysis. In our research we identified the influence of culturally conditioned rules that is part of the Japanese value system, such as Traditional Class Order and Fear of Failure. Such rules are commonly associated with disciplines such as social psychology or the history of ideas.

While venturing beyond disciplinary boundaries may be a stimulating experience to the aspiring economist, familiarising oneself with another school of thought does present an additional challenge. Much depends on the individual researcher. Accordingly, we suggest that rule-based analysis will represent a more enjoyable and—as a corollary—a more successful experience for researchers with strong interdisciplinary curiosity.

To bring our discussion of empirical practice in rule-based economics to a conclusion, we suggest a "qualitative cost–benefit analysis". In terms of costs: first, crossing disciplinary boundaries translates into more demanding reasoning; second, there are potential risks associated with a relatively more open analytical framework; and third, empirical work in rule-based economics involves additional investment of time and effort. On the other hand, important benefits can be reaped by the researcher willing to bear these costs or, rather, by the scientific entrepreneur deciding to invest in such inquiry: greater explanatory power, more consistent models and smoother integration of insights across disciplinary boundaries.

The author's own positive experience with exploring the empirical practice of rule-based economics can be condensed into a single statement by transforming the line by Francis Edgeworth quoted at the beginning of this volume: "There is a discipline *not yet* adapted to the schools, but which is profitable to have studied, as it *does* have a direct bearing upon action". Significantly, our judgment extends beyond Edgeworth's understanding of "action" as representing economic operations. In our view, it also includes the "rule action" of policymakers.

References

Blind GD (2012a) Investigating entrepreneurial spirit with the rule approach: why self-employment is on the decline in Japan. Evol Inst Econ Rev 9(1):183–198

Blind GD (2012b) Culture and economic explanation: economics in the US and Japan. By Donald W. Katzner. New York: Routledge, 2008. 184 pp. $39.95 (paper). J East Asian Stud 12(1):150–153

Blind GD (2016) Behavioral rules: Veblen, Nelson-Winter, Oström and beyond. In: Frantz R, Chen S-H, Dopfer K, Heukelom F, Mousavi S (eds) Routledge handbook of behavioral economics. Routledge, Milton Park, pp 139–151

Blind G, Pyka A (2014) The rule approach in evolutionary economics: a methodological template for empirical research. J Evol Econ 24(5):1085–1105

Blind GD, Pyka A (2015) Erich Schneider: the admiring disciple who did not become a follower. J Evol Econ 25(1):239–252

Blind G, Ziltener P (2014) Free trade live: insights from the Switzerland-Japan free trade and economic partnership agreement. In: Mottini R (ed) Yearbook 2014. Swiss Japanese Chamber of Commerce, Zurich, pp 53–63

Chiavacci D, Blind G et al (2012) Ist das Freihandels- und wirtschaftliche Partnerschaftsabkommen (FHWPA) zwischen der Schweiz und Japan (bereits) eine Erfolgsgeschichte? Hauptergebnisse einer empirischen Analyse zu Umsetzung und Wirkung. Asiat Stud 66(1):19–56

Dopfer K (2004) The economic agent as rule maker and rule user: Homo sapiens oeconomicus. J Evol Econ 14:177–195

Dopfer K, Potts J (2008) The general theory of economic evolution. Routledge, London

Dopfer K, Foster J et al (2004) Micro-meso-macro. J Evol Econ 14:263–279

Harada N (2005) Potential entrepreneurship in Japan. Small Bus Econ 25(3):293–304

Katzner DW (2008) Culture and economic explanation: economics in the US and Japan. Routledge, New York

Masuda T (2006) The determinants of latent entrepreneurship in Japan. Small Bus Econ 26:227–240

Ostrom E (1986) An agenda for the study of institutions. Public Choice 48(1):3–25

Oström E, Basurto X (2011) Crafting analytical tools to study institutional change. J Inst Econ 7 (3):317–343

Schneider E (1953[1949]) Einführung in die Wirtschaftstheorie II. 2nd edn. JCB Mohr (Paul Siebeck), Tübingen

Veblen T (1925) Economic theory in the calculable future. Am Econ Rev 15(1 Suppl):48–55

Chapter 17
Appendices

Table 17.1 Data matrix for analysis of ENTREPRENEURIAL SPIRIT

Year	ES (%)	BizSent (DI)	FUe98 (%)	SFI (%)	PCoC (%)	Real interest (%)
1992	0.60	12	45.0	0.42	3.75	1.32
1993	3.80	−26	46.6	0.37	2.50	1.57
1994	3.80	−36	50.0	0.43	1.75	0.93
1995	4.20	−18	54.0	0.46	1.00	1.20
1996	3.90	−19	54.0	0.47	0.50	0.30
1997	2.80	−7	56.5	0.46	0.50	−1.42
1998	3.00	−22	58.8	0.51	0.50	0.10
1999	2.90	−49	63.8	0.53	0.50	0.60
2000	3.00	−26	62.4	0.51	0.50	1.29
2001	2.60	−14	68.5	0.49	0.25	0.95
2002	1.60	−40	72.0	0.54	1.75	2.86
2003	1.60	−28	71.0	0.59	0.10	0.20
2004	1.30	−15	71.1	0.54	0.10	0.51
2005	0.90	1	67.0	0.56	0.10	0.30
2006	0.70	5	67.6	0.58	0.10	0.20
2007	1.40	8	62.2	0.60	0.75	0.75

Table 17.2 Correlation matrix and VIFs for regression on ENTREPRENEURIAL SPIRIT

Correlation coefficients	BizSent	FUe98	PCoC	SFI
BizSent	1.00	−0.11	0.06	0.13
FUe98		1.00	−0.35	0.61
PCoC			1.00	−0.67
SFI				1.00
Variance inflation factors	1.14	1.71	1.95	2.86

G.D. Blind, *The Entrepreneur in Rule-Based Economics*, Economic Complexity and Evolution, DOI 10.1007/978-3-319-62779-3_17

Table 17.3 Differentials in BIC values through inclusion of additional factor rules

		Change upon introduction of additional factor rule			
Prior model variables	Reference value	BizSent	FUe98	PCoC	SFI
BizSent; FUe98; PCoC	−0.07				−1.01
BizSent; FUe98; SFI	−0.31			−1.39	
BizSent; PCoC; SFI	−0.45		−1.53		
FUe98; PCoC; SFI	−0.85	−1.93			
Four factor rules	−1.08				

Table 17.4 OLS and ridge confidence intervals of parameter estimates in analysis of Entrepreneurial Spirit

Parameter estimates [90% conf. intervals]	BizSent	FUe98	PCoC	SFI
OLS	−0.49 [−0.70,−0.30]	−0.44 [−0.69,−0.20]	−0.51 [−0.77,−0.25]	−0.60 [−0.92,−0.29]
Ridge ($\lambda_{hkb} = 0.32$)	−0.49 [−0.69,−0.31]	−0.44 [−0.67,−0.21]	−0.48 [−0.73,−0.23]	−0.57 [−0.87,−0.28]

Table 17.5 Size of Individual Entrepreneurship rule population in dependently employed men and for non-working individuals

	Population size of Individual Entrepreneurship (1000)									
	Dependently employed male individuals					Non-working individuals				
Prefecture	1992	1997	2002	2007	2012	1992	1997	2002	2007	2012
Hokkaido	34.0	39.0	26.6	17.4	12.0	12.0	13.0	23.1	14.8	11.8
Aomori	8.0	10.0	5.9	5.3	2.6	3.0	3.0	5.5	2.9	2.4
Iwate	9.0	10.0	5.2	3.8	2.1	2.0	3.0	5.2	3.1	3.1
Miyagi	17.0	19.0	10.9	9.5	6.1	6.0	7.0	11.3	5.1	7.1
Akita	6.0	7.0	4.2	4.0	2.3	2.0	2.0	3.7	1.5	2.6
Yamagata	5.0	6.0	4.5	3.6	3.0	1.0	3.0	4.4	2.5	1.6
Fukushima	13.0	15.0	9.5	7.5	4.5	4.0	4.0	7.9	4.1	3.9
Ibaraki	21.0	22.0	12.9	11.0	4.7	6.0	9.0	12.4	7.0	5.8
Tochigi	13.0	16.0	10.2	8.6	5.7	4.0	7.0	9.2	4.7	4.3
Gunma	14.0	16.0	12.4	8.0	6.1	7.0	5.0	8.0	4.8	4.9
Saitama	55.0	66.0	39.1	32.2	17.9	23.0	27.0	28.1	23.2	23.4
Chiba	43.0	51.0	28.2	25.3	17.0	17.0	21.0	27.0	16.3	15.4
Tokyo	118.0	140.0	90.1	73.1	56.5	58.0	65.0	80.1	64.4	57.4
Kanagawa	76.0	89.0	47.7	39.0	23.2	26.0	32.0	50.0	37.3	39.1
Niigata	14.0	11.0	10.7	7.5	4.3	3.0	4.0	6.4	2.9	2.5
Toyama	6.0	6.0	4.3	4.0	2.0	2.0	2.0	3.9	1.4	1.5
Ishikawa	8.0	7.0	4.5	4.2	2.5	3.0	2.0	5.2	3.2	1.8
Fukui	5.0	6.0	3.3	2.3	2.0	1.0	2.0	2.6	1.6	0.8
Yamanashi	6.0	8.0	4.7	3.0	2.3	2.0	2.0	4.2	2.9	2.1
Nagano	15.0	14.0	12.8	8.5	5.3	4.0	5.0	9.0	3.3	4.8
Gifu	16.0	18.0	10.9	6.9	6.1	5.0	4.0	7.2	4.1	3.6
Shizuoka	30.0	25.0	20.1	16.5	11.5	8.0	11.0	13.0	7.8	6.4
Aichi	56.0	65.0	42.1	23.8	19.2	18.0	22.0	26.9	17	17.1
Mie	9.0	10.0	8.7	7.0	3.4	4.0	4.0	6.7	3.5	2.9

(continued)

Table 17.5 (continued)

	Population size of Individual Entrepreneurship (1000)									
	Dependently employed male individuals					Non-working individuals				
Prefecture	1992	1997	2002	2007	2012	1992	1997	2002	2007	2012
Shiga	9.0	9.0	7.0	4.8	3.9	3.0	3.0	7.2	2.5	5.1
Kyoto	22.0	20.0	13.8	10.4	7.9	11.0	11.0	19	13.3	11.7
Osaka	84.0	91.0	54.1	32.5	34.2	37.0	40.0	54.7	32.7	36.6
Hyogo	36.0	42.0	27.7	18.5	15.5	20.0	22.0	29.1	18.2	17.1
Nara	10.0	10.0	6.2	5.5	3.2	7.0	6.0	8.2	4.8	4.7
Wakayama	6.0	6.0	3.2	2.9	2.3	4.0	4.0	5.7	2.3	2.4
Tottori	3.0	3.0	3.3	1.7	0.8	1.0	2.0	1.9	0.8	1.2
Shimane	3.0	3.0	3.1	2.0	1.5	1.0	1.0	2.2	0.7	1.3
Okayama	10.0	12.0	6.2	5.8	3.8	5.0	5.0	10.3	4.7	5.1
Hiroshima	22.0	19.0	12.6	10.8	7.8	8.0	8.0	13.5	5.2	6.2
Yamaguchi	9.0	7.0	5.5	3.3	3.4	4.0	4.0	6.2	2.3	2.1
Tokushima	6.0	4.0	3.5	2.6	1.4	2.0	3.0	4.2	2.9	2.0
Kagawa	5.0	6.0	4.0	3.0	2.3	2.0	3.0	4.5	3.2	1.7
Ehime	9.0	10.0	6.6	4.4	3.2	6.0	5.0	6.0	2.6	2.9
Kochi	6.0	5.0	4.5	2.9	1.5	3.0	3.0	4.0	2.1	2.1
Fukuoka	34.0	43.0	28.8	23.0	14.4	17.0	17.0	30.3	19.7	22.9
Saga	4.0	5.0	2.8	2.5	1.6	2.0	2.0	3.7	1.6	1.3
Nagasaki	7.0	7.0	5.7	4.9	2.4	3.0	4.0	5.8	2.7	2.8
Kumamoto	11.0	10.0	6.6	6.3	5.1	4.0	4.0	7.7	4.2	4.0
Oita	7.0	8.0	4.9	4.6	3.0	4.0	3.0	5.4	3.1	3.2
Miyazaki	7.0	5.0	4.9	2.8	3.5	2.0	3.0	4.8	3.2	2.8
Kagoshima	8.0	10.0	6.3	6.4	3.8	3.0	5.0	7.1	4.3	3.7
Okinawa	10.0	10.0	6.2	7.0	5.6	6.0	5.0	9.7	7.7	7.4
Kolmogorov–Smirnov (for % of pop.)	>0.20	>0.20	>0.20	>0.20	>0.20	0.01	>0.20	0.14	0.03	0.05

Table 17.6 Number of start-up operations in dependently employed men and for non-working individuals

Prefecture	Number of start-up operations (1000)									
	Dependently employed male individuals					Non-working individuals				
	1992	1997	2002	2007	2012	1992	1997	2002	2007	2012
Hokkaido	12.0	17.0	7.8	7.3	5.4	7.0	8.0	11.1	8.3	5.2
Aomori	3.0	3.0	2.4	2.0	1.1	1.0	2.0	2.5	1.5	1.3
Iwate	4.0	4.0	1.4	1.9	1.0	1.0	1.0	1.9	1.4	1.8
Miyagi	8.0	7.0	4.1	4.1	2.9	3.0	3.0	4.9	2.9	3.8
Akita	3.0	2.0	1.4	1.6	1.1	1.0	1.0	1.8	0.6	1.4
Yamagata	2.0	3.0	1.4	1.1	1.3	1.0	1.0	1.5	1.5	1.0
Fukushima	4.0	6.0	3.5	3.2	2.2	2.0	2.0	3.7	2.3	2.1
Ibaraki	8.0	11.0	5.0	4.4	2.0	3.0	5.0	6.2	4.4	3.2
Tochigi	7.0	7.0	4.3	4.3	2.7	2.0	4.0	3.4	2.4	1.8
Gunma	6.0	7.0	5.5	3.5	3.4	4.0	2.0	3.7	2.3	2.0
Saitama	23.0	32.0	15.7	17.8	7.5	12.0	16.0	15.0	13.0	11.4
Chiba	17.0	24.0	11.2	12.4	6.7	10.0	12.0	13.1	8.8	7.2
Tokyo	52.0	70.0	46.2	43.0	31.7	31.0	36.0	39.4	37.6	26.8
Kanagawa	35.0	43.0	18.7	20.0	12.7	13.0	16.0	22.0	21.4	22.9
Niigata	7.0	4.0	3.4	3.0	2.5	1.0	2.0	2.2	1.3	1.4
Toyama	2.0	2.0	1.5	1.1	0.9	1.0	1.0	1.3	0.7	0.9
Ishikawa	3.0	3.0	1.6	2.0	1.0	2.0	1.0	1.8	1.8	1.1
Fukui	2.0	3.0	0.9	1.0	0.8	1.0	1.0	0.9	0.8	0.5
Yamanashi	2.0	3.0	1.6	1.5	1.0	1.0	1.0	1.5	1.6	1.2
Nagano	7.0	6.0	4.7	3.6	2.5	2.0	2.0	3.3	2.4	2.9
Gifu	7.0	8.0	4.7	3.0	2.7	2.0	2.0	2.6	2.8	2.0
Shizuoka	15.0	12.0	8.3	9.2	5.4	5.0	6.0	6.4	5.2	3.5
Aichi	22.0	32.0	17.0	13.3	8.7	10.0	12.0	14.4	10.3	9.8
Mie	4.0	5.0	3.8	3.2	1.7	2.0	2.0	2.4	1.4	1.5

(continued)

Table 17.6 (continued)

Prefecture	Number of start-up operations (1000)									
	Dependently employed male individuals					Non-working individuals				
	1992	1997	2002	2007	2012	1992	1997	2002	2007	2012
Shiga	4.0	4.0	2.3	2.2	2.0	2.0	2.0	3.4	1.6	2.8
Kyoto	9.0	10.0	4.3	4.8	4.7	5.0	6.0	9.0	7.9	5.7
Osaka	35.0	38.0	23.2	14.5	15.9	18.0	23.0	22.9	16.4	18.9
Hyogo	15.0	18.0	12.6	8.9	4.9	9.0	12.0	13.8	7.9	10.7
Nara	5.0	5.0	2.3	2.6	1.7	4.0	3.0	3.4	2.0	2.4
Wakayama	2.0	3.0	1.1	1.3	0.7	2.0	2.0	2.5	1.3	1.1
Tottori	1.0	1.0	1.5	0.7	0.3	1.0	1.0	0.8	0.3	0.6
Shimane	1.0	1.0	1.2	0.9	0.5	1.0	1.0	0.9	0.4	0.6
Okayama	4.0	5.0	3.1	2.4	1.9	3.0	2.0	4.9	2.0	2.8
Hiroshima	8.0	8.0	5.8	6.0	4.2	4.0	4.0	7.3	2.7	3.5
Yamaguchi	4.0	3.0	2.7	1.5	1.2	2.0	2.0	2.9	1.8	1.0
Tokushima	2.0	2.0	1.5	1.2	0.6	1.0	1.0	1.7	1.2	1.0
Kagawa	2.0	2.0	1.6	1.4	0.7	1.0	2.0	1.7	2.2	0.8
Ehime	4.0	5.0	2.5	2.5	0.9	3.0	3.0	2.1	1.6	1.3
Kochi	2.0	2.0	1.6	1.3	0.4	1.0	1.0	1.9	1.1	1.4
Fukuoka	14.0	17.0	10.0	9.3	7.3	9.0	9.0	13.2	9.9	13.0
Saga	2.0	1.0	1.2	1.0	0.8	1.0	1.0	1.3	0.8	0.9
Nagasaki	3.0	3.0	1.9	1.8	1.0	2.0	2.0	1.7	1.4	1.5
Kumamoto	5.0	4.0	2.6	2.6	2.0	2.0	3.0	4.0	2.3	2.3
Oita	3.0	4.0	1.7	2.6	1.2	1.0	2.0	2.6	1.7	0.9
Miyazaki	3.0	3.0	1.6	1.0	2.0	1.0	2.0	2.1	1.6	1.5
Kagoshima	3.0	4.0	1.9	2.6	2.2	2.0	3.0	3.7	2.1	2.0
Okinawa	4.0	4.0	2.7	3.9	2.9	3.0	3.0	5.0	4.6	3.6
Kolmogorov–Smirnov (for % of pop.)	>0.20	>0.20	>0.20	0.02	>0.20	0.10	>0.20	>0.20	0.00	0.03

Table 17.7 Male and total population aged 15–64

	Population age 15–64 (1000)									
	Male					Total				
Prefecture	1992	1997	2002	2007	2012	1992	1997	2002	2007	2012
Hokkaido	1893	1890	1825	1755	1658	3926	3927	3799	3608	3398
Aomori	471	472	460	435	406	990	986	950	886	823
Iwate	457	452	439	416	393	938	919	884	832	777
Miyagi	776	803	798	769	750	1556	1605	1595	1536	1491
Akita	388	378	359	335	307	803	774	730	676	618
Yamagata	401	395	383	367	345	806	791	762	728	680
Fukushima	689	691	679	652	613	1381	1373	1342	1283	1198
Ibaraki	1020	1049	1034	998	957	1991	2048	2023	1944	1855
Tochigi	681	693	690	684	654	1332	1359	1349	1321	1266
Gunma	689	693	682	659	627	1355	1363	1345	1294	1229
Saitama	2495	2588	2556	2476	2408	4826	5031	4991	4817	4686
Chiba	2124	2186	2160	2094	2028	4123	4254	4229	4103	3966
Tokyo	4534	4419	4427	4494	4565	8818	8639	8675	8757	8923
Kanagawa	3134	3168	3159	3130	3072	5988	6106	6125	6040	5943
Niigata	812	812	789	753	718	1628	1616	1563	1489	1415
Toyama	371	370	360	345	326	755	747	722	689	646
Ishikawa	389	396	387	375	361	794	797	776	746	716
Fukui	271	267	263	254	245	544	538	524	505	483
Yamanashi	290	298	290	281	266	575	586	573	552	523
Nagano	707	716	704	672	638	1416	1422	1396	1333	1260
Gifu	703	703	686	665	626	1424	1427	1388	1336	1259
Shizuoka	1288	1291	1276	1246	1176	2557	2568	2524	2444	2302
Aichi	2489	2515	2511	2533	2459	4862	4933	4924	4908	4781
Mie	612	617	604	598	568	1233	1242	1214	1189	1128
Shiga	424	449	461	466	457	846	890	912	917	898
Kyoto	904	907	879	847	814	1825	1833	1788	1717	1646
Osaka	3203	3172	3036	2861	2772	6391	6355	6126	5793	5605
Hyogo	1876	1841	1834	1764	1698	3815	3753	3753	3608	3467
Nara	481	488	470	438	411	982	1002	973	911	855
Wakayama	348	343	327	303	283	718	702	675	624	582
Tottori	194	191	190	185	176	393	387	381	372	346
Shimane	240	233	228	216	208	485	470	456	431	404
Okayama	635	634	618	605	579	1289	1286	1253	1216	1167
Hiroshima	964	961	936	915	875	1950	1945	1900	1832	1746
Yamaguchi	499	487	466	440	413	1036	1004	955	895	833
Tokushima	267	262	254	243	231	548	538	519	493	463
Kagawa	335	333	323	309	297	681	673	653	623	590
Ehime	478	472	457	439	413	999	976	944	893	841
Kochi	256	251	247	232	214	531	515	503	471	437
Fukuoka	1609	1651	1648	1608	1564	3318	3399	3392	3294	3213

(continued)

Table 17.7 (continued)

	Population age 15–64 (1000)									
	Male					Total				
Prefecture	1992	1997	2002	2007	2012	1992	1997	2002	2007	2012
Saga	273	273	267	259	249	564	562	549	529	511
Nagasaki	477	469	453	432	411	1005	986	950	891	838
Kumamoto	573	577	565	546	529	1193	1192	1166	1120	1081
Oita	386	381	370	361	346	808	794	768	736	704
Miyazaki	362	364	354	339	326	759	759	733	700	671
Kagoshima	541	538	530	508	488	1131	1116	1092	1044	1003
Okinawa	406	427	440	447	457	813	857	880	891	910

Table 17.8 Share of non-regular employment in male and total economically active population

	Non-regular employment in economically active population (percent)									
	Male					Total				
Prefecture	1992	1997	2002	2007	2012	1992	1997	2002	2007	2012
Hokkaido	5.3	10.8	16.6	19.4	23.3	18.2	25.9	32.8	35.4	40.2
Aomori	3.9	10.7	14.5	17.9	20.9	14.5	22.8	28.1	32.3	36.0
Iwate	4.4	9.6	13.5	18.1	21.4	13.8	20.6	27.5	31.8	35.9
Miyagi	5.3	10.0	16.4	19.0	22.4	15.1	21.7	30.3	33.7	37.2
Akita	3.7	10.0	15.3	17.5	19.5	12.6	20.0	27.7	32.1	33.7
Yamagata	3.6	9.6	12.4	17.2	19.9	10.4	17.5	24.3	29.9	33.5
Fukushima	4.0	8.3	12.0	16.6	18.8	13.0	18.4	25.2	31.7	32.7
Ibaraki	3.8	8.8	13.0	17.3	20.5	16.3	21.7	28.6	33.3	36.8
Tochigi	3.8	7.6	12.1	16.6	18.5	15.7	21.2	27.3	32.5	34.6
Gunma	4.0	8.9	14.2	17.5	19.9	15.7	22.2	29.6	32.9	35.7
Saitama	4.9	10.3	15.8	18.0	20.7	17.5	24.6	31.2	34.1	37.2
Chiba	5.7	9.8	14.3	18.7	21.5	17.7	23.4	30.5	35.3	37.4
Tokyo	6.7	12.8	16.7	18.8	19.8	15.8	24.2	30.1	31.2	32.7
Kanagawa	5.8	10.7	15.8	17.8	20.3	17.4	23.4	30.7	32.5	36.0
Niigata	3.6	7.8	12.7	14.6	16.8	12.4	18.4	25.8	29.0	32.0
Toyama	3.8	8.5	11.4	15.2	18.0	12.6	18.3	23.8	27.6	31.0
Ishikawa	5.3	8.5	13.6	16.1	18.5	13.1	19.5	26.0	29.7	33.4
Fukui	3.5	7.7	12.3	14.9	16.2	11.1	16.0	23.4	27.5	30.4
Yamanashi	4.5	8.8	13.3	17.4	19.3	14.8	21.6	28.3	33.5	36.9
Nagano	3.5	8.4	14.0	16.9	18.9	15.3	20.2	29.0	32.6	36.5
Gifu	3.8	8.7	12.8	16.7	18.6	16.4	21.9	28.9	33.7	35.4
Shizuoka	4.0	8.4	13.7	17.5	18.2	16.6	22.7	29.3	33.6	35.4
Aichi	5.3	9.7	13.4	16.6	18.6	17.8	23.7	29.0	32.7	35.2
Mie	3.3	9.0	13.9	18.0	19.0	16.2	23.5	29.9	34.0	36.6

(continued)

Table 17.8 (continued)

Prefecture	Non-regular employment in economically active population (percent)									
	Male					Total				
	1992	1997	2002	2007	2012	1992	1997	2002	2007	2012
Shiga	4.3	10.2	14.2	20.7	19.9	16.4	23.9	30.4	35.7	36.7
Kyoto	6.8	12.9	17.7	21.3	23.5	18.3	26.5	32.8	37.3	39.2
Osaka	5.7	11.3	18.4	21.2	22.7	17.3	23.9	32.6	35.8	38.6
Hyogo	4.8	10.2	14.5	18.7	20.6	16.9	24.0	30.3	34.5	36.9
Nara	5.2	10.4	14.5	18.6	21.4	15.9	22.3	28.5	34.4	37.4
Wakayama	3.8	9.7	12.7	18.0	17.8	15.9	24.0	28.3	33.3	36.2
Tottori	3.6	7.5	12.5	16.7	19.2	11.8	17.9	25.3	30.6	34.1
Shimane	2.9	9.4	12.4	16.2	18.6	12.3	19.8	25.5	30.2	32.9
Okayama	3.6	8.4	12.6	14.0	18.8	14.1	20.9	26.2	28.4	34.5
Hiroshima	3.8	9.1	13.8	17.5	18.3	15.1	21.6	29.0	32.5	34.6
Yamaguchi	3.8	8.1	13.0	14.7	19.1	16.4	22.2	28.3	30.8	34.1
Tokushima	2.8	8.2	10.9	15.2	17.4	11.6	18.7	23.1	27.3	31.0
Kagawa	4.1	7.1	11.5	13.7	17.8	13.9	19.5	25.8	28.2	33.1
Ehime	4.1	9.2	12.0	14.4	17.8	15.5	21.4	26.6	30.6	34.3
Kochi	3.6	10.7	16.2	18.9	21.3	13.5	21.8	27.5	31.1	34.9
Fukuoka	5.7	10.8	15.2	19.2	22.5	16.9	24.3	30.5	34.4	37.8
Saga	4.0	9.4	15.0	16.3	18.4	14.2	21.4	28.8	30.7	33.1
Nagasaki	4.5	8.8	13.8	17.1	19.1	15.3	21.6	29.2	32.0	33.9
Kumamoto	5.1	8.5	14.4	18.2	20.0	14.8	20.8	29.5	32.5	34.5
Oita	2.7	8.6	11.7	15.7	17.6	13.6	22.2	27.3	30.8	33.4
Miyazaki	4.3	10.2	14.6	16.7	20.9	14.3	22.1	29.0	31.1	37.0
Kagoshima	4.8	9.8	12.8	16.8	20.7	16.3	24.4	28.3	32.7	37.6
Okinawa	8.3	15.9	21.0	24.0	28.9	17.7	26.7	34.5	38.9	43.0
Kolmogorov–Smirnov	0.03	0.09	0.04	>0.20	>0.20	>0.20	>0.20	>0.20	>0.20	>0.20

Table 17.9 Indicator variable for Filial Piety and control variable for urban–rural divide

	Intergenerational cohabitation (indicator variable; percent)					Residential surface per capita (control variable; m^2)				
Prefecture	1992	1997	2002	2007	2012	1992	1997	2002	2007	2012
Hokkaido	16.4	15.5	14.8	11.0	7.0	84	89	92	97	99
Aomori	34.9	37.0	40.0	32.2	20.8	111	118	125	135	141
Iwate	40.9	43.4	47.2	38.1	25.1	129	138	148	159	167
Miyagi	34.9	36.3	38.9	30.4	18.5	98	103	108	115	117
Akita	46.2	49.3	53.1	41.8	26.9	120	129	139	150	158
Yamagata	53.9	59.2	66.1	52.7	32.6	115	120	127	134	140
Fukushima	42.4	45.2	49.0	38.8	24.4	105	113	121	130	137
Ibaraki	34.2	36.0	38.6	30.0	17.8	126	133	142	149	151
Tochigi	36.0	37.9	40.4	31.2	18.6	117	124	133	140	141
Gunma	31.3	32.1	33.2	25.0	14.6	109	116	124	131	133
Saitama	19.0	19.0	19.3	14.9	8.7	61	62	64	66	65
Chiba	20.4	20.4	20.7	15.8	9.3	68	72	75	78	77
Tokyo	10.8	9.8	8.9	6.6	3.9	32	32	33	32	31
Kanagawa	13.8	13.3	12.8	9.8	5.7	43	44	45	46	45
Niigata	45.4	48.8	53.4	42.2	25.8	94	99	106	112	115
Toyama	46.4	49.0	52.6	41.2	25.3	109	115	123	128	131
Ishikawa	37.5	38.5	40.4	30.9	18.6	81	86	92	97	97
Fukui	46.4	50.3	55.6	44.0	27.3	87	95	105	112	114
Yamanashi	32.7	33.2	34.5	26.7	16.2	103	107	119	128	131
Nagano	38.1	39.5	42.0	32.5	19.6	109	117	127	137	140
Gifu	38.7	42.0	45.7	35.4	21.2	83	88	97	103	105
Shizuoka	34.1	36.5	39.3	30.7	18.7	73	76	82	87	88
Aichi	25.0	25.9	27.0	20.5	11.6	62	64	67	69	68
Mie	33.7	34.1	34.9	26.0	15.2	89	95	103	107	109

(continued)

Table 17.9 (continued)

Prefecture	Intergenerational cohabitation (indicator variable; percent)					Residential surface per capita (control variable; m^2)				
	1992	1997	2002	2007	2012	1992	1997	2002	2007	2012
Shiga	36.2	37.6	39.3	29.4	16.4	83	85	88	92	90
Kyoto	20.7	20.0	19.5	14.5	8.4	48	51	53	55	56
Osaka	12.9	12.4	11.9	9.0	5.4	31	32	34	35	35
Hyogo	20.8	20.6	20.3	15.3	9.0	51	55	58	60	60
Nara	27.5	27.6	28.3	21.5	12.2	63	66	71	76	77
Wakayama	27.9	27.7	28.0	21.2	12.6	69	73	80	87	90
Tottori	43.0	45.2	48.2	37.8	23.7	94	99	107	115	119
Shimane	42.7	44.9	48.6	38.9	25.1	101	108	117	126	130
Okayama	31.4	31.7	32.6	24.6	14.6	91	97	103	108	108
Hiroshima	21.5	21.0	20.7	15.6	9.7	66	71	75	79	79
Yamaguchi	24.1	22.9	22.3	16.7	10.6	95	101	108	115	119
Tokushima	35.6	35.8	36.8	27.9	17.2	87	91	100	108	111
Kagawa	32.1	32.0	32.0	23.7	14.2	94	100	107	113	115
Ehime	23.9	22.8	22.0	16.4	10.5	83	88	93	98	101
Kochi	21.8	20.5	19.7	15.2	10.2	68	74	80	87	90
Fukuoka	20.2	19.8	19.8	15.2	9.1	69	72	75	78	77
Saga	39.2	41.4	45.1	35.7	21.9	92	98	108	116	119
Nagasaki	24.5	25.0	26.3	20.7	13.0	76	83	89	96	99
Kumamoto	31.7	32.5	34.4	26.7	16.3	100	106	113	120	121
Oita	27.9	27.3	27.3	20.6	12.8	93	100	108	114	116
Miyazaki	20.3	19.3	19.0	14.5	9.4	119	126	132	139	141
Kagoshima	11.3	9.9	9.1	7.1	5.0	119	127	136	146	149
Okinawa	14.0	12.8	12.1	9.7	6.9	65	67	69	70	68
Kolmogorov–Smirnov	>0.20	>0.20	>0.20	0.14	>0.20	0.15	>0.20	>0.20	>0.20	>0.20

Table 17.10 SME business sentiment and jobs-per-applicant ratio

	SME business sentiment (diffusion index)					Jobs per applicant (ratio)				
Prefecture	1992	1997	2002	2007	2012	1992	1997	2002	2007	2012
Hokkaido	−30.0	−44.4	−43.7	25.8	25.3	1.19	0.54	0.47	0.56	0.62
Aomori	−25.4	−48.6	−46.9	37.0	28.0	1.71	0.43	0.29	0.47	0.61
Iwate	−12.4	−33.7	−31.6	21.4	17.4	2.42	0.88	0.40	0.73	0.90
Miyagi	−27.1	−41.6	−51.9	31.8	19.6	2.06	0.85	0.58	0.93	1.11
Akita	−19.4	−41.2	−47.5	22.2	27.7	2.21	0.86	0.41	0.61	0.69
Yamagata	−25.8	−28.5	−51.8	20.1	22.8	2.84	1.17	0.51	0.94	0.92
Fukushima	−25.9	−46.1	−48.4	27.6	15.5	2.96	0.87	0.45	0.89	1.06
Ibaraki	−40.2	−40.7	−43.7	17.4	23.7	3.19	0.82	0.51	0.98	0.78
Tochigi	−38.3	−41.6	−38.4	20.0	21.2	3.39	0.99	0.64	1.45	0.81
Gunma	−33.9	−45.6	−42.3	20.5	25.5	2.63	0.98	0.73	1.63	0.96
Saitama	−44.8	−46.3	−49.1	16.5	25.9	1.93	0.56	0.45	1.01	0.57
Chiba	−28.9	−47.1	−40.2	14.2	24.9	2.02	0.55	0.47	0.94	0.68
Tokyo	−45.3	−40.5	−37.2	15.9	18.1	1.89	0.64	0.70	1.38	1.14
Kanagawa	−43.7	−40.5	−36.5	20.7	20.7	2.39	0.52	0.49	0.95	0.59
Niigata	−34.0	−47.0	−48.3	30.9	23.7	3.37	1.11	0.51	1.12	0.84
Toyama	−31.9	−42.6	−44.0	25.1	25.2	3.38	1.01	0.57	1.19	0.99
Ishikawa	−31.3	−45.1	−48.2	19.6	34.2	3.53	0.95	0.62	1.35	0.94
Fukui	−12.9	−45.0	−46.7	15.3	26.0	3.76	1.35	0.74	1.40	1.19
Yamanashi	−35.9	−42.0	−42.8	27.3	34.0	3.75	1.23	0.83	1.07	0.63
Nagano	−33.6	−33.0	−50.1	17.3	28.0	4.08	1.23	0.66	1.18	0.82
Gifu	−33.0	−35.6	−44.6	19.1	26.5	3.54	1.15	0.71	1.35	0.96
Shizuoka	−37.1	−43.3	−45.1	14.9	21.8	3.32	1.00	0.77	1.21	0.77
Aichi	−39.1	−46.6	−45.9	21.2	26.3	3.14	0.92	0.75	1.95	1.10
Mie	−28.6	−44.7	−42.8	25.6	28.4	2.43	0.80	0.66	1.40	0.88

(continued)

Table 17.10 (continued)

Prefecture	SME business sentiment (diffusion index)					Jobs per applicant (ratio)				
	1992	1997	2002	2007	2012	1992	1997	2002	2007	2012
Shiga	−40.6	−50.5	−58.1	28.1	29.9	1.96	0.83	0.53	1.31	0.67
Kyoto	−40.7	−42.4	−50.2	26.3	24.4	1.67	0.56	0.49	0.95	0.81
Osaka	−50.1	−50.8	−45.8	21.4	25.5	1.64	0.58	0.46	1.26	0.80
Hyogo	−41.1	−44.0	−48.4	23.6	16.2	1.60	0.58	0.42	0.94	0.68
Nara	−35.5	−50.7	−41.2	27.6	27.7	1.89	0.63	0.42	0.81	0.70
Wakayama	−30.4	−48.1	−42.6	23.1	31.5	2.55	0.69	0.44	0.90	0.85
Tottori	−31.4	−29.4	−40.4	31.7	25.1	3.23	1.22	0.60	0.75	0.73
Shimane	−29.3	−39.9	−36.3	27.4	29.4	3.36	1.16	0.61	0.92	0.95
Okayama	−37.5	−48.7	−44.2	26.4	34.4	3.09	1.13	0.76	1.43	1.08
Hiroshima	−33.4	−36.9	−44.5	22.3	23.1	2.89	0.87	0.63	1.19	0.91
Yamaguchi	−30.7	−43.8	−48.5	27.5	34.5	2.49	1.02	0.63	1.07	0.89
Tokushima	−36.4	−46.9	−44.7	30.1	24.5	3.04	0.71	0.53	0.89	0.87
Kagawa	−33.9	−50.9	−50.9	24.3	30.4	3.14	1.35	0.79	1.29	1.06
Ehime	−23.9	−46.3	−40.8	28.6	30.8	1.86	0.91	0.63	0.87	0.83
Kochi	−20.9	−37.6	−38.7	34.9	26.9	1.45	0.48	0.43	0.50	0.62
Fukuoka	−31.4	−44.6	−42.0	23.2	27.3	1.77	0.54	0.41	0.85	0.71
Saga	−25.9	−48.8	−41.4	22.6	31.6	2.13	0.70	0.42	0.70	0.74
Nagasaki	−25.9	−50.4	−46.0	32.7	31.5	2.00	0.64	0.42	0.62	0.66
Kumamoto	−19.4	−35.6	−32.3	19.1	30.4	1.82	0.57	0.41	0.82	0.69
Oita	−16.8	−37.5	−34.1	31.2	29.2	1.86	0.75	0.54	1.03	0.75
Miyazaki	−18.5	−46.2	−40.1	33.5	15.9	1.67	0.61	0.42	0.67	0.71
Kagoshima	−13.6	−38.4	−32.8	25.7	22.7	1.08	0.60	0.41	0.61	0.66
Okinawa	−13.4	−27.8	−15.7	10.9	8.4	0.32	0.24	0.30	0.42	0.42
Kolmogorov–Smirnov	>0.20	>0.20	0.11	>0.20	>0.20	0.19	0.10	0.15	>0.20	>0.20

Table 17.11 Regression output for analysis of Individual Entrepreneurship in dependently employed men

	Parameter estimates	S.E.	Confidence interval of parameter estimate (90%)		t value	p-level	H_0 rejected? (5%)
Intercept	−1.225	0.225	−1.596	−0.853	−5.446	0.000	Yes
BizSent	−0.338	0.146	−0.579	−0.097	−2.314	0.022	Yes
Cohab	−0.101	0.045	−0.176	−0.027	−2.246	0.026	Yes
NonRegmale	0.328	0.113	0.142	0.515	2.910	0.004	Yes
Surfpercap	−0.119	0.040	−0.186	−0.053	−2.950	0.004	Yes
Dum92	2.371	0.398	1.714	3.028	5.958	0.000	Yes
Dum97	2.174	0.373	1.558	2.79	5.832	0.000	Yes
Dum02	0.808	0.337	0.252	1.364	2.399	0.017	Yes
Dum07	0.770	0.106	0.596	0.945	7.284	0.000	Yes
R	0.897	Adjusted R^2		0.797	# of observations		235
R^2	0.804	S.E.		0.45	d.f.		8

Table 17.12 Regression output for analysis of INDIVIDUAL ENTREPRENEURSHIP in non-working individuals

	Parameter estimates	S.E.	Confidence interval of parameter estimate (90%)		t value	p-level	H_0 rejected? (5%)
Intercept	−0.867	0.181	−1.165	−0.568	−4.789	0.000	Yes
NonRegall	0.321	0.159	0.058	0.583	2.018	0.045	Yes
Surfpercap	−0.316	0.048	−0.395	−0.236	−6.545	0.000	Yes
Cohab	−0.231	0.065	−0.338	−0.124	−3.556	0.000	Yes
JpA	−0.201	0.077	−0.328	−0.075	−2.624	0.009	Yes
Dum92	1.216	0.412	0.536	1.896	2.952	0.003	Yes
Dum97	0.827	0.283	0.360	1.295	2.922	0.004	Yes
Dum02	1.979	0.185	1.673	2.285	10.682	0.000	Yes
Dum07	0.310	0.129	0.097	0.523	2.409	0.017	Yes
R	0.835	Adjusted R^2		0.687	# of observations		235
R^2	0.697	S.E.		0.56	d.f.		8

Table 17.13 Correlation matrices and VIFs by agent subgroup (including subsets)

Subgroup DE (1992–2012)	NonRegall	Surfpercap	Cohab	BizSent
NonRegmale		0.10	−0.46	0.69
Surfpercap			0.42	0.24
Cohab				−0.42
VIFs	2.08	1.64	2.00	2.27
Subgroup NA (1992–2012)				
NonRegall		0.10	−0.47	−0.65
Surfpercap			0.42	−0.07
Cohab				0.25
VIFs	2.50	1.46	1.93	1.76
Subgroup NA (1992–1997)				
NonRegall		−0.20	−0.39	−0.82
Surfpercap			0.62	0.10
Cohab				0.32
VIFs	3.22	1.68	1.85	3.09
Subgroup NA (2002–2012)				
NonRegall		−0.186	−0.72	0.17
Surfpercap			0.45	0.02
Cohab				−0.07
VIFs	2.22	1.33	2.64	1.03

Table 17.14 Regression output for analysis of INDIVIDUAL ENTREPRENEURSHIP in non-working individuals, 1992 and 1997

	Parameter estimates	S.E.	Confidence interval of parameter estimate (90%)		t value	p-level	H_0 rejected? (5%)
Intercept	−0.042	0.226	−0.418	0.333	−0.187	0.852	No
Surfpercap	−0.463	0.088	−0.608	−0.317	−5.289	0.000	Yes
NonRegall	−0.110	0.201	−0.444	0.223	−0.550	0.584	No
JpA	−0.332	0.140	−0.565	−0.100	−2.374	0.020	Yes
Cohab	−0.297	0.130	−0.513	−0.082	−2.291	0.024	Yes
Dum97	0.084	0.431	−0.633	0.801	0.195	0.845	No
R	0.77084	Adjusted R^2		0.57114	# of observations		94
R^2	0.59419	S.E.		0.65488	d.f.		5

Table 17.15 Regression output for analysis of INDIVIDUAL ENTREPRENEURSHIP in non-working individuals, 2002, 2007 and 2012

	Parameter estimates	S.E.	Confidence interval of parameter estimate (90%)		t value	p-level	H_0 rejected? (5%)
Intercept	−0.756	0.113	−0.943	−0.568	−6.667	0.000	Yes
Surfpercap	−0.271	0.060	−0.370	−0.172	−4.528	0.000	Yes
NonRegall	0.194	0.089	0.047	0.342	2.180	0.031	Yes
JpA	−0.129	0.065	−0.236	−0.022	−1.989	0.049	Yes
Cohab	−0.241	0.077	−0.369	−0.114	−3.134	0.002	Yes
Dum02	1.881	0.222	1.513	2.248	8.471	0.000	Yes
Dum07	0.386	0.133	0.165	0.607	2.899	0.004	Yes
R	0.847	Adjusted R^2		0.704	# of observations		141
R^2	0.717	S.E.		0.544	d.f.		6

Table 17.16 Regression output for actual entrepreneurship in dependently employed men

	Parameter estimates	S.E.	Confidence interval of parameter estimate (90%)		t value	p-level	H_0 rejected? (5%)
Intercept	−0.897	0.286	−1.370	−0.424	−3.132	0.002	Yes
BizSent	−0.455	0.186	−0.763	−0.148	−2.450	0.015	Yes
Cohab	−0.155	0.057	−0.250	−0.060	−2.697	0.008	Yes
NonRegmale	0.310	0.144	0.072	0.547	2.155	0.032	Yes
Surfpercap	−0.169	0.052	−0.254	−0.084	−3.279	0.001	Yes
Dum92	1.800	0.507	0.963	2.637	3.553	0.000	Yes
Dum97	1.696	0.475	0.912	2.480	3.573	0.000	Yes
Dum02	0.195	0.429	−0.514	0.903	0.454	0.650	No
Dum07	0.793	0.135	0.570	1.015	5.884	0.000	Yes
R	0.826	Adjusted R^2		0.671	# of observations		235
R^2	0.683	S.E.		0.573	d.f.		8

Table 17.17 Regression output for actual entrepreneurship in non-working individuals

	Parameter estimates	S.E.	Confidence interval of parameter estimate (90%)		t value	p-level	H_0 rejected? (5%)
Intercept	−1.067	0.218	−1.427	−0.707	−4.892	0.000	Yes
NonRegall	0.570	0.192	0.254	0.887	2.977	0.003	Yes
Surfpercap	−0.310	0.058	−0.406	−0.214	−5.338	0.000	Yes
Cohab	−0.311	0.078	−0.440	−0.181	−3.969	0.000	Yes
JpA	−0.042	0.093	−0.195	0.111	−0.451	0.652	No
Dum92	1.640	0.496	0.820	2.460	3.303	0.001	Yes
Dum97	1.391	0.341	0.827	1.954	4.075	0.000	Yes
Dum02	1.800	0.223	1.431	2.169	8.06	0.000	Yes
Dum07	0.503	0.155	0.247	0.759	3.241	0.001	Yes
R	0.749	Adjusted R^2		0.545	# of observations		235
R^2	0.56	S.E.		0.675	d.f.		8

Table 17.18 Regression output for actual entrepreneurship in non-working individuals 1992 and 1997

	Parameter estimates	S.E.	Confidence interval of parameter estimate (90%)		t value	p-level	H_0 rejected? (5%)
Intercept	−0.108	0.247	−0.519	0.302	−0.439	0.662	No
Surfpercap	−0.401	0.096	−0.560	−0.242	−4.193	0.000	Yes
NonRegall	0.080	0.220	−0.285	0.445	0.364	0.717	No
JpA	−0.041	0.153	−0.296	0.213	−0.270	0.788	No
Cohab	−0.330	0.142	−0.566	−0.094	−2.322	0.023	Yes
Dum97	0.217	0.472	−0.567	1.001	0.460	0.647	No
R	0.717	Adjusted R^2		0.487	# of observations		94
R^2	0.515	S.E.		0.716	d.f.		5

Table 17.19 Regression output for actual entrepreneurship in non-working individuals 2002, 2007 and 2012

	Parameter estimates	S.E.	Confidence interval of parameter estimate (90%)		t value	p-level	H_0 rejected? (5%)
Intercept	−0.767	0.138	−0.996	−0.539	−5.555	0.000	Yes
Surfpercap	−0.274	0.073	−0.395	−0.154	−3.765	0.000	Yes
NonRegall	0.300	0.109	0.120	0.480	2.762	0.007	Yes
JpA	−0.099	0.079	−0.229	0.032	−1.254	0.212	No
Cohab	−0.329	0.094	−0.485	−0.174	−3.505	0.001	Yes
Dum02	1.719	0.271	1.271	2.167	6.352	0.000	Yes
Dum07	0.583	0.162	0.314	0.852	3.591	0.000	Yes
R	0.847	Adjusted R^2		0.704	# of observations		141
R^2	0.717	S.E.		0.544	d.f.		6

List of Abbreviations

BOJ	Bank of Japan	*Nihon ginkō*	日本銀行
CabO	Cabinet Office	*Naikakufu*	内閣府
CSS	Changing subsystem		
DE	Dependently employed (subgroup)		
ES	Entrepreneurial spirit (rule)		
FUe	Fear of unemployment (rule)		
FF	Founder force		
GEM	Global Entrepreneurship Monitor		
GTEE	General Theory of Economic Evolution (Dopfer and Potts 2008)		
HSO	*Homo sapiens oeconomicus* (Dopfer 2004)		
ISIF	Industrial Structure Improvement Fund (integrated into SMRJ 2004)	*Sangyō kiban seibi kikin*	産業基盤整備基金
IStM	Institute for Statistical Mathematics	*Tōkei sūri kenkyūjo*	統計数理研究所
JASMEC	Japan Small and Medium Enterprise Corporation (integrated into SMRJ in 2004)	*Chūshō kigyō sōgō jigyōdan*	中小企業総合事業団
JFC	Japan Finance Corporation	*Nihon seisaku kin'yū kōko*	日本政策金融公庫
JIWE	Japan Institute of Workers' Evolution	*Nijū'isseiki shokugyō zaidan*	21世紀職業財団
JRDC	Japan Regional Development Corporation (integrated into SMRJ in 2004)	*Chi'iki shinkō seibi kōdan*	地域振興整備公団

(continued)

G.D. Blind, *The Entrepreneur in Rule-Based Economics*, Economic Complexity and Evolution, DOI 10.1007/978-3-319-62779-3

JSBRI	Japan Small Business Research Institute	*Chūshō kigyō sōgō kenkyū kikō*	中小企業総合研究機構
LTB	Local Tax Bureau	*Jichii zei'mu kyoku*	自治税務局
METI	Ministry of Economy, Trade and Industry	*Kei'zai sangyōshō*	経済産業省
MIAC	Ministry of Internal Affairs and Communications	*Sōmushō*	総務省
MHLW	Ministry of Health, Labor and Welfare	*Kōsei'rōdōshō*	厚生労働省
MoF	Ministry of Finance	*Zai'mushō*	財務省
MRI	Mitsubishi Research Institute	*Mitsubishi sōgō kenkyūjo*	三菱総合研究所
MSSS	Metastable subsystem		
NA	Economically non-active (subgroup)		
NLFC	National Life Finance Corporation	*Kokumin sei'katsu kin'yū kōko*	国民生活金融公庫
NRE	Non-regular employment (rule)		
NRI	Nippon Research Institute	*Nippon risāchi sōgō kenkyūjo*	日本リサーチ 総合研究所
NVCA	National Venture Capital Association		
RBA	Rule-based approach (Dopfer 2004)		
SE	Self-employed (subgroup)		
SFR	System of factor rules		
SMEA	Small and Medium Enterprise Agency	*Chūshō kigyōchō*	中小企業庁
SMRJ	Organization for Small & Medium Enterprises and Regional Innovation, Japan	*Chūshō kigyō kiban seibi kikō* or briefly *chūshō kikō*	中小企業基盤整備機構; or briefly 中小機構
VEC	Venture Enterprise Center	*Benchā entāpuraisu sentā*	ベンチャーエンタープライスセンター

Glossary

By Japanese pronunciation (in alphabetic order)

アルバイト	*Arubaito*	Jobbing; short-term non-regular work
ビジネス	*Bijinesu*	Business
中小企業信用保険	*Chūshō kigyō shin'yō hoken*	SME credit insurance
企業投資促進税制	*Chūshō kigyō tōshi sokushin zei'sei*	Tax regulations for the promotion of small and medium enterprises; official title of the "Angel Tax" *enjeru zei'sei*
脱サラ	*Datsusara*	Resigning from a regular job in order to become self-employed. The term does *not* refer to layoffs, family business succession or parenting activities
エンジェル税制	*Enjeru zei'sei*	Angel tax; tax exemption of gains from Venture Capital investments; colloquial term for "Tax regulations for the promotion of small and medium enterprises" *Chūshō kigyō tōshi sokushin zei'sei*
フリーター	*Furītā*	Jobber; individual making a living from alternating jobs aged below 35
行政指導	*Gyōsei shidō*	Administrative guidance
業績主義	*Gyōseki shugi*	Performance principle; refers to the consideration of performance measures for wage determination in dependent employment (compare: → Management by objectives)
派遣	*Haken*	Temporary work
派遣会社	*Haken gaisha*	Temporary employment agency
破産法	*Hasanhō*	Bankruptcy law
平成	*Hei'sei*	Era of Emperor Akihito (since 1989)
非正社員	*Hisei'sha'in*	Non-regular employee
自営業	*Ji'eigyō*	Self-employment; sole trading
自己破産	*Jiko hasan*	Personal bankruptcy
株式会社	*Kabushiki gai'sha*	Joint stock company; also PLC

(continued)

G.D. Blind, *The Entrepreneur in Rule-Based Economics*, Economic Complexity and Evolution, DOI 10.1007/978-3-319-62779-3

会社法	*Kai'sha hō*	Corporate Law (until Dec. 31, 2005)
企業内組合	*Kigyōnai kumiai*	In-house labour union. A post-war characteristic of Japanese industrial relations; one of the "Three Sacred Treasures" (compare: → Treasures, Three Sacred)
起業家	*Kigyōka*	Business founder; refers to the individual at the time of business commencement
企業家	*Kigyōka*	Entrepreneur; refers to the individual leading an established business
金融庁	*Kin'yūchō*	Financial Services Agency
目標による管理	*Moku'hyō ni yoru kanri*	Management by objectives
年功序列	*Nenkō joretsu*	Seniority principle; refers to positions and wages being overwhelmingly a function of tenure, particularly in traditionally managed firms. The principle relates to the esteem of older individuals in Confucian tradition (compare: → Filial piety); one of the "Three Sacred Treasures" (compare: → Treasures, Three Sacred)
親孝行	*Oyakōkō*	Filial piety; refers to respect for and good relations with parents and senior attachment figures; relates to Confucian tradition (compare: (vgl. → Seniority principle)
パート	*Pāto*	Part-time work, part-timer
連帯保証	*Rentai hoshō*	Joint guarantee; characteristics of Japanese law of obligations that allows for including subsidiary bailsmen in credit contracts
三種の神器	*Sanshu no jingi*	The Three Sacred Treasures (lit.); originally refers to three objects mentioned in Japan's foundation myth but is frequently used to label three characteristics of post-war employment practices in large Japanese corporations (compare: → Seniority principle; → Lifetime employment; → In-house trade unions)
成果主義	*Seika shugi*	Performance principle; increasingly used in corporate human resource management to decide on wages and career advancement since the 1990s
生活保護	*Seikatsu hogo*	Social security
正社員	*Sei'sha'in*	Regular employee
新会社法	*Shinkai'sha hō*	New Corporate Law (since 2006)
士農工商	*Shinōkōshō*	Four Occupations (The); an order of social rank based on Confucian tradition: warriors, peasants, craftsmen and merchants; particularly strongly prevailing during the Edo period (1603–1868)
信用保証協会	*Shin'yō hoshō kyōkai*	Credit guarantee association
失業保険	*Shitsugyō hoken*	Unemployment insurance
少子高齢化	*Shōshi kōrei'ka*	Population ageing (lit. low birth rates and population ageing)

(continued)

商業登記簿	*Shōgyōtōkibo*	Commercial register
終身雇用	*Shūshin koyō*	*Lifetime employment*; often cited as a specific element of human resource management in large Japanese firms until the 1990s; term coined by American anthropologist and later business consultant James Abegglen (Abegglen 1958); one of the "Three Sacred Treasures" (compare: → Treasures, Three Sacred)
就職活動	*Shūshoku katsudō*	Job hunting; refers to all activities related to the search of work, typically between May and October during the last year of formal education aiming at employment from April 1st of the following year (beginning of Japanese fiscal year)
創業者	*Sōgyōsha*	Business founder; frequently referring to a historically important entrepreneur
転職	*Tenshoku*	Change of employment, voluntary; since the late 1990s increasingly common among younger employees, typically motivated by higher wages, by a more diverse work experience or by discontent with current employment conditions
有限会社	*Yūgen gai'sha*	Limited liability company

By English pronunciation (in alphabetic order)

行政指導	*Gyōsei shidō*	Administrative guidance
エンジエル税制	*Enjeru zei'sei*	Angel tax; tax exemption of gains from Venture Capital investments; colloquial term for "Tax regulations for the promotion of small and medium enterprises" *Chūshō kigyō tōshi sokushin zei'sei*
破産法	*Hasanhō*	Bankruptcy law
ビジネス	*Bijinesu*	Business
創業者	*Sōgyōsha*	Business founder; frequently referring to a historically important entrepreneur
起業家	*Kigyōka*	Business founder; refers to the individual at the time of business commencement
転職	*Tenshoku*	Change of employment, voluntary; since the late 1990s increasingly common among younger employees, typically motivated by higher wages, by a more diverse work experience or by discontent with current employment conditions
商業登記簿	*Shōgyōtōkibo*	Commercial register
会社法	*Kai'sha hō*	Corporate Law (until Dec. 31, 2005)
信用保証協会	*Shin'yō hoshō kyōkai*	Credit guarantee association
企業家	*Kigyōka*	Entrepreneur; refers to the individual leading an established business
平成	*Hei'sei*	Era of Emperor Akihito (since 1989)

(continued)

親孝行	*Oyakōkō*	Filial piety; refers to respect for and good relations with parents and senior attachment figures; relates to Confucian tradition (compare: (vgl. è Seniority principle).
金融庁	*Kin'yūchō*	Financial Services Agency
士農工商	*Shinōkōshō*	Four Occupations (The); an order of social rank based on Confucian tradition: warriors, peasants, craftsmen and merchants; particularly strongly prevailing during the Edo period (1603–1868)
企業内組合	*Kigyōnai kumiai*	In-house labour union. A post-war characteristic of Japanese industrial relations; one of the "Three Sacred Treasures" (compare: è Treasures, Three Sacred)
就職活動	*Shūshoku katsudō*	Job hunting; refers to all activities related to the search of work, typically between May and October during the last year of formal education aiming at employment from April 1st of the following year (beginning of Japanese fiscal year)
フリーター	*Furītā*	Jobber; individual making a living from alternating jobs aged below 35
アルバイト	*Arubaito*	Jobbing; short-term non-regular work
連帯保証	*Rentai hoshō*	Joint guarantee; characteristics of Japanese law of obligations that allows for including subsidiary bailsmen in credit contracts
株式会社	*Kabushiki gai'sha*	Joint stock company; also PLC
終身雇用	*Shūshin koyō*	*Lifetime employment*; often cited as a specific element of human resource management in large Japanese firms until the 1990s; term coined by American anthropologist and later business consultant James Abegglen (Abegglen 1958); one of the "Three Sacred Treasures" (compare: è Treasures, Three Sacred)
有限会社	*Yūgen gai'sha*	Limited liability company
目標による管理	*Moku'hyō ni yoru kanri*	Management by objectives
新会社法	*Shinkai'sha hō*	New Corporate Law (since 2006)
非正社員	*Hisei'sha'in*	Non-regular employee
パート	*Pāto*	Part-time work, part-timer
成果主義	*Seika shugi*	Performance principle; increasingly used in corporate human resource management to decide on wages and career advancement since the 1990s
業績主義	*Gyōseki shugi*	Performance principle; refers to the consideration of performance measures for wage determination in dependent employment (compare: è Management by objectives)
自己破産	*Jiko hasan*	Personal bankruptcy
少子高齢化	*Shōshi kōrei'ka*	Population ageing (lit. low birth rates and population ageing)
正社員	*Sei'sha'in*	Regular employee

(continued)

脱サラ	*Datsusara*	Resigning from a regular job in order to become self-employed. The term does *not* refer to layoffs, family business succession or parenting activities
自営業	*Ji'eigyō*	Self-employment; sole trading
年功序列	*Nenkō joretsu*	Seniority principle; refers to positions and wages being overwhelmingly a function of tenure, particularly in traditionally managed firms. The principle relates to the esteem of older individuals in Confucian tradition (compare: è Filial piety); one of the "Three Sacred Treasures" (compare: è Treasures, Three Sacred)
中小企業信用保険	*Chūshō kigyō shin'yō hoken*	SME credit insurance
生活保護	*Seikatsu hogo*	Social security
企業投資促進税制	*Chūshō kigyō tōshi sokushin zei'sei*	Tax regulations for the promotion of small and medium enterprises; official title of the "Angel Tax" *enjeru zei'sei*
派遣会社	*Haken gaisha*	Temporary employment agency
派遣	*Haken*	Temporary work
三種の神器	*Sanshu no jingi*	The Three Sacred Treasures (lit.); originally refers to three objects mentioned in Japan's foundation myth, but is frequently used to label three characteristics of post-war employment practices in large Japanese corporations (compare: è Seniority principle; è Lifetime employment; è In-house trade unions)
失業保険	*Shitsugyō hoken*	Unemployment insurance

Bibliography

Abe Y, Oshi A (2007) The role of married women's labor supply on family earnings distribution in Japan. J Income Distrib 16(3–4):110–127
Abegglen J (1958) The Japanese factory: aspects of its social organization. Free Press, Glencoe, IL
Addleson M (2002) Equilibrium versus understanding: towards the rehumanizing of economics within social theory. Routledge, London
Aldrich HE, Hodgson GM (2008) In defence of generalized Darwinism. J Evol Econ 18:577–596
Aoki T (1990) Nihon Bunka-Ron [Theorizing on Japanese culture]. Chūō Kōronsha, Tokyo
Aoyama Y (1999) Policy interventions for industrial network formation: contrasting historical underpinnings of the small business policy in Japan and the United States. Small Bus Econ 12:217–231
Armour J, Cumming D (2008) Bankruptcy law and entrepreneurship. European Corporate Governance Institute, Law working papers, vol 105, pp 1–36
Asogawa S (2008) Dr. Asogawa on the lending practices of Japanese banks. Interview with author. Kyoto, 17 April
Asogawa S (2009) Dr. Asogawa on occupations preferences in contemporary Japan. Interview with author. Kyoto, 2 April
Audretsch DB (2004) Sustaining innovation and growth: public policy support for entrepreneurship. Ind Innov 11(3):167–191
Audretsch DB, Yamawaki H (1988) R&D Rivalry, industrial policy, and U.S.-Japanese trade. Rev Econ Stat 70:438–447
Baumol W (1968) Entrepreneurship in economic theory. Am Econ Rev 58(2):64–71
Beck T, Demirgüc-Kunt A (2008) Access to finance: an unfinished agenda. World Bank Econ Rev 22(3):383–396
Beinhocker E (2011) Evolution as computation: integrating self-organization with generalized Darwinism. J Inst Econ 7(3):393–423
Berger LA (1989) Economics and hermeneutics. Econ Philos 5(02):209–234
Bird A, Mitsuhashi H (2003) Entrepreneurs and entrepreneurial processes: historical and theoretical perspectives on entrepreneurship in the Japanese contexts. Asian Perspect 27(3):125–175
Blind GD (2003) Statistical methods for a dynamic analysis of meso-trajectories in evolutionary systems. M.A. thesis, St. Gallen University
Blind G (2012a) Unternehmensgründer in Japan seit 1992. Evidenz zur Evolution gegensätzlicher Gründergruppen. Bonn Japanstudien 29:19–68
Blind GD (2012b) Investigating entrepreneurial spirit with the rule approach: why self-employment is on the decline in Japan. Evol Inst Econ Rev 9(1):183–198

G.D. Blind, *The Entrepreneur in Rule-Based Economics*, Economic Complexity and Evolution, DOI 10.1007/978-3-319-62779-3

Blind GD (2012c) Culture and economic explanation: economics in the US and Japan. By Donald W. Katzner. New York: Routledge, 2008. 184 pp. $39.95 (paper). J East Asian Stud 12(1):150–153

Blind GD (2012d) Unternehmensgründer in Japan seit 1991: Evidenz zur Evolution gegensätzlicher Gründergruppen. In: Distelrath G, Menkhaus H, Ölschleger HD (eds) Bonner Japanforschungen 29. Bier'sche Verlagsanstalt, Bonn, pp 19–68

Blind GD (2016) Behavioral rules: Veblen, Nelson-Winter, Oström and beyond. In: Frantz R, Chen S-H, Dopfer K, Heukelom F, Mousavi S (eds) Routledge handbook of behavioral economics. Routledge, Milton Park, pp 139–151

Blind GD, Lottanti von Mandach S (2012) Ansichtssache: Zum Zustand der japanischen Wirtschaft nach Doppelschlag und Dreifachkatastrophe. In: Chiavacci D, Wiezcorek I (eds) Japan 2012: Politik, Wirtschaft und Gesellschaft. Vereinigung für sozialwissenschaftliche Japanforschung, Berlin, pp 131–149

Blind G, Lottanti von Mandach S (2013a) Bescheidene Managementgehälter und sich schliessende Lohnscheren: Neue Einblicke in den japanischen Arbeitsmarkt. In: Chiavacci D, Wieczorek I (eds) Japan 2013. VSJF, Berlin, pp 203–228

Blind G, Lottanti von Mandach S (2013b) Ansichtssache: Zum Zustand der japanischen Wirtschaft nach Doppelschlag und Dreifach-Katastrophe. In: Chiavacci D, Wiezcorek I (eds) Japan 2013. VSJF, Berlin, pp 131–149

Blind GD, Lottanti von Mandach S (2013c) Bescheidene Managementgehälter und sich schliessende Lohnscheren: Neue Einblicke in den japanischen Arbeitsmarkt. In: Chiavacci D, Wiezcorek I (eds) Japan 2013: Politik, Wirtschaft und Gesellschaft. Vereinigung für sozialwissenschaftliche Japanforschung, Berlin

Blind GD, Lottanti von Mandach S (2015) Decades not lost, but won: increased employment, higher wages, and more equal opportunities in the Japanese labour market. Soc Sci Jpn J 18 (1):63–88

Blind G, Lottanti von Mandach S (2017a) Modeling the "Visitors to Rome" effect: reputation building in anglo-saxon buyout funds in Japan. MPRA working paper 7761. Munich University, Munich

Blind G, Lottanti von Mandach S (2017b) Secular trends in the Japanese labour market during the lost decades: a reply to Andrew Gordon. MPRA working paper 80812. University of Munich, Munich

Blind G, Lottanti von Mandach S (2017c) When vultures bring blessings: employment growth in Japanese businesses under private equity ownership. MPRA working paper 80816. University of Munich, Munich

Blind GD, Lottanti von Mandach S (2017d) Not a coincidence: sons-in-law as successors in successful Japanese family firms. Crit Finance Rev (forthcoming)

Blind G, Pyka A (2014) The rule approach in evolutionary economics: a methodological template for empirical research. J Evol Econ 24(5):1085–1105

Blind GD, Pyka A (2015) Erich Schneider: the admiring disciple who did not become a follower. J Evol Econ 25(1):239–252

Blind G, Ziltener P (2014) Free trade live: insights from the Switzerland-Japan free trade and economic partnership agreement. In: Mottini R (ed) Yearbook 2014. Swiss Japanese Chamber of Commerce, Zurich, pp 53–63

Brandes W, Weise P (1999) Team performance as a constellation of forces: a general model. Kyklos 52(4):573–590

Brockhaus RH (1987) Entrepreneurial Folklore. J Small Bus Manag 25(3):1–6

Bushimata T, Shiro Y (2002) Chūshō kigyō kin'yū nyūmon [Introduction to small business finance]. Tōyō Keizai, Tokyo

CabO (2007) Heisei jū'nana nendo kenmin keizai keisan [2005 Prefectural economic statistics]. Cabinet Office, Tokyo

Cavelaars P (2005) Has the tradeoff between productivity gains and job growth disappeared? Kyklos 58(1):45–64

Chen P (2005) A biological perspective of macro dynamics and division of labor: persistent cycles, disruptive technology, and the trade-off between stability and complexity. In: Dopfer K (ed) The evolutionary foundations of economics. Cambridge University Press, Cambridge
Chen K, İmrohoroğlu A et al (2006) The Japanese saving rate. Am Econ Rev 96(5):1850–1858
Chiavacci D (2010) Divided society model and social cleavages in Japanese politics: no alignment by social class, but dealignment of rural-urban division. Contemporary Jpn 22(1–2):47–74
Chiavacci D, Blind G et al (2012) Ist das Freihandels- und wirtschaftliche Partnerschaftsabkommen (FHWPA) zwischen der Schweiz und Japan (bereits) eine Erfolgsgeschichte? Hauptergebnisse einer empirischen Analyse zu Umsetzung und Wirkung. Asiat Stud 66(1):19–56
Cressy R (2002) Funding gaps: a symposium. Econ J 112:F1–F16
Daly GG (1998) Entrepreneurship and business culture in Japan and the U.S. Jpn World Econ 10:487–494
Davidsson P, Honig B (2003) The role of social and human capital among nascent entrepreneurs. J Bus Ventur 18:301–331
De Long JB (1988) Productivity growth, convergence, and welfare: comment. Am Econ Rev 78 (5):1138–1154
Debroux P (2006) Trends in female entrepreneurship in Japan. In: Gan X, Jaussaud J, Dzever S (eds) Economic dynamism and business strategies for firms in Asia. China Economic Publishing, Beijing, pp 326–356
Dennis WJ (1996) Self-employment: when nothing else is available? J Lab Res XVII(4):645–661
Di Iorio F (2015) Hayek and the hermeneutics of mind. Soc Sci Inf 54(2):177–191
Diamond J, Schaede U (2013) Self-employment in Japan. A microanalysis of personal profiles. Soc Sci Jpn J 16(1):1–27
Dilthey W (1900) Die Entstehung der Hermeneutik. Mohr (Paul Siebeck), Tübingen
Dopfer K (2001) Evolutionary economics – framework for analysis. In: Dopfer K (ed) The evolutionary foundations of economics. Kluwer Academic Publishers, Boston, pp 1–44
Dopfer K (2004) The economic agent as rule maker and rule user: Homo sapiens oeconomicus. J Evol Econ 14:177–195
Dopfer K (ed) (2005) The evolutionary foundations of economics. Cambridge University Press, Cambridge
Dopfer K (2006) The origins of meso economics – Schumpeter's legacy. Papers on economics and evolution. Max Planck Institute, Jena, p 610
Dopfer K (2011) Economics in a cultural key: complexity and evolution revisited. In: Davis JB, Hands DW (eds) The Elgar companion to recent economic methodology. Edward Elgar, Cheltenham, pp 319–340
Dopfer K (2012) The origins of meso economics. J Evol Econ 22(1):133–160
Dopfer K, Potts J (2008) The general theory of economic evolution. Routledge, London
Dopfer K, Foster J et al (2004) Micro-meso-macro. J Evol Econ 14-3:263–279
Dosi G (1982) Technological paradigms and technological trajectories. Res Policy 11:147–162
Douhan R, Eliasson G et al (2007) Israel M. Kirzner: an outstanding Austrian contributor to the economics of entrepreneurship. Small Bus Econ 29:213–223
Drucker PF (1954) The practice of management. Harper & Brothers, New York
Drucker PF (2002[1985]) Innovation and entrepreneurship: practice and principles, Ebook edn. Harper & Row, New York
Egashira S (2006) A present appreciation of evolutionary economics – a historical characterization of the alternative thoughts of economics in the light of evolutionism. Evol Inst Econ Rev 3 (1):47–69
Engelhardt WW (2008) Johann Heinrich von Thünen als Vordenker einer Sozialen Marktwirtschaft. Metropolis, Marburg
Eucken W (1932) Staatliche Strukturwandlungen und die Krisis des Kapitalismus. Weltwirtschaftliches Arch 36(2):299–321
Farmer JD, Foley D (2009) The economy needs agent-based modelling. Nature 460:685–686

Fehr E, Gächter S (2002) Altruistic punishment in humans. Nature 415(6868):137–140
Foster J (1987) Evolutionary Macroeconomics. Georg Allen Unwin, London
Foster J, Potts J (2009) A micro-meso-macro perspective on the methodology of evolutionary economics: integrating history, simulation and econometrics. In: Canter U, Gaffard J-L, Nesta L (eds) Schumpeterian perspectives on innovation, competition and growth. Springer, Berlin, pp 53–68
Foster J, Wild P (1999) Econometric modelling in the presence of evolutionary change. Camb J Econ 23:749–770
Futagami S, Helms MM (2009) Emerging female entrepreneurship in Japan: a case study of Digimom workers. Thunderbird Int Bus Rev 51(1):71–85
Gadamer H-G (1960) Wahrheit und Methode [Truth and method]. Mohr, Tübingen
Geels FW (2002) Technological transitions as evolutionary reconfiguration processes: a multi-level perspective and a case-study. Res Policy 31(8):1257–1274
GEM (2001–2013) GEM Global Report. Global Entrepreneurship Research Association, London Business School, London
GEM (2007) GEM 2007 Global Report. Global Entrepreneurship Research Association, London Business School, London
GEM (2008) GEM 2008 global report. Global Entrepreneurship Research Association, London Business School, London
GEM (2010) Adult population survey: micro data for Japan, Global Entrepreneurship Monitor. http://www.gemconsortium.org/docs/download/3132 Accessed 28 Mar 2014
Genda Y, Kambayashi R (2002) Declining self-employment in Japan. J Jpn Int Econ 16:73–91
George G, Zahra SA (2002) Culture and its consequences for entrepreneurship. Entrep Theory Pract 26(4):5–7
Gilbert NG (2008) Agent-based models. Sage, Thousand Oaks
Global Entrepreneurship Monitor (1999–2013) Global entrepreneurship monitor executive reports 1999–2013. London Business School and Babson College, London
Grebel T (2013) On the tradeoff between similarity and diversity in the creation of novelty in basic science. Struct Chang Econ Dyn 27(0):66–78
Grebel T, Pyka A (2003) Agent-based modelling : a methodology for the analysis of qualitative development processes. Discussion paper series, Institute of Economics at University of Augsburg, vol 251
Grebel T, Pyka A et al (2003) An evolutionary approach to the theory of entrepreneurship. Ind Innov 10(4):493–514
Grilo I, Thurik R (2008) Determinants of entrepreneurial engagement levels in Europe and the US. Ind Corp Chang 17(6):1113–1145
Habermas J (1973) Zur Logik der Sozialwissenschaften (Materials on logic in social sciences), 3rd edn. Suhrkamp, Frankfurt
Hagemann H (2008) Capital, growth, and production disequilibria: on the employment consequences of new technologies. In: Scazzieri R, Sen A, Zamagni S (eds) Markets, money and capital. Cambridge University Press, Cambridge, pp 346–366
Hamada Y (2008) Prof. Hamada on entepreneurial finance. Interview with author. Kyoto, 10 July
Harada N (2002) Potential entrepreneurship in Japan. JCER discussion paper, vol 81
Harada N (2005) Potential entrepreneurship in Japan. Small Bus Econ 25(3):293–304
Harayama Y (2003) Industry-University linkage in Japan. In: International conference on "New trends and challenges of science and technological innovation in a critical era", Taipei
Hayami Y, Dasgupta P (1996) The International economic association's roundtable conference on cultural consequences on growth and development. Yomiuri Morning Edition, Tokyo, p 13
Hayek FA (1948) Individualism and economic order. Routledge, London
Hayek FA (1973) Law, legislation, and liberty: rules and order. The University of Chicago Press, Chicago
Hirooka M (2006) Innovation dynamism and economic growth: a nonlinear perspective. Edward Elgar, Cheltenham

Hodgson GM (1993) Economics and evolution: bringing life back into economics. Polity, Cambridge

Hodgson GM (1997) The ubiquity of habits and rules. Camb J Econ 21:663–684

Hofstede G (1980) Culture's consequences. International differences in work-related values. Sage, Beverly Hills

Hofstede G, Bond MH (1988) The confucius connection: from cultural roots to economic growth. Organ Dyn 16(4):5–21

Honjo Y, Harada N (2006) SME policy, financial structure and firm growth: evidence from Japan. Small Bus Econ 27(4–5):289–300

Hughes A, Burchell B (2006). The stigma of failure: an international comparison of failure tolerance and second chancing. Centre for Business Research, University of Cambridge working paper, vol 334

Imai M (1986) Kaizen: the key to Japan's competitive success. McGraw-Hill, New York

Imai Y, Kawagoe M (2000) Business start-ups in Japan: problems and policies. Oxf Rev Econ Policy 16(2):114–123

Ishida T (2008) Die Entdeckung der Gesellschaft [Sociology in Japan] – Edited and translated by Wolfgang Seifert (Nihon no shakai kagaku, Tōkyō Daigaku shuppansha, 1984). Suhrkamp, Frankfurt am Main

Isobe T (2003) Sekai kara mita Nihon no benchā katsudō [Japan's venture activities from a global]. Ryūtsū kagaku kenkyū 3(1):145–159

IStM (1993–2013) Kokuminsei no kenkyū. Daijūichiji nisensan'nen zenkoku chōsa [A study of the Japanese national character—the 12th nationwide survey 2008]. Research Report. Institute of Statistical Mathematics, Tokyo

IStM (2009) Kokuminsei no kenkyū. Daijūichiji nisensan'nen zenkoku chōsa [A study of the Japanese National character – the 12th nationwide survey 2008]. Research report. Institute of Statistical Mathematics, Tokyo

Jimenez JC, Carbonell F (2006) Local linear approximation of jump diffusion processes. J Appl Probab 43:185–194

JIWE (2006) Kigyō ni kan suru genjō oyobi ishiki ni kan suru ankēto (Opinion poll and status survey on start-up conditions). Nijū'isseiki shokugyō zaidan (Japan Institute of Worker's Evolution), Tokyo

Kaldor N (1975) Economic growth and the verdoorn law – a comment on Mr Rowthorn's article. Econ J 85:891–896

Kanaya A, Woo D (2000) The Japanese banking crisis of the 1990: sources and lessons. International Monetary Fund, Washington

Katzner DW (2002) What are the questions. J Post-Keynesian Econ 25(1):51–68

Katzner DW (2008) Culture and economic explanation: economics in the US and Japan. Routledge, New York

Kawai H, Urata S (2002) Entry of small and medium enterprises and economic dynamism in Japan. Small Bus Econ 18(1):41–51

Kiyokawa Y, Yamane H (2004) Nihonjin no rōdōkan: ishiki chōsa ni miru sono hensen [The Japanese appreciation of work: developments as found by opinion polls]. Ōhara shakai mondai kenkyūjo zasshi 524(1):14–33

Knight FH (1964[1921]). Risk, uncertainty and profit. Augustus M. Kelley, New York

kuraray Co. (1992–2007) 'Shōrai tsukitai shokugyō' ankēto [Survey on desired future profession], from http://www.kuraray.co.jp/enquete/index.html

Kuroda Y, Suzuki T (1991) A comparative analysis of the Arab culture: Arabic, English and Japanese languages and values. Behaviormetrika 18(30):35–53

Lachmann L (1971) The legacy of Max Weber. Glendessary Press, Berkeley

Lavoie D (1990a) Hermeneutics, subjectivity, and the Lester/Machlup debate: toward a more anthropological approach to empirical economics, Economics as discourse. Springer, Berlin, pp 167–187

Lavoie D (1990b) Introduction, Economics and hermeneutics. Routledge, London and New York, pp 1–15

Lavoie D (2011) The interpretive dimension of economics: science, hermeneutics, and praxeology. Rev Austrian Econ 24(2):91–128

Lee S-H, Peng MW et al (2007) Bankruptcy law and entrepreneurship development: a real options perspective. Acad Manag Rev 32(1):257–272

Lee L, Wong PK et al (2009) Entrepreneurial intentions: the influence of organizational and individual factors. J Bus Ventur 26:124–136

Leibenstein H (1968) Entrepreneurship and development. Am Econ Rev 58(2):72–83

Leombruni R, Richiardi M (2005) Why are economists sceptical about agent-based simulations? Physica A 335(1):103–109

Loasby B (1991) Equilibrium and evolution: an exploration of connecting principles in economics. Manchester University Press, Manchester

LTB (1992–2012) Kotei shisan no kakakura no gaiyô chôsho [Summary report on real estate value and other aspects]. Ministry of Internal Affairs Communications, Local Tax Bureau, Tokyo

Madison G (1990) Getting beyond objectivism: the philosophical hermeneutics of Gadamer and Ricoeur. In: Lavoie D (ed) Economics and hermeneutics. Routledge, London and New York, pp 32–57

Makino K (2008) Dr. Makino on job preferences and filial piety. Interview with author. Kyoto, 14 May

Marshall A (1920[1890]) Principles of economics. London, Macmillan.

Marx K (2004) Das Kapital – Kritik der politischen Ökonomie Dritter Band, Hamburg 1894. Akademie Verlag, Berlin

Masuda T (2006) The determinants of latent entrepreneurship in Japan. Small Bus Econ 26(3):227–240

Masuda T (2010) Entrepreneurial re-starters in Japan. Int J Entrep Small Bus 11(2):145–163

Mayer C, Schoors K et al (2005) Sources of funds and investment activities of venture capital funds: evidence from Germany, Israel, Japan and the United Kingdom. J Corp Finan 11:586–608

Meager N (1992) The fall and rise of self-employment (again): a comment on Bogenhold and Staber. Work Employ Soc 6:127

Metcalfe JS (1998) Evolutionary economics and creative destruction. Routledge, London

Metcalfe S (2004) The entrepreneur and the style of modern economics. J Evol Econ 14(2):157–175

Metcalfe S (2005) Evolutionary concepts in relation to evolutionary economics. In: Dopfer K (ed) The evolutionary foundation of economics. Cambridge University Press, Cambridge, pp 391–430

METI (2015) Dai 1kai zenkoku sōgyō suku-ru senshuken jisshi hōkoku [Press release for 1st national business plan contest]. Small and Medium Enterprise Agency, Ministry of Economy, Trade and Industry, Tokyo

MEXT (2007) Heisei jūkyū nendo gakkō kihon chōsa (2007 fundamental schooling survey). Ministry of Education, Culture, Sports, Science and Technology, Tokyo

MEXT (2013) Heisei nijūgo nendo gakkō kihon chōsa (2013 fundamental schooling survey). Ministry of Education, Culture, Sports, Science and Technology, Tokyo

Meyer W (1975) Der Nationalökonom und die Wissenschaftstheorie. Public Finan Anal (New Series) 33(3):536–545

MHLW (1992–2012) The labour force survey [Rōdōryoku chōsa]. Ministry for Health, Labour and Welfare, Tokyo

MHLW (1997–2012) Koyō hoken jigyō nenpō [Employment insurance annual report]. Ministry of Health, Labor and Welfare, Tokyo

MHLW (2001–2009) Shūgyō jōken sōgō chōsa [Survey on employment conditions]. Ministry of Health, Labor and Welfare, Tokyo

MHLW (2013a) Heisei 25nen rōdō kumiai kisō chōsa (The 2013 labour union survey). Ministry of Health, Labour and Welfare, Tokyo
MHLW (2013b) The labour force survey. Ministry for Health, Labour and Welfare, Tokyo
MIAC (1992–2012) Shūgyō kōsō kihon chōsa (The employment status survey). Ministry of Internal Affairs and Communications, Tokyo
MIAC (2013) The labour force survey: 2011 annual averages. Ministry of Internal Affairs and Communications, Statistics Bureau, Tokyo
Mirowski P (1987) The philosophical bases of institutionalist economics. J Econ Issues 21 (3):1001–1038
Mises L (1998[1949]) Human action. Ludwig von Mises Institute, Auburn, AL
Mitchell RK, Smith B et al (2000) Cross-cultural cognitions and the venture creation decision. Acad Manag J 43(5):974–993
Mitsuhashi H, Bird A (2011) The stigma of failure and limited opportunities for ex-failed entrepreneurs' redemption in Japan. In: Usui C (ed) Comparative entrepreneurship initiatives: studies in China, Japan, and the USA. Palgrave Macmillan, New York, pp 222–246
Miyauchi Y (2001) Management theory (kei'ei ron). Tōyō Keizai Shuppansha, Tokyo
Modigliani F, Brumberg R (1954) Utility analysis and the aggregate consumption function: an interpretation of cross-section data. In: Kurihara KK (ed) Post-Keynesian economics. Rutgers University Press, New Brunswick
MoF (2007) Current Japanese fiscal conditions and issues to be considered. Ministry of Finance, Tokyo. Available at: http://www.mof.go.jp/english/budget/budget/fy2007/cjfc2007.pdf
MPMHA (2008) Heisei jūnana-nen kokusei chōsa [2005 National Census]. Ministry of Public Management, Home Affairs, Posts and Telecommunications, Tokyo
MRI (2005) 'Wagakuni no monozukuri wo sasaete iru "jinzai" no kongo' dai'ikkai chōsa kekka hōkoku [First news release reporting results from the survey "Present and future of the human resources supporting manufacturing in our country"]. Mitsubishi Research Institute, Tokyo
Muzyka DF, Kets de Vries M et al (1991) Cross cultural aspects of entrepreneurship: a european view. In: Churchill NC, Birley S, Doutriaux J et al (eds) Frontiers of entrepreneurship research 1993. Babson College, Babson Park, pp 545–561
Nakamura Y (2008) Bushidō-Diskurs. Die analyse der Diskrepanz zwischen Ideal und Realität im Bushidō-Diskurs aus dem Jahr 1904. PhD Thesis. Faculty of Philosophy. Vienna, University of Vienna
National Family Research Committee (1999, 2004). Zenkoku kazoku chōsa [National family survey]. Tokyo, Japan Society of Family Sociology.
Nelson R, Winter S (1982) An evolutionary theory of economic change. Harvard University Press, Cambridge
Nishibe M (2006) Redefining evolutionary economics. Evol Inst Econ Rev 3(1):3–25
NLFC (1987–2008) Zenkoku kigyō dōkō chōsa kekka [Results of the national small enterprise trend survey]. National Life Finance Corporation, Tokyo
NLFC (1991–2012) Shinki kaigyō jittai chōsa [Fact-finding survey on newly opened businesses]. National Life Finance Corporation, Tokyo
NLFC (2001) 'Nidome no kaigyō' ni kan suru jittai chōsa kekka ni tsuite [Survey on second chancing: results]. National Life Finance Corporation, Tokyo
NLFC (2007) Annual report 2007. National Life Finance Corporation, Tokyo
Nojima N (2008) Dr. Nojima on psychological aspects of entrepreneurship in Japan. Interview with author. Kyoto, 12 September
NRI (1992–2009) Consumer sentiment index. Nippon Research Institute, Tokyo
NVCA (2013) 2013 Yearbook. National Venture Capital Association, Arlington, VA
Obschonka M, Silbereisen RK, Cantner U, Goethner M (2015) Entrepreneurial self-identity: predictors and effects within the theory of planned behavior framework. J Bus Psychol 30 (4):773–794
OECD (2006) OECD economic surveys: Japan. OECD, Paris

Ohe S, Ohe T (1996) Three key experiences of Japanese entrepreneurs during their elementary and secondary school years. Frontiers of entrepreneurship research (Conference Proceedings). Wellesley (MA). Available at: http://fusionmx.babson.edu/entrep/fer/papers96/ohe/

Ohe T, Honjo S et al (1990) Japanese entrepreneurs and corporate managers: a comparison. J Bus Ventur 6(2):135–144

Ohno T (1988) Toyota production system: beyond large-scale production. Productivity Press, New York

Okuno-Fujiwara M (1991) Industrial policy in Japan: a political economy view. In: Krugman P (ed) Trade with Japan: has the door opened wider? University of Chicago Press, Chicago, pp 271–296

Ostrom E (1986) An agenda for the study of institutions. Public Choice 48(1):3–25

Osträm E, Basurto X (2011) Crafting analytical tools to study institutional change. J Inst Econ 7(3):317–343

Ōtake F (2005) Nihon no fubyōdō: kakusa shakai no gensō to mirai [Inequality in Japan – illusion and future of the disparate society]. Nikkei, Tokyo

Ozaki M (2002) Jibun no kaisha wo motsu. seikō ma'nyuaru [Owning one's own company – a guide to success]. Kodansha, Tokyo

Parker SC (2009) The economics of entrepreneurship. Cambridge University Press, Cambridge

Patrick HT, Rohlen TP (1987) Small-scale family enterprises. In: Yamamura K, Yasuba Y (eds) The political economy of Japan, Part 1: The domestic transformation. Stanford University Press, Stanford, pp 331–384

Prencipe A (1997) Technological competencies and product's evolutionary dynamics a case study from the aero-engine industry. Res Policy 25(8):1261–1276

Rengō Sōken (2001–2013) Kinrôsha no shigoto to kurashi ni tsuite no ankêto [Survey on work and life of the dependently employed]. Research Institute for Advancement of Living Standards, Tokyo

Reynolds PD, Bygrave WD et al (2002) Global entrepreneurship monitor 2002 executive report. Babson College, Wellesley, MA

Ripsas S (1998) Towards an interdisciplinary theory of entrepreneurship. Small Bus Econ 10:103–115

Robbins L (1945[1932]) An essay on the nature and significance of economic science, 1st edn. MacMillan, London

Roininen S, Ylinenpää H (2009) Schumpeterian versus Kirznerian entrepreneurship. J Small Bus Enterp Dev 16(3):504–520

Runde J (2009) Ontology and the foundations of evolutionary economic theory: on Dopfer and Potts' general theory of economic evolution. J Inst Econ 5(3):361–378

Sakuta K i (1967) Haji no bunka saikō [Reflection on the culture of shame]. Shikuma Shobo, Tokyo

Samila S, Sorenson O (2011) Venture capital, entrepreneurship, and economic growth. Rev Econ Stat 93(1):338–349

Satō T (2000) Fubyōdō shakai nihon: sayonara sōchūryū [Japan's unequal society – a farewell to the general middle class]. Chūkō, Tokyo

Saviotti PP (ed) (2003) Applied evolutionary economics – new empirical methods and simulation techniques. Edward Elgar, Cheltenham

Schneider E (1953[1949]) Einführung in die Wirtschaftstheorie II. 2nd edn. JCB Mohr (Paul Siebeck), Tübingen

Schultz TW (1975) The value of the ability to deal with disequilibria. J Econ Lit 13:827–846

Schumpeter JA (1912) Theorie der wirtschaftlichen Entwicklung. Duncker & Humblot, Leipzig

Schumpeter JA (1939) Business cycles: a theoretical, historical and statistical analysis of the capitalist process. McGraw-Hill, New York and London

Semba T (2008) Semba Takahiro on attractiveness of corporate careers. Interview with author. Kyoto, 13 May

Shackle GLS (1979) Imagination and the nature of choice. Edinburgh University Press, Edinburgh

Shane S, Kolvereid L et al (1991) An exploratory examination of the reasons leading to new firm formation across country and gender. J Bus Ventur 6:431–446

Shapero A, Sokol L (1982) The social dimensions of entrepreneurship. In: Kent CA, Sexton DL, Vesper KH (eds) The encyclopedia of entrepreneurship. Prentice-Hall, Englewood Cliffs, NJ, pp 72–90

SMEA (2007) 2007 White paper on small and medium enterprises. Small and Medium Enterprise Agency, Ministry of Economy, Trade and Industry

SMEA (2012) 2012 White paper on small and medium enterprises. Small and Medium Enterprise Agency, Ministry of Economy, Trade and Industry

SMRJ (1992–2012) Chūshō kigyō keikyō chōsa [Business conditions in smaller enterprises]. Ministry of Economy, Trade and Industry, Small and Medium Enterprise Agency, Organization for Small & Medium Enterprises and Regional Innovation, Tokyo

SMRJ (2011) Incubation report, vol 2. Ministry of Economy, Trade and Industry, Small and Medium Enterprise Agency, Organization for Small & Medium Enterprizes and Regional Innovation, Tokyo

Sombart W, Stoltenberg HL (1924) Soziologie. Pan-Verlag, Berlin

Steineck C (2013) Truth, time, and the extended umwelt principle: conceptual limits and methodological constraints. In: Parker JA, Harris PA, Steineck C (eds) Time: limits and constraints. Brill, Leiden, Boston, pp 350–365

Storey DJ, Johnson S (1987) Regional variations in entrepreneurship in the U.K. Scot J Polit Econ 34(2):161–173

Strohmaier R (2010) The general theory of economic evolution [Book review]. Eur J Hist Econ Thought 17(2):352–356

Sugiman T (2008) Prof. Sugiman on sociological aspects of business formation. Interview with author. Kyoto, 30 April

Suzuki K-i, Kim S-H et al (2002) Entrepreneurship in Japan and Silicon Valley: a comparative study. Technovation 22:595–606

Swett Mansfield M (1927) Why women fail in business. North Am Rev 223(883):638–644

Tachibanaki T (1998) Nihon no keizai kakusa: shotoku to shisan kara kangaeru [Japan's economic disparities – thoughts on income and assets]. Iwanami, Tokyo

Tachibanaki T (2006) Kakusa shakai: nani ga mondai nano ka [Disparate society – what is the problem about it?]. Iwanami, Tokyo

Tagaya M (2008) Venture capital investments in Japan. Interview with author. Nippon Venture Capital Co., Ltd. Osaka

Takagi T (2008) Venture capital investments. Interview with author. Ibis Capital Partners. Tokyo, 6 June

Takahashi N (2005) Kigyōka purofairu [Entrepreneur profiles]. In: Kutsuna K, Yasuda T (eds) Nihon no shinki kaigyō kigyō [Japan's new ventures]. Hakutō Shobō, Tokyo

Takahashi N, Isobe T et al (2013) Kigyō katsudō ni ei'kyō o ataeru yō'in no kokusai hikaku bunseki [International comparison on factors influencing business formation]. RIETI discussion paper series, vol 13(J-15)

Tanioka F (2008) Mrs. Tanioka on self-employment out of non-regular dependent employment. Interview with author. Kyoto, 4 April

Thomas AS, Mueller SL (2000) A case for comparative entrepreneurship: assessing the relevance of culture. J Int Bus Stud 31(2):287–301

Thünen JH v (1990) Der isolierte Staat in Beziehung auf Landwirtschaft und Nationalökonomie (1826). Akademie, Berlin

Tuttle CA (1927) The function of the entrepreneur. Am Econ Rev 17:13–25

Uematsu T (1997) Shinōkōshō: jukyō shisō to kanryō shihai [Warriors, farmers, craftsmen and merchants: confucianist thought and bureaucratic rule]. Dōbunkan, Tokyo

Veblen T (1899) The theory of the leisure class. Macmillan, New York

Veblen T (1925) Economic theory in the calculable future. Am Econ Rev 15(1 Suppl):48–55

VEC (2002–2013) 2001–2012 surveys on trends in venture capital investments. Venture Enterprise Center, commissioned by METI, Tokyo

von Mandach SL (2014) Neo-confucianism and industrial relations in Meiji Japan. J Manag Hist 20(4):387–408

Wäckerle M (2013) On the bottom-up foundations of the banking-macro nexus. Econom: Open Access Open Assess E J 7(2013–40):1

Waldenberger F (2000) Japans Finanzkrise [Japan's financial crisis]. Jpn Mag 12:12–14

Walsh ST (2004) Roadmapping a disruptive technology: a case study: the emerging microsystems and top-down nanosystems industry. Technol Forecast Soc Chang 71(1–2):161–185

Watanabe T (2008) Interview on start-up organization: emotional intelligence research, inc. G. D. Blind, Tokyo

Weber M (1904/1905) Die protestantische ethik und der 'Geist' des Kapitalismus. Archiv für Sozialwissenschaft und Sozialpolitik 20, 21(1):1–54, 51–110

Wennekers S, Uhlaner LM et al (2002) Entrepreneurship and its conditions: a macro perspective. Int J Entrep Educ 1(1):25–64

Witt U (1993) Evolutionary economics. Edward Elgar, Aldershot

Witt U (2000) Changing cognitive frames – changing organizational forms: an entrepreneurial theory of organizational development. Ind Corp Chang 9:733–755

Witt U (2001) Learning to consume – a theory of wants and the growth of demand. J Evol Econ 11(1):23–36

Womack JP, Jones DT et al (1990) The machine that changed the world: the story of lean production. Rawson Associates, New York

Printed by Printforce, the Netherlands